THE
NEW WEBSTER
QUOTATION
DICTIONARY

THE
NEW WEBSTER
QUOTATION
DICTIONARY

Compiled By

Donald O. Bolander, M.A., Litt. D.

LEXICON PUBLICATIONS, INC.

ISBN 0-7172-4565-9

QUOTATION DICTIONARY

ABILITY *Also see:* ACTION, CHARACTER, DISCRETION, FORCE, GENIUS, PERSEVERANCE, POWER, STRENGTH, SUCCESS.

There is something that is much more scarce, something finer far, something rarer than ability. It is the ability to recognize ability.

ELBERT HUBBARD

Consider the postage stamp: its usefulness consists in the ability to stick to one thing till it gets there.

JOSH BILLINGS

The question, "Who ought to be boss?" is like asking "Who ought to be the tenor in the quartet?" Obviously, the man who can sing tenor.

HENRY FORD

Executive ability is deciding quickly and getting somebody else to do the work.

JOHN G. POLLARD

They are able because they think they are able.

VERGIL

Ability is of little account without opportunity.

NAPOLEON BONAPARTE

Natural abilities are like natural plants; they need pruning by study.

FRANCIS BACON

The wind and the waves are always on the side of the ablest navigators.

EDWARD GIBBON

ABSENCE *Also see:* LONELINESS, MEMORY, WANT.

Is not absence death to those who love?

ALEXANDER POPE

Absence diminishes little passions and increases great ones, as wind extinguishes candles and fans a fire.

FRANÇOIS DE LA ROCHEFOUCALD

The absent are never without fault. Nor the present without excuse.

BENJAMIN FRANKLIN

Taken from Instant Quotation Dictionary compiled by Donald O. Bolander, M.A., LITT.D. ©Copyrighted and Reprinted by Permission of Career Publishing, Inc.

When a man is out of sight, it is not too long before he is out of mind.
THOMAS À KEMPIS

The absent are like children, helpless to defend themselves.
CHARLES READE

The absent are always in the wrong.
ENGLISH PROVERB

Absence and death are the same—only that in death there is no suffering.
WALTER S. LANDOR

ABSTINENCE *Also see:* DRUNKENNESS, MODERATION, SACRIFICE.

Complete abstinence is easier than perfect moderation.
ST. AUGUSTINE

Always rise from the table with an appetite, and you will never sit down without one.
WILLIAM PENN

All philosophy lies in two words, sustain and abstain.
EPICTETUS

The only way for a rich man to be healthy is by exercise and abstinence, to live as if he were poor.
WILLIAM TEMPLE

Abstaining is favorable both to the head and the pocket.
HORACE GREELEY

ABSURDITY *Also see:* RIDICULE, SARCASM.

In politics, an absurdity is not a handicap.
NAPOLEON BONAPARTE

There is nothing so absurd or ridiculous that has not at some time been said by some philosopher.
OLIVER GOLDSMITH

It is the height of absurdity to sow little but weeds in the first half of one's lifetime and expect to harvest a valuable crop in the second half.
PERCY JOHNSTON

ABUSE *Also see:* CRUELTY, INJURY, POLLUTION, SLANDER.

Abuse is the weapon of the vulgar.

SAMUEL GRISWOLD GOODRICH

The best security against revolution is in constant correction of abuses and the introduction of needed improvements.

RICHARD WHATELY

I never yet heard man or woman much abused that I was not inclined to think the better of them, and to transfer the suspicion or dislike to the one who found pleasure in pointing out the defects of another.

JANE PORTER

There is none more abusive to others than they that lie most open to it themselves.

SENECA

Anyone entrusted with power will abuse it if not also animated with the love of truth and virtue.

JEAN DE LA FONTAINE

ACCURACY *Also see:* FACTS, FIDELITY, PUNCTUALITY, SCIENCE.

Accuracy is the twin brother of honesty; inaccuracy, of dishonesty.

CHARLES SIMMONS

Accuracy is to a newspaper what virtue is to a lady, but a newspaper can always print a retraction.

ADLAI E. STEVENSON

Accuracy of statement is one of the first elements of truth; inaccuracy is a near kin to falsehood.

TRYON EDWARDS

Even a stopped clock is right twice a day.

ANONYMOUS

From principles is derived probability, but truth or certainty is obtained only from facts.

NATHANIEL HAWTHORNE

ACHIEVEMENT *Also see:* ACTION, AIM, AMBITION, DECISION, LABOR, PURPOSE, SUCCESS, WORK.

Mere longevity is a good thing for those who watch Life from the side lines. For those who play the game, an hour may be a year, a single day's work an achievement for eternity.

GABRIEL HEATTER

Do not attempt to do a thing unless you are sure of yourself; but do not relinquish it simply because someone else is not sure of you.

STEWART E. WHITE

Every man who is high up loves to think that he has done it all himself; and the wife smiles, and lets it go at that.

JAMES MATTHEW BARRIE

Life affords no higher pleasure than that of surmounting difficulties, passing from one step of success to another, forming new wishes and seeing them gratified.

SAMUEL JOHNSON

ACTION *Also see:* ACHIEVEMENT, DESIRE, LABOR, PROGRESS, WORK.

Thought is the blossom; language the bud; action the fruit behind it.
RALPH WALDO EMERSON

Positive anything is better than negative nothing.

ELBERT HUBBARD

Our grand business is not to see what lies dimly at a distance, but to do what lies clearly at hand.

THOMAS CARLYLE

The actions of men are the best interpreters of their thoughts.

JOHN LOCKE

Think like a man of action and act like a man of thought.

HENRI BERGSON

What you do speaks so loud that I cannot hear what you say.
RALPH WALDO EMERSON

Action may not always bring happiness; but there is no happiness without action.

BENJAMIN DISRAELI

It is by acts and not by ideas that people live.

ANATOLE FRANCE

Thought and theory must precede all salutary action; yet action is nobler in itself than either thought or theory.

WILLIAM WORDSWORTH

Action to be effective must be directed to clearly conceived ends.

JAWAHARLAL NEHRU

Indolence is a delightful but distressing state; we must be doing something to be happy. Action is no less necessary than thought to the instinctive tendencies of the human frame.

MAHATMA GANDHI

ADAPTABILITY See also: CONFORMITY.

Make yourself necessary to somebody.

RALPH WALDO EMERSON

Complete adaptation to environment means death. The essential point in all response is the desire to control environment.

JOHN DEWEY

One learns to itch where one can scratch.

ERNEST BRAMAH

Adaptability is not imitation. It means power of resistance and assimilation.

MAHATMA GANDHI

ADMIRATION Also see: FAME, FOOL, LOVE, PRAISE RESPECT.

We always love those who admire us; we do not always love those whom we admire.

FRANÇOIS DE LA ROCHEFOUCAULD

The only things one can admire at length are those one admires without knowing why.

JEAN ROSTAND

Fools admire, but men of sense approve.

ALEXANDER POPE

A fool always finds a greater fool to admire him.

NICOLAS BOLLEAU-DESPRÉAUX

Admiration is a very short-lived passion, that immediately decays upon growing familiar with its object.

JOSEPH ADDISON

ADVANCEMENT . . . See PROGRESS.

ADVENTURE Also see: DANGER, DISCOVERY, INVENTION, SPACE, TRAVEL.

Without adventure civilization is in full decay.

ALFRED NORTH WHITEHEAD

Who dares nothing, need hope for nothing.

JOHANN VON SCHILLER

You can't cross the sea merely by standing and staring at the water. Don't let yourself indulge in vain wishes.

RABINDRANATH TAGORE

We live in a wonderful world that is full of beauty, charm and adventure. There is no end to the adventures that we can have if only we seek them with our eyes open.

JAWAHARLAL NEHRU

ADVERSITY Also see: AFFLICTION, CALAMITY, MISERY, PROSPERITY.

By trying we can easily learn to endure adversity—another man's I mean.

MARK TWAIN

Adversity makes men, and prosperity makes monsters.

VICTOR HUGO

Little minds are tamed and subdued by misfortune; but great minds rise above them.

WASHINGTON IRVING

Prosperity is not without many fears and distastes; adversity not without many comforts and hopes.

FRANCIS BACON

The good things of prosperity are to be wished; but the good things that belong to adversity are to be admired.

SENECA

Prosperity is a great teacher; adversity is a greater. Possession pampers the mind; privation trains and strengthens it.

WILLIAM HAZLITT

ADVERTISING Also see: ART, BUSINESS, PUBLICITY.

The business that considers itself immune to the necessity for advertising sooner or later finds itself immune to business.

DERBY BROWN

Advertising is the foot on the accelerator, the hand on the throttle, the spur on the flank that keeps our economy surging forward.

ROBERT W. SARNOFF

Doing business without advertising is like winking at a girl in the dark. You know what you are doing, but nobody else does.

STEUART H. BRITT

The product that will not sell without advertising will not sell profitably with advertising.

ALBERT LASKER

Advertising promotes that divine discontent which makes people strive to improve their economic status.

RALPH S. BUTLER.

ADVICE *Also see:* CAUTION, EXPERIENCE, HELP, WISDOM.

Advice is like snow; the softer it falls the longer it dwells upon, and the deeper it sinks into the mind.

SAMUEL TAYLOR COLERIDGE

Advice is seldom welcome, and those who need it the most, like it the least.

LORD CHESTERFIELD

It is easy when we are in prosperity to give advice to the afflicted.

AESCHYLUS

In those days he was wiser than he is now—he used frequently to take my advice.

WINSTON CHURCHILL

Men give away nothing so liberally as their advice.

FRANÇOIS DE LA ROCHEFOUCAULD

No man is so foolish but he may sometimes give another good counsel, and no man so wise that he may not easily err if he takes no other counsel than his own. He that is taught only by himself has a fool for a master.

BEN JONSON

It is only too easy to make suggestions and later try to escape the consequences of what we say.

JAWAHARLAL NEHRU

The only thing to do with good advice is to pass it on. It is never of any use to oneself.

OSCAR WILDE

He that won't be counselled can't be helped.

BENJAMIN FRANKLIN

There is as much difference between the counsel that a friend giveth, and that a man giveth himself, as there is between the counsel of a friend and a flatterer.

FRANCIS BACON

AFFECTION *Also see:* ADMIRATION, FRIENDSHIP, KISS, LOVE

A slight touch of friendly malice and amusement towards those we love keeps our affections for them from turning flat.

LOGAN P. SMITH

Talk not of wasted affection; affection never was wasted.

HENRY WADSWORTH LONGFELLOW

Caresses, expressions of one sort or another, are necessary to the life of the affections as leaves are to the life of a tree.

NATHANIEL HAWTHORNE

The affections are like lightning: you cannot tell where they will strike till they have fallen.

JOHN BAPTISTE LACORDAIRE

A woman's life is a history of the affections.

WASHINGTON IRVING

I never met a man I didn't like.

WILL ROGERS

AFFLICTION *See also:* ADVERSITY, CALAMITY, DISEASE, PAIN, SORROW, SUFFERING.

The gem cannot be polished without friction, nor man perfected without trials.

CHINESE PROVERB

Strength is born in the deep silence of long-suffering hearts; not amid joy.

FELICIA HEMANS

Affliction, like the iron-smith, shapes as it smites.

CHRISTIAN NESTELL BOVEE

I thank God for my handicaps, for through them, I have found myself, my work and my God.

HELEN KELLER

As threshing separates the wheat from the chaff, so does affliction purify virtue.

RICHARD E. BURTON

Affliction comes to us, not to make us sad but sober; not to make us sorry but wise.

HENRY WARD BEECHER

AGE *Also see:* AVARICE, YOUTH.

I refuse to admit I'm more than fifty-two, even if that does make my sons illegitimate.

LADY ASTOR

If wrinkles must be written upon our brows, let them not be written upon the heart. The spirit should never grow old.

JAMES A. GARFIELD

Age . . . is a matter of feeling, not of years.

GEORGE WILLIAM CURTIS

Age does not depend upon years, but upon temperament and health. Some men are born old, and some never grow so.

TRYON EDWARDS

A man is not old as long as he is seeking something.

JEAN ROSTAND

The woman who tells her age is either too young to have anything to lose or too old to have anything to gain.

CHINESE PROVERB

The older I grow the more I distrust the familiar doctrine that age brings wisdom.

H. L. MENCKEN

AGGRESSION *Also see:* ANGER, ENEMY, WAR.

The truth is often a terrible weapon of aggression. It is possible to lie, and even to murder, with the truth.

ALFRED ADLER

It is the habit of every aggressor nation to claim that it is acting on the defensive.

JAWAHARLAL NEHRU

Civilized society is perpetually menaced with disintegration through this primary hostility of men towards one another . . .

SIGMUND FREUD

AGITATION *Also see:* ARGUMENT, DISSENT.

Agitation is that part of our intellectual life where vitality results; there ideas are born, breed and bring forth.

GEORGE EDWARD WOODBERRY

Those who profess to favor freedom, and yet depreciate agitation, are men who want rain without thunder and lightning. They want the ocean without the roar of its many waters.

FREDERICK DOUGLASS

Agitation is the marshalling of the conscience of a nation to mold its laws.

ROBERT PEEL

AGNOSTICISM *Also see:* ATHEISM, GOD, SKEPTICISM.

Agnosticism simply means that a man shall not say he knows or believes that for which he has no grounds for professing to believe.

THOMAS HUXLEY

Agnosticism is the philosophical, ethical and religious dry-rot of the modern world.

F. E. ABBOT

There is only one greater folly than that of the fool who says in his heart there is no God, and that is the folly of the people that says with its head that it does not know whether there is a God or not.

OTTO VON BISMARK

I am an agnostic; I do not pretend to know what many ignorant men are sure of.

CLARENCE DARROW

AGREEMENT *Also see:* COMPROMISE, CONFORMITY, UNDER-STANDING, UNITY.

We hardly find any persons of good sense save those who agree with us.

FRANÇOIS DE LA ROCHEFOUCAULD

When two men in business always agree, one of them in unnecessary.

WILLIAM .pa WRIGLEY, JR.

There is no conversation more boring than the one where everybody agrees.

MICHEL DE MONTAIGNE

I have never in my life learned anything from any man who agreed with me.

DUDLEY FIELD MALONE

You may easily play a joke on a man who likes to argue—agree with him.

ED HOWE

AIM *Also see:* AMBITION, DESIRE, END, IDEAL, PURPOSE, PURSUIT.

Aim at the sun, and you may not reach it; but your arrow will fly far higher than if aimed at an object on a level with yourself.

JOEL HAWES

In great attempts it is glorious even to fall.

CASSIUS

Not failure, but low aim, is crime.

JAMES RUSSELL LOWELL

High aims form high characters, and great objects bring out great minds.

TRYON EDWARDS

AMBIGUITY *Also see:* DOUBT.

Those who write clearly have readers, those who write obscurely have commentators.

ALBERT CAMUS

I fear explanations explanatory of things explained.

ABRAHAM LINCOLN

Clearly spoken, Mr. Fogg; you explain English by Greek.

BENJAMIN FRANKLIN

That must be wonderful; I have no idea of what it means.

MOLIÈRE

AMBITION *Also see:* AIM, CONSCIENCE, DESIRE, EFFORT, GLORY, IDEAL, PURPOSE, SUCCESS, WORTH, ZEAL.

You can't hold a man down without staying down with him.

BOOKER T. WASHINGTON

Ambition is the last refuge of failure.

OSCAR WILDE

We grow small trying to be great.

E. STANLEY JONES

Hitch your wagon to a star.

RALPH WALDO EMERSON

Most people would succeed in small things if they were not troubled with great ambitions.

HENRY WADSWORTH LONGFELLOW

He who surpasses or subdues mankind, must look down on the hate of those below.

LORD BYRON

Ambition is so powerful a passion in the human breast, that however high we reach we are never satisfied.

NICCOLÒ MACHIAVELLI

All ambitions are lawful except those which climb upward on the miseries or credulities of mankind.

JOSEPH CONRAD

If you wish to reach the highest, begin at the lowest.

PUBLILIUS SYRUS

When you are aspiring to the highest place, it is honorable to reach the second or even the third rank.

CICERO

Some folks can look so busy doing nothin' that they seem indispensable.

KIN HUBBARD

The men who succeed are the efficient few. They are the few who have the ambition and will power to develop themselves.

HERBERT N. CASSON

No bird soars too high if he soars with his own wings.

WILLIAM BLAKE

It seems to me we can never give up longing and wishing while we are thoroughly alive. There are certain things we feel to be beautiful and good, and we must hunger after them.

GEORGE ELIOT

The very substance of the ambitious is merely the shadow of a dream.

WILLIAM SHAKESPEARE

AMERICA *Also see:* DEMOCRACY, NATION, PARTY, PATRI-OTISM, PRESIDENT.

America has believed that in differentiation, not in uniformity, lies the path of progress. It acted on this belief; it has advanced human happiness, and it has prospered.

LOUIS D. BRANDEIS

America is not a mere body of traders; it is a body of free men. Our greatness is built upon our freedom—is moral, not material. We have a great ardor for gain; but we have a deep passion for the rights of man.

WOODROW WILSON

A citizen of America will cross the ocean to fight for democracy, but won't cross the street to vote in a national election.

BILL VAUGHAN

If there is one word that describes our form of society in America, it may be the word—voluntary.

LYNDON BAINES JOHNSON

Intellectually I know that America is no better than any other country; emotionally I know she is better than every country.

SINCLAIR LEWIS

I am certain that, however great the hardships and the trials which loom ahead, our America will endure and the cause of human freedom will triumph.

CORDELL HULL

I would rather see the United States respected than loved by other nations.

HENRY CABOT LODGE

Wake up, America.

AUGUSTUS P. GARDNER

America lives in the heart of every man everywhere who wishes to find a region where he will be free to work out his destiny as he chooses.

WOODROW WILSON

Our country is still young and its potential is still enormous. We should remember, as we look toward the future, that the more fully we believe in and achieve freedom and equal opportunity—not simply for ourselves but for others—the greater our accomplishments as a nation will be.

HENRY FORD II

The interesting and inspiring thing about America is that she asks nothing for herself except what she has a right to ask for humanity itself.

WOODROW WILSON

If the American dream is for Americans only, it will remain our dream and never be our destiny.

RENÉ DE VISME WILLIAMSON

Our country, right or wrong. When right, to be kept right; when wrong, to be put right.

CARL SCHURZ

The country's honor must be upheld at home and abroad.

THEODORE ROOSEVELT

In the field of world policy, I would dedicate this nation to the policy of the good neighbor.

FRANKLIN DELANO ROOSEVELT

Let our object be our country, our whole country, and nothing but our country.

DANIEL WEBSTER

America . . . a great social and economic experiment, noble in motive and far-reaching in purpose.

HERBERT HOOVER

America is not merely a nation but a nation of nations.

LYNDON BAINES JOHNSON

AMIABILITY *Also see:* AGREEMENT, CHEERFULNESS, COURTESY, HAPPINESS.

Natural amiableness is too often seen in company with sloth, with uselessness, with the vanity of fashionable life.

WILLIAM ELLERY CHANNING

How easy to be amiable in the midst of happiness and success.

ANNE SOPHIE SWETCHINE

An inexhaustible good nature is one of the most precious gifts of heaven, spreading itself like oil over the troubled sea of thought, and keeping the mind smooth and equable in the roughest weather.

WASHINGTON IRVING

AMUSEMENT *Also see:* ENJOYMENT, JOY, PLEASURE, REVERIE.

. . . the happiness of those who cannot think.

ALEXANDER POPE

The only way to amuse some people is to slip and fall on an icy pavement.

ED HOWE

True enjoyment comes from activity of the mind and exercise of the body; the two are ever united.

HUMBOLDT

You can't live on amusement. It is the froth on water—an inch deep and then the mud.

GEORGE MACDONALD

I am a great friend to public amusements, for they keep people from vice.

SAMUEL JOHNSON

If those who are the enemies of innocent amusements had the direction of the world, they would take away the spring, and youth, the former from the year, the latter from human life.

HONORÉ DE BALZAC

The real character of a man is found out by his amusements.

JOSHUA REYNOLDS

Life is worth living, but only if we avoid the amusements of grown-up people.

ROBERT LYND

The mind ought sometimes to be diverted, that it may return the better to thinking.

PHAEDRUS

ANCESTRY *Also see:* ARISTOCRACY.

Everyone has ancestors and it is only a question of going back far enough to find a good one.

HOWARD KENNETH NIXON

Whoever serves his country well has no need of ancestors.

VOLTAIRE

Every man is his own ancestor, and every man his own heir. He devises his own future, and he inherits his own past.

H. F. HEDGE

Everyone has something ancestral, even if it is nothing more than a disease.

ED HOWE

Some men by ancestry are only the shadow of a mighty name.

LUCAN

The man who has nothing to boast of but his illustrious ancestry, is like the potato—the best part under ground.

THOMAS OVERBURY

It is of no consequence of what parents a man is born, so he be man of merit.

HORACE

It is indeed a desirable thing to be well descended, but the glory belongs to our ancestors.

PLUTARCH

We are all omnibuses in which our ancestors ride, and every now and then one of them sticks his head out and embarrasses us.

OLIVER WENDELL HOLMES

ANGER *Also see:* AGGRESSION, QUARREL, TEMPER.

When angry count four; when very angry, swear.

MARK TWAIN

Men often make up in wrath what they want in reason.

WILLIAM ROUNSEVILLE ALGER

Anger blows out the lamp of the mind.

ROBERT GREEN INGERSOLL

To rule one's anger is well; to prevent it is still better.

TRYON EDWARDS

Beware the fury of a patient man.

JOHN DRYDEN

An angry man opens his mouth and shuts up his eyes.

CATO

Anger is seldom without argument but seldom with a good one.

HALIFAX

Anger and intolerance are the twin enemies of correct understanding.

MAHATMA GANDHI

An angry man is again angry with himself when he returns to reason.

PUBLILIUS SYRUS

Anger is a momentary madness, so control your passion or it will control you.

HORACE

Anger begins with folly, and ends with repentance.

H. G. BOHN

Keep cool; anger is not an argument.

DANIEL WEBSTER

When a man is wrong and won't admit it, he always gets angry.

HALIBURTON

ANTICIPATION *Also see:* ANXIETY, DISAPPOINTMENT, HOPE.

Nothing is so good as it seems beforehand.

GEORGE ELIOT

If pleasures are greatest in anticipation, just remember that this is also true of trouble.

ELBERT HUBBARD

What we anticipate seldom occurs, what we least expected generally happens.

BENJAMIN DISRAELI

Few enterprises of great labor or hazard would be undertaken if we had not the power of magnifying the advantages we expect from them.

SAMUEL JOHNSON

Our desires always disappoint us; for though we meet with something that gives us satisfaction, yet it never thoroughly answers our expectation.

FRANÇOIS DE LA ROCHEFOUCAULD

Nothing is so wretched or foolish as to anticipate misfortunes. What madness is it to be expecting evil before it comes.

SENECA

ANXIETY *Also see:* ANTICIPATION, FEAR, WORRY.

The natural role of twentieth-century man is anxiety.

NORMAN MAILER

The thinner the ice, the more anxious is everyone to see whether it will bear.

JOSH BILLINGS

We have a lot of anxieties, and one cancels out another very often.

WINSTON CHURCHILL

Do not anticipate trouble, or worry about what may never happen. Keep in the sunlight.

BENJAMIN FRANKLIN

God never built a Christian strong enough to carry today's duties and tomorrow's anxieties piled on the top of them.

THEODORE LEDYARD CUYLER

The misfortunes hardest to bear are those which never came.

JAMES RUSSELL LOWELL

Borrow trouble for yourself, if that's your nature, but don't lend it to your neighbors.

RUDYARD KIPLING

APATHY *Also see:* IDLENESS, NEGLECT, WORK.

Apathy is a sort of living oblivion.

HORACE GREELEY

There is no calamity which a great nation can invite which equals that which follows a supine submission to wrong and injustice.

GROVER CLEVELAND

The apathy of the people is enough to make every statue leap from its pedestal and hasten the resurrection of the dead.

WILLIAM LLOYD GARRISON

The tyranny of a prince in an oligarchy is not so dangerous to the public welfare as the apathy of a citizen in a democracy.

MONTESQUIEU

Most people are on the world, not in it—having no conscious sympathy or relationship to anything about them—undiffused, separate, and rigidly alone like marbles of polished stone, touching but separate.

JOHN MUIR

Nothing for preserving the body like having no heart.

JOHN PETIT-SENN

APPEARANCE *Also see:* DRESS, FASHION, ILLUSION, REALITY.

How little do they see what is, who frame their hasty judgments upon that which seems.

ROBERT SOUTHEY

The world is governed more by appearances than by realities, so that it is fully as necessary to seem to know something as to know it.

DANIEL WEBSTER

You are only what you are when no one is looking.

ROBERT C. EDWARDS

Half the work that is done in this world is to make things appear what they are not.

ELIAS ROOT BEADLE

You may turn into an archangel, a fool, or a criminal—no one will see it. But when a button is missing—everyone sees that.

ERICH M. REMARQUE

When I see a bird that walks like a duck and swims like a duck and quacks like a duck, I call that a bird a duck.

RICHARD CARDINAL CUSHING

APPETITE Also see: DESIRE, EATING, GLUTTON, HUNGER.

Reason should direct and appetite obey.

CICERO

Let the stoics say what they please, we do not eat for the good of living, but because the meat is savory and the appetite is keen.

RALPH WALDO EMERSON

Animals feed; man eats. Only the man of intellect and judgment knows how to eat.

ANTHELME BRILLAT-SAVARIN

A well-governed appetite is a great part of liberty.

SENECA

ARGUMENT Also see: DIFFERENCE, DISSENT, QUARREL.

Debate is the death of conversation.

EMIL LUDWIG

People generally quarrel because they cannot argue.

GILBERT K. CHESTERTON

A long dispute means both parties are wrong.

VOLTAIRE

Behind every argument is someone's ignorance.

LOUIS D. BRANDEIS

The best way I know of to win an argument is to start by being in the right.

LORD HALLSHAM

He who establishes his argument by noise and command shows that his reason is weak.

MICHEL DE MONTAIGNE

Weak arguments are often thrust before my path; but although they are most unsubstantial, it is not easy to destroy them. There is not a more difficult feat known than to cut through a cushion with a sword.

RICHARD WHATELY

Any fact is better established by two or three good testimonies than by a thousand arguments.

NATHANIEL EMMONS

The sounder your argument, the more satisfaction you get out of it.

ED HOWE

Argument, as usually managed, is the worst sort of conversation.

JONATHAN SWIFT

ARISTOCRACY *Also see:* ANCESTRY, KING, RANK.

What is aristocracy? A corporation of the best, of the bravest.

THOMAS CARLYLE

I am an aristocrat. I love liberty; I hate equality.

JOHN RANDOLPH

Democracy means government by the uneducated, while aristocracy means government by the badly educated.

GILBERT K. CHESTERTON

There is a natural aristocracy among men. The grounds of this are virtue and talent.

THOMAS CARLYLE

Aristocracy is always cruel.

WENDELL PHILLIPS

Some will always be above others. Destroy the equality today, and it will appear again tomorrow.

RALPH WALDO EMERSON

The aristocrat is the democrat ripe and gone to seed.

RALPH WALDO EMERSON

ART *Also see:* ARTIST.

If art is to nourish the roots of our culture, society must set the artist free to follow his vision wherever it takes him.

JOHN FITZGERALD KENNEDY

Art, like morality, consists in drawing the line somewhere.

GILBERT K. CHESTERTON

Art is an effort to create, beside the real world, a more human world.

ANDRÉ MAUROIS

Art is the most intense mode of individualism that the world has known.

OSCAR WILDE

The art of a people is a true mirror of their minds.

JAWAHARLAL NEHRU

The course of Nature is the art of God.

EDWARD YOUNG

Art is a form of catharsis.

DOROTHY PARKER

In art the hand can never execute anything higher than the heart can inspire.

RALPH WALDO EMERSON

Science and art belong to the whole world, and before them vanish the barriers of nationality.

JOHANN WOLFGANG VON GOETHE

Art is a collaboration between God and the artist, and the less the artist does the better.

ANDRÉ GIDE

Supreme art is a traditional statement of certain heroic and religious truth, passed on from age to age, modified by individual genius, but never abandoned.

WILLIAM BUTLER YEATS

The true work of art is but a shadow of the divine perfection.

MICHELANGELO

Nothing is so poor and melancholy as art that is interested in itself and not in its subject.

GEORGE SANTAYANA

Art is the desire of a man to express himself, to record the reactions of his personality to the world he lives in.

AMY LOWELL

We must never forget that art is not a form of propaganda, it is a form of truth.

JOHN FITZGERALD KENNEDY

ARTIST Also see: ART.

The artist does not illustrate science (but) he frequently responds to the same interests that a scientist does.

LEWIS MUMFORD

The work of art may have a moral effect, but to demand moral purpose from the artist is to make him ruin his work.

JOHANN WOLFGANG VON GOETHE

One puts into one's art what one has not been capable of putting into one's existence. It is because he was unhappy that God created the world.

HENRI DE MONTHERLANT

Every artist dips his brush in his own soul, and paints his own nature into his pictures.

HENRY WARD BEECHER

ASPIRATION ... *See* AMBITION.

ASSASSINATION *Also see:* MURDER, SLANDER.

Assassination: the extreme form of censorship.

GEORGE BERNARD SHAW

Assassination has never changed the history of the world.

BENJAMIN DISRAELI

Woe to the hand that shed this costly blood.

WILLIAM SHAKESPEARE

Yet each man kills the thing he loves, By each let his be heard, Some do it with a bitter look, Some with a flattering word, The coward does it with a kiss, The brave man with a sword!

OSCAR WILDE

Some men are alive simply because it is against the law to kill them.

ED HOWE

I'm proud of the fact that I never invented weapons to kill.

THOMAS A. EDISON

ATHEISM *Also see:* AGNOSTICISM, DOUBT, GOD, SKEPTICISM, SOUL.

I am an atheist, thank God!

ANONYMOUS

I don't believe in God because I don't believe in Mother Goose.

CLARENCE DARROW

Nobody talks so constantly about God as those who insist that there is no God.

HEYWOOD BROUN

There are no atheists in the foxholes of Bataan.

DOUGLAS MACARTHUR

Atheism is rather in the life than in the heart of man.

FRANCIS BACON

An atheist is a man who has no invisible means of support.

FULTON J. SHEEN

AUTHORITY *Also see:* DEMOCRACY, GOVERNMENT, KING, POWER, PRESIDENT.

Nothing is more gratifying to the mind of man than power or dominion.

JOSEPH ADDISON

Every great advance in natural knowledge has involved the absolute rejection of authority.

THOMAS HUXLEY

The wisest have the most authority.

PLATO

All authority belongs to the people.

THOMAS JEFFERSON

If you wish to know what a man is, place him in authority.

YUGOSLAV PROVERB

Authority without wisdom is like a heavy ax without an edge, fitter to bruise than polish.

ANNE BRADSTREET

Authority is no stronger than the man who wields it.

DOLORES E. MCGUIRE

AUTOMATION *Also see:* MACHINE, SCIENCE, WORK.

The Christian notion of the possibility of redemption is incomprehensible to the computer.

VANCE PACKARD

If it keeps up, men will atrophy all his limbs but the pushbutton finger.

FRANK LLOYD WRIGHT

Jobs are physically easier, but the worker now takes home worries instead of an aching back.

HOMER BIGART

We live in a time when automation is ushering in a second industrial revolution.

ADLAI E. STEVENSON

AVARICE *Also see:* GREED, MISER, MONEY, SELFISHNESS, WEALTH.

If you would abolish avarice, you must abolish its mother, luxury.

CICERO

Avarice increases with the increasing pile of gold.

JUVENAL

Avarice in old age is foolish; for what can be more absurd than to increase our provisions for the road the nearer we approach to our journey's end.

CICERO

The avaricious man is like the barren sandy ground of the desert which sucks in all the rain and dew with greediness, but yields no fruitful herbs or plants for the benefit of others.

ZENO

Avarice is always poor.

SAMUEL JOHNSON

AVERAGE *Also see:* CONFORMITY, MAJORITY, MODERATION.

The average person puts only 25% of his energy and ability into his work. The world takes off its hat to those who put in more than 50% of their capacity, and stands on its head for those few and far between souls who devote 100%.

ANDREW CARNEGIE

I am only an average man but, by George, I work harder at it than the average man.

THEODORE ROOSEVELT

Not doing more than the average is what keeps the average down.

WILLIAM M. WINANS

A jury is a group of twelve people of average ignorance.

HERBERT SPENCER

BABY *Also see:* BIRTH, CHILDREN, FAMILY.

A baby is God's opinion that the world should go on.

CARL SANDBURG

The worst feature of a new baby is its mother's singing.

KIN HUBBARD

Babies are such a nice way to start people.

DON HEROLD

When the first baby laughed for the first time, the laugh broke into a thousand pieces and they all went skipping about, and that was the beginning of fairies.

JAMES MATTHEW BARRIE

BACHELOR

By persistently remaining single a man converts himself into a permanent public temptation.

OSCAR WILDE

Bachelors know more about women than married men; if they didn't, they'd be married too.

H. L. MENCKEN

A bachelor never quite gets over the idea that he is a thing of beauty and a boy forever.

HELEN ROWLAND

Bachelors have consciences, married men have wives.

H. L. MENCKEN

The only good husbands stay bachelors: They're too considerate to get married.

FINLEY PETER DUNNE

A single man has not nearly the value he would have in a state of union. He is an incomplete animal. He resembles the odd half of a pair of scissors.

BENJAMIN FRANKLIN

BARGAIN Also see: ADVERTISING, ECONOMY, GAIN, SALES-MANSHIP.

. . . anything a customer thinks a store is losing money on.

KIN HUBBARD

Sometimes one pays most for the things one gets for nothing.

ALBERT EINSTEIN

Nothing is cheap which is superfluous, for what one does not need, is dear at a penny.

PLUTARCH

There are very honest people who do not think that they have had a bargain unless they have cheated a merchant.

ANATOLE FRANCE

BEAUTY Also see: APPEARANCE, ART, ARTIST, BLUSH, CHARM.

Beauty is not caused. It is.

EMILY DICKINSON

There is no cosmetic for beauty like happiness.

COUNTESS OF BLESSINGTON

Nothing's beautiful from every point of view.

HORACE

Beauty is power; a smile is its sword.

CHARLES READE

Truth exists for the wise, beauty for the feeling heart.

JOHANN VON SCHILLER

Beauty is the first present nature gives to women and the first it takes away.

GEORGE BROSSIN MÉRÉ

In every man's heart there is a secret nerve that answers to the vibrations of beauty.

CHRISTOPHER MORLEY

Beauty is only skin deep, but it's a valuable asset if you're poor or haven't any sense.

KIN HUBBARD

BEHAVIOR Also see: CHARM, COURTESY, MANNERS, MORAL-ITY.

Behavior is a mirror in which every one displays his image.

JOHANN WOLFGANG VON GOETHE

Be nice to people on your way up because you'll meet them on your way down.

WILSON MIZNER

As a rule, there is no surer way to the dislike of men than to behave well where they have behaved badly.

LEW WALLACE

With a gentleman I am always a gentleman and a half, and with a fraud I try to be a fraud and a half.

OTTO VON BISMARCK

The reason the way of the transgressor is hard is because it's so crowded.

KIN HUBBARD

When man learns to understand and control his own behavior as well as he is learning to understand and control the behavior of crop plants and domestic animals, he may be justified in believing that he has become civilized.

E. C. STAKMAN

BELIEF Also see: ATHEISM, BUSINESS, CALAMITY, CONFI-

DENCE, CREDULITY, FAITH, HOPE, OPIN-
ION, PREJUDICE, RELIGION, THEORY,
TRUST.

Nothing is so firmly believed as that which we least know.

MICHEL DE MONTAIGNE

It is always easier to believe than to deny. Our minds are naturally affirmative.

JOHN BURROUGHS

One person with a belief is equal to a force of ninety-nine who have only interests.

JOHN STUART MILL

Every time a child says "I don't believe in fairies" there is a little fairy somewhere that falls down dead.

JOHN MATTHEW BARRIE

Believe that life is worth living, and your belief will help create the fact.

WILLIAM JAMES

The practical effect of a belief is the real test of its soundness.

JAMES A. FROUDE

BENEVOLENCE . . . *See* GENEROSITY.

BIBLE *Also see:* GOD.

The Bible is a window in this prison of hope, through which we look into eternity.

JOHN SULLIVAN DWIGHT

The total absence of humor from the Bible is one of the most singular things in all literature.

ALFRED NORTH WHITEHEAD

All human discoveries seem to be made only for the purpose of confirming more and more strongly the truths that come on high and are contained in the sacred writings.

JOHN F. HERSCHEL

To say nothing of its holiness or authority, the Bible contains more specimens of genius and taste than any other volume in existence.

WALTER S. LANDOR

Most people are bothered by those passages of Scripture they do not understand, but the passages that bother me are those I do understand.

MARK TWAIN

The Bible may be the truth, but it is not the whole truth and nothing but the truth.

SAMUEL BUTLER

BIGOTRY *Also see:* INTOLERANCE, OPINION, PERSECUTION, PREJUDICE, RACE, REASON, ZEAL.

Wisdom has never made a bigot, but learning has.

JOSH BILLINGS

A man must be both stupid and uncharitable who believes there is no virtue or truth but on his own side.

JOSEPH ADDISON

The mind of the bigot is like the pupil of the eye; the more light you pour upon it, the more it will contract.

OLIVER WENDELL HOLMES

Bigotry dwarfs the soul by shutting out the truth.

EDWIN HUBBEL CHAPIN

BIRTH *Also see:* ANCESTRY, BABY, BIRTH CONTROL, CHILDREN, DEATH, FAMILY.

About the only thing we have left that actually discriminates in favor of the plain people is the stork.

KIN HUBBARD

There is (sic) two things in life for which we are never fully prepared, and that is—twins.

JOSH BILLINGS

The fate of nations is intimately bound up with their powers of reproduction. All nations and all empires first felt decadence gnawing at them when their birth rate fell off.

BENITO MUSSOLINI

If nature had arranged that husbands and wives should have children alternatively, there would never be more than three in a family.

LAURENCE HOUSMAN

BIRTH CONTROL *Also see:* BIRTH, POPULATION, SEX.

Prevention of birth is a precipitation of murder.

TERTULLIAN

However we may pity the mother whose health and even life is imperiled by the performance of her natural duty, there yet remains no sufficient reason for condoning the direct murder of the innocent.

PIUS XI

No woman can call herself free who does not own and control her body.

No woman can call herself free until she can choose consciously whether she will or will not be a mother.

MARGARET H. SANGER

BLINDNESS *Also see:* EYE.

In the country of the blind the one-eyed man is king.

ERASMUS

A blind man will not thank you for a looking-glass.

THOMAS FULLER

There's none so blind as they that won't see.

JONATHAN SWIFT

My darkness has been filled with the light of intelligence, and behold, the outer day-lit world was stumbling and groping in social blindness.

HELEN KELLER

Hatred is blind, as well as love.

THOMAS FULLER

What a blind person needs is not a teacher but another self.

HELEN KELLER

BLOOD *Also see:* ANCESTRY, CHILDREN, REVOLUTION, WAR.

Blood will tell, but often it tells too much.

DON MARQUIS

No one need think that the world can be ruled without blood. The civil sword shall and must be red and bloody.

MARTIN LUTHER

The future can be anything we want it to be, providing we have the faith and that we realize that peace, no less than war, required "blood and sweat and tears."

CHARLES F. KETTERING

The blood of the martyrs is the seed of the church.

TERTULLIAN

Peace, above all things, is to be desired, but blood must sometimes be spilled to obtain it on equable and lasting terms.

ANDREW JACKSON

Blood is a cleansing and sanctifying thing, and the nation that regards it as the final horror has lost its manhood . . . there are many things more horrible than bloodshed, and slavery is one of them!

PADRAIC PEARSE

BLUSH *Also see:* CRIME.

Man is the only animal that blushes. Or needs to.

MARK TWAIN

When a girl ceases to blush, she has lost the most powerful charm of her beauty.

GREGORY I

The man that blushes is not quite a brute.

EDWARD YOUNG

BOASTING . . . *See* VANITY.

BODY *Also see:* HEALTH, MORALITY, SOUL.

A healthy body is a guest chamber for the soul: a sick body is a prison.

FRANCIS BACON

A human being is an ingenious assembly of portable plumbing.

CHRISTOPHER MORLEY

We are bound to our bodies like an oyster is to its shell.

PLATO

All of us have mortal bodies, composed of perishable matter, but the soul lives forever: it is a portion of the Deity housed in our bodies.

FLAVIUS JOSEPHUS

Our body is a well-set clock, which keeps good time, but if it be too much or indiscreetly tampered with, the alarm runs out before the hour.

JOSEPH HALL

BOLDNESS *Also see:* CONFIDENCE, COURAGE, COWARDICE, GALLANTRY.

Fortune befriends the bold.

JOHN DRYDEN

Who bravely dares must sometimes risk a fall.

TOBIAS G. SMOLLETT

Fools rush in where angels fear to tread.

ALEXANDER POPE

When you cannot make up your mind which of two evenly balanced courses of action you should take—choose the bolder.

W. J. SLIM

Boldness is ever blind, for it sees not dangers and inconveniences; whence it is bad in council though good in execution.

FRANCIS BACON

It is wonderful what strength of purpose and boldness and energy of will are roused by the assurance that we are doing our duty.

WALTER SCOTT

In great straits and when hope is small, the boldest counsels are the safest.

LIVY

BOOK *Also see:* BIBLE, CENSORSHIP, HISTORY, LEARNING, LITERATURE, READING, WORD.

If I have not read a book before, it is, for all intents and purposes, new to me whether it was printed yesterday or three hundred years ago.

WILLIAM HAZLITT

That is a good book which is opened with expectation and closed in profit.

AMOS BRONSON ALCOTT

Some books leave us free and some books make us free.

RALPH WALDO EMERSON

The books that help you the most are those which make you think the most.

THEODORE PARKER

A book is a mirror: If an ass peers into it, you can't expect an apostle to look out.

G. C. LICHTENBERG

Read the best books first, or you may not have a chance to read them all.

HENRY DAVID THOREAU

This is the best book ever written by any man on the wrong side of a question of which he is profoundly ignorant.

THOMAS B. MACAULAY

A house is not a home unless it contains food and fire for the mind as well as the body.

MARGARET FULLER

Some books are to be tasted; others swallowed; and some to be chewed and digested.

FRANCIS BACON

The man who does not read good books has no advantage over the man who can't read them.

MARK TWAIN

Books, like friends, should be few and well chosen.

SAMUEL PATERSON

BORE and BOREDOM *Also see:* COMMUNICATION, CONVERSATION, LOQUACITY.

Bore, n. A person who talks when you wish him to listen.

AMBROSE BIERCE

There are few wild beasts more to be dreaded than a communicative man having nothing to communicate.

CHRISTIAN NESTELL BOVEE

The capacity of human beings to bore one another seems to be vastly greater than that of any other animal.

H. L. MENCKEN

Any subject can be made interesting, and therefore any subject can be made boring.

HILAIRE BELLOC

The man who lets himself be bored is even more contemptible than the bore.

SAMUEL BUTLER

A man who spends so much time talking about himself that you can't talk about yourself.

MELVILLE D. LANDON

A guy who wraps up a two-minute idea in a two-hour vocabulary.

WALTER WINCHELL

BORROWING *Also see:* CREDIT, DEBT.

The shoulders of a borrower are always a little straighter than those of a beggar.

MORRIS LEOPOLD ERNST

If you would know the value of money, go try to borrow some; for he that goes a-borrowing goes a-sorrowing.

BENJAMIN FRANKLIN

The human species, according to the best theory I can form of it, is composed of two distinct races: the men who borrow, and the men who lend.

CHARLES LAMB

Only an inventor knows how to borrow, and every man is or should be an inventor.

RALPH WALDO EMERSON

Live within your income, even if you have to borrow money to do so.

JOSH BILLINGS

Lots of fellows think a home is only good to borrow money on.

KIN HUBBARD

He who borrows sells his freedom.

GERMAN PROVERB

Creditors have better memories than debtors.

PROVERB

BOYS *Also see:* AGE, BACHELOR, CHILDREN, GIRLS, YOUTH.

I am convinced that every boy, in his heart, would rather steal second base than an automobile.

THOMAS CAMBELL CLARK

When you can't do anything else to a boy, you can make him wash his face.

ED HOWE

Boys will be boys, and so will a lot of middle-aged men.

KIN HUBBARD

Boys are beyond the range of anybody's sure understanding, at least when they are between the ages of 18 months and 90 years.

JAMES THURBER

A man can never quite understand a boy, even when he has been a boy.

GILBERT K. CHESTERTON

Of all wild beasts, the most difficult to manage.

PLATO

A boy is a magical creature—you can lock him out of your workshop, but you can't lock him out of your heart.

ALLAN BECK

BREVITY *Also see:* CONVERSATION, LOQUACITY, SIMPLICITY, WORDS.

The more you say, the less people remember. The fewer the words, the greater the profit.

FÉNELON

Brevity is the best recommendation of speech, whether in a senator or an orator.

CICERO

If you would be pungent, be brief; for it is with words as with sunbeams—the more they are condensed, the deeper they burn.

ROBERT SOUTHEY

The fewer the words, the better the prayer.

MARTIN LUTHER

Brevity is a great charm of eloquence.

CICERO

BROTHERHOOD *Also see:* CITIZENSHIP, EQUALITY, FAMILY, FRIENDSHIP, HUMANITY, MAN, SELFISHNESS.

On this shrunken globe, men can no longer live as strangers.

ADLAI E. STEVENSON

We must learn to live together as brothers or perish together as fools.

MARTIN LUTHER KING

We do not want the men of another color for our brothers-in-law, but we do want them for our brothers.

BOOKER T. WASHINGTON

Brotherhood is the very price and condition of man's survival.

CARLOS P. ROMULO

We live in a world that has narrowed into a neighborhood before it has broadened into a brotherhood.

LYNDON BAINES JOHNSON

It is easier to love humanity than to love one's neighbor.

ERIC HOFFER

BUSINESS *Also see:* ACTION, ADVERTISING, EMPLOYMENT, INDUSTRY, FINANCE, PURSUIT, SPECULATION, WORK.

There are two times in a man's life when he should not speculate: when he can't afford it, and when he can.

MARK TWAIN

All business proceeds on beliefs, or judgments of probabilities, and not on certainties.

CHARLES ELIOT

It is not the crook in modern business that we fear but the honest man who does not know what he is doing.

OWEN D. YOUNG

The successful business man sometimes makes his money by ability and experience; but he generally makes it by mistake.

GILBERT K. CHESTERTON

Business is a combination of war and sport.

ANDRÉ MAUROIS

A man to carry on a successful business must have imagination. He must see things as in a vision, a dream of the whole thing.

CHARLES M. SCHWAB

The best mental effort in the game of business is concentrated on the major problem of securing the consumer's dollar before the other fellow gets it.

STUART CHASE

A friendship founded on business is better than a business founded on friendship.

JOHN D. ROCKEFELLER

BUSY *Also see:* BUSINESS, INDUSTRY, PERSEVERANCE, WORK.

It is not enough to be busy; so are the ants. The question is: What are we busy about?

HENRY DAVID THOREAU

The busy have no time for tears.

LORD BYRON

Whoever admits that he is too busy to improve his methods has acknowledged himself to be at the end of his rope. And that is always the saddest predicament which anyone can get into.

J. OGDEN ARMOUR

What we hope ever to do with ease, we must learn first to do with diligence.

SAMUEL JOHNSON

The successful people are the ones who can think up things for the rest of the world to keep busy at.

DON MARQUIS

Who makes quick use of the moment, is a genius of prudence.

JOHANN KASPAR LAVATER

Occupation is the necessary basis of all enjoyment.

LEIGH HUNT

Busy souls have no time to be busybodies.

AUSTIN O'MALLEY

CALAMITY *Also see:* ADVERSITY, AFFLICTION, ANTICIPA-
TION, CRISIS, DEBT, MISERY, WAR.

Calamities are of two kinds. Misfortune to ourselves, and good fortune
to others.

AMBROSE BIERCE

He who forsees calamities, suffers them twice over.

BEILBY PORTEUS

Calamity is the perfect glass wherein we truly see and know ourselves.

WILLIAM DAVENANT

Calamity is the test of integrity.

SAMUEL RICHARDSON

It is only from the belief of the goodness and wisdom of a supreme being,
that our calamities can be borne in the manner which becomes a man.

HENRY MACKENZIE

CANDOR *Also see:* HONESTY, SINCERITY, TRUTH.

Candor is the brightest gem of criticism.

BENJAMIN DISRAELI

Examine what is said, not him who speaks.

ARABIAN PROVERB

Friends, if we be honest with ourselves, we shall be honest with each
other.

GEORGE MACDONALD

Frank and explicit—that is the right line to take when you wish to conceal
your own mind and confuse the minds of others.

BENJAMIN DISRAELI

Nothing astonishes men so much as common sense and plain dealing.

RALPH WALDO EMERSON

There is no wisdom like frankness.

BENJAMIN DISRAELI

A "No" uttered from deepest conviction is better and greater than a "Yes" merely uttered to please, or what is worse, to avoid trouble.

MAHATMA GANDHI

CAPITALISM *Also see:* BUSINESS, FINANCE, MONEY.

The fundamental idea of modern capitalism is not the right of the individual to possess and enjoy what he has earned, but the thesis that the exercise of this right redounds to the general good.

RALPH BARTON PERRY

Capital is that part of wealth which is devoted to obtaining further wealth.

ALFRED MARSHALL

The dynamo of our economic system is self-interest which may range from mere petty greed to admirable types of self-expression.

FELIX FRANKFURTER

The inherent vice of capitalism is the unequal sharing of blessings; the inherent virtue of socialism is the equal sharing of miseries.

WINSTON CHURCHILL

Capitalism and communism stand at opposite poles. Their essential difference is this: The communist, seeing the rich man and his fine home, says: "No man should have so much." The capitalist, seeing the same thing, says: "All men should have as much."

PHELPS ADAMS

CATASTROPHE ... *See* CALAMITY.

CAUSE *Also see:* EFFICIENCY, MOTIVE, PURPOSE, RESULT.

That cause is strong, which has not a multitude, but a strong man behind it.

JAMES RUSSELL LOWELL

We are all ready to be savage in some cause. The difference between a good man and a bad one is the choice of the cause.

WILLIAM JAMES

No cause is helpless if it is just. Errors, no matter how popular, carry the seeds of their own destruction.

JOHN W. SCOVILLE

No man is worth his salt who is not ready at all times to risk his well-being, to risk his body, to risk his life, in a great cause.

THEODORE ROOSEVELT

The humblest citizen of all the land, when clad in the armor of a righteous cause, is stronger than all the hosts of Error.

WILLIAM JENNINGS BRYAN

The mark of the immature man is that he wants to die nobly for a cause, while the mark of a mature man is that he wants to live humbly for one.

WILHELM STEKEL

The probability that we may fail in the struggle ought not to deter us from the support of a cause we believe to be just.

ABRAHAM LINCOLN

Ours is an abiding faith in the cause of human freedom. We know it is God's cause.

THOMAS E. DEWEY

Men are blind in their own cause.

HEYWOOD BROUN

It is not a field of a few acres of ground, but a cause, that we are defending, and whether we defeat the enemy in one battle, or by degrees, the consequences will be the same.

THOMAS PAINE

Respectable men and women content with good and easy living are missing some of the most important things in life. Unless you give yourself to some great cause you haven't even begun to live.

WILLIAM P. MERRILL

CAUTION Also see: ADVICE, COWARDICE, DISCRETION, PRUDENCE, SAFETY, VIGILANCE.

I don't like these cold, precise perfect people, who, in order not to speak wrong, never speak at all, and in order not to do wrong, never do anything.

HENRY WARD BEECHER

Among mortals second thoughts are wisest.

EURIPIDES

The chief danger in life is that you may take too many precautions.

ALFRED ADLER

Deliberate with caution, but act with decision; and yield with graciousness, or oppose with firmness.

CHARLES HOLE

Be slow of tongue and quick of eye.

MIGUEL DE CERVANTES

It is a good thing to learn caution from the misfortunes of others.

PUBLILIUS SYRUS

CENSORSHIP Also see: ASSASSINATION, FREEDOM, FREEDOM

OF PRESS, FREEDOM OF SPEECH, NEWSPAPER.

Only the suppressed word is dangerous.

LUDWIG BÖRNE

I am opposed to censorship. Censors are pretty sure fools. I have no confidence in the suppression of everyday facts.

JAMES ROBINSON

Censorship reflects a society's lack of confidence in itself.

POTTER STEWART

He is always the severest censor of the merit of others who has the least worth of his own.

ELIAS LYMAN MAGGON

Every burned book enlightens the world.

RALPH WALDO EMERSON

Pontius Pilate was the first great censor, and Jesus Christ the first great victim of censorship.

BEN LINDSAY

If there had been a censorship of the press in Rome we should have had today neither Horace nor Juvenal, nor the philosophical writings of Cicero.

VOLTAIRE

CENSURE *Also see:* ABUSE, CRITICISM.

Censure is the tax a man pays to the public for being eminent.

JONATHAN SWIFT

The readiest and surest way to get rid of censure, is to correct ourselves.

DEMOSTHENES

He who would acquire fame must not show himself afraid of censure. The dread of censure is the death of genius.

WILLIAM GILMORE SIMMS

The censure of those who are opposed to us, is the highest commendation that can be given us.

SEIGNEUR DE SAINT-EVREMOND

It is folly for an eminent man to think of escaping censure, and a weakness to be affected with it. All the illustrious persons of antiquity, and indeed of every age in the world, have passed through this fiery persecution.

JOSEPH ADDISON

I find that the pain of a little censure, even when it is unfounded, is more acute than the pleasure of much praise.

THOMAS JEFFERSON

CERTAINTY *Also see:* CONFIDENCE, DOUBT, FACT, KNOWL-
EDGE, QUESTION, SUCCESS.

To be absolutely certain about something, one must know everything or
nothing about it.

OLIN MILLER

Convictions are more dangerous foes of truth than lies.

NIETZSCHE

In these matters the only certainty is that there is nothing certain.

PLINY THE ELDER

If we begin with certainties, we shall end in doubts; but if we begin with
doubts, and are patient in them, we shall end in certainties.

FRANCIS BACON

There is nothing certain in a man's life but that he must lose it.

OWEN MEREDITH

CHANGE *Also see:* IMPROVEMENT, PROGRESS, REFORM, REV-
OLUTION, VARIETY.

All change is not growth; all movement is not forward.

ELLEN GLASGOW

He that will not apply new remedies must expect new evils.

FRANCIS BACON

The world hates change, yet it is the only thing that has brought progress.

CHARLES F. KETTERING

Everyone thinks of changing the world, but no one thinks of changing
himself.

LEO TOLSTOI

We are restless because of incessant change, but we would be frightened
if change were stopped.

LYMAN LLOYD BRYSON

There is nothing permanent except change.

HERACLITUS

Things do not change, we do.

HENRY DAVID THOREAU

Christians are supposed not merely to endure change, nor even to profit
by it, but to cause it.

HARRY EMERSON FOSDICK

I've never met a person, I don't care what his condition, in whom I could not see possibilities. I don't care how much a man may consider himself a failure, I believe in him, for he can change the thing that is wrong in his life any time he is ready and prepared to do it. Whenever he develops the desire, he can take away from his life the thing that is defeating it. The capacity for reformation and change lies within.

PRESTON BRADLEY

Life belongs to the living, and he who lives must be prepared for changes.

JOHANN WOLFGANG VON GOETHE

We emphasize that we believe in change because we were born of it, we have lived by it, we prospered and grew great by it. So the status quo has never been our god, and we ask no one else to bow down before it.

CARL T. ROWAN

CHARACTER Also see: FAME, INDIVIDUALITY, MORALITY, PERSONALITY, QUALITY, REPUTATION, TEMPER.

Let us not say, Every man is the architect of his own fortune; but let us say, Every man is the architect of his own character.

GEORGE DANA BOARDMAN

Weakness of character is the only defect which cannot be amended.

FRANÇOIS DE LA ROCHEFOUCAULD

Characters do not change. Opinions alter, but characters are only developed.

BENJAMIN DISRAELI

You must look into people, as well as at them.

LORD CHESTERFIELD

Make the most of yourself, for that is all there is of you.

RALPH WALDO EMERSON

Character is not made in a crisis—it is only exhibited.

ROBERT FREEMAN

A man never discloses his own character so clearly as when he describes another's.

JEAN PAUL RICHTER

The four cornerstones of character on which the structure of this nation was built are: Initiative, Imagination, Individuality and Independence.

EDWARD RICKENBACKER

There is no such thing as a "self-made" man. We are made up of thousands of others. Everyone who has ever done a kind deed for us, or spoken one word of encouragement to us, has entered into the make-up of our character and of our thoughts, as well as our success.

GEORGE MATTHEW ADAMS

Every man has three characters—that which he exhibits, that which he has, and that which he thinks he has.

ALPHONSE KARR

CHARITY *Also see:* GENEROSITY, HEART, HELP, HUMANITY, KINDNESS, LOVE, OSTENTATION, TOLERANCE.

Charity: a thing that begins at home, and usually stays there.

ELBERT HUBBARD

Not he who has much is rich, but he who gives much.

ERICH FROMM

As the purse is emptied, the heart is filled.

VICTOR HUGO

He who waits to do a great deal of good at once, will never do anything.

SAMUEL JOHNSON

The truly generous is the truly wise, and he who loves not others, lives unblest.

HENRY HOME

A bone to the dog is not charity. Charity is the bone shared with the dog, when you are just as hungry as the dog.

JACK LONDON

Though I speak with the tongues of men and angels and have not charity, I am become as sounding brass, or a tinkling cymbal.

I CORINTHIANS 13:1-3

Charity sees the need, not the cause.

GERMAN PROVERB

With malice toward none, with charity for all, with firmness in the right as God gives us to see the right, let us finish the work we are in.

ABRAHAM LINCOLN

Every charitable act is a stepping stone towards heaven.

HENRY WARD BEECHER

If you haven't got any charity in your heart, you have the worst kind of heart trouble.

BOB HOPE

What we frankly give, forever is our own.

GEORGE GRANVILLE

One must be poor to know the luxury of giving.

GEORGE ELIOT

It is more blessed to give than to receive.

ACTS.20:35

CHARM *Also see:* BEAUTY, BLUSH, GRACE.

A really plain woman is one who, however beautiful, neglects to charm.

EDGAR SALTUS

There is no personal charm so great as the charm of a cheerful temperament.

HENRY VAN DYKE

Charm is more than beauty.

YIDDISH PROVERB

CHEERFULNESS *Also see:* CHARM, HAPPINESS, HUMOR, JOY, OPTIMISM, SMILE.

A good laugh is sunshine in a house.

WILLIAM MAKEPEACE THACKERAY

The best way to cheer yourself up is to try to cheer somebody else up.

MARK TWAIN

So of cheerfulness, or a good temper, the more it is spent, the more it remains.

RALPH WALDO EMERSON

The true source of cheerfulness is benevolence.

P. GODWIN

Wondrous is the strength of cheerfulness, and its power of endurance—the cheerful man will do more in the same time, will do it better, will preserve it longer, than the sad or sullen.

THOMAS CARLYLE

I feel an earnest and humble desire, and shall till I die, to increase the stock of harmless cheerfulness.

CHARLES DICKENS

Health is the condition of wisdom, and the sign is cheerfulness—an open and noble temper.

RALPH WALDO EMERSON

Cheer up! The worst is yet to come!

PHILANDER JOHNSON

The cheerful live longest in years, and afterwards in our regards. Cheerfulness is the off-shoot of goodness.

CHRISTIAN NESTELL BOVEE

CHILDREN Also see: BIRTH, BOYS, FAMILY, FATHER, GIRLS, YOUTH.

It is dangerous to confuse children with angels.

DAVID FYFE

Childhood sometimes does pay a second visit to man; youth never.

ANNA JAMESON

The best way to make children good is to make them happy.

OSCAR WILDE

The child is father of the man.

WILLIAM WORDSWORTH

The potential possibilities of any child are the most intriguing and stimulating in all creation.

RAY L. WILBUR

Pretty much all the honest truth telling there is in the world is done by children.

OLIVER WENDELL HOLMES

Don't take up a man's time talking about the smartness of your children; he wants to talk to you about the smartness of his children.

ED HOWE

Children are our most valuable natural resource.

HERBERT HOOVER

Better to be driven out from among men than to be disliked of children.

RICHARD HENRY DANA

A child is a curly, dimpled lunatic.

RALPH WALDO EMERSON

Children in a family are like flowers in a bouquet: there's always one determined to face in an opposite direction from the way the arranger desires.

MARCELENE COX

We've had bad luck with our kids—they've all grown up.

CHRISTOPHER MORELY

Children are poor men's riches.

ENGLISH PROVERB

If a child annoys you, quiet him by brushing his hair. If this doesn't work, use the other side of the brush on the other end of the child.

ANONYMOUS

CHOICE Also see: DECISION, DESIRE, DESTINY, FREEDOM, LIBERTY.

Between two evils, choose neither; between two goods, choose both.

TRYON EDWARDS

Life often presents us with a choice of evils rather than of goods.

CHARLES CALEB COLTON

When you have to make a choice and don't make it, that in itself is a choice.

WILLIAM JAMES

He who chooses the beginning of a road chooses the place it leads to. It is the means that determine the end.

HARRY EMERSON FOSDICK

A man is too apt to forget that in this world he cannot have everything. A choice is all that is left him.

K. MATHEWS

CHRISTIANITY Also see: BROTHERHOOD, CHURCH, FAITH, RELIGION.

Christianity is a battle, not a dream.

WENDELL PHILLIPS

Christian: one who believes that the New Testament is a divinely inspired book admirably suited to the spiritual needs of his neighbors.

AMBROSE BIERCE

Christianity has not been tried and found wanting; it has been found difficult and not tried.

GILBERT K. CHESTERTON

No man ever repented of being a Christian on his death bed.

HANNAH MORE

Christianity does not remove you from the world and its problems; it makes you fit to live in it, triumphantly and usefully.

CHARLES TEMPLETON

If a man cannot be a Christian in the place where he is, he cannot be a Christian anywhere.

HENRY WARD BEECHER

Christianity is a missionary religion, converting, advancing, aggressive, encompassing the world; a non-missionary church is in the band of death.

FRIEDRICH MAX MÜLLER

CHURCH and STATE *Also see:* CHRISTIANITY, RELIGION.

The church is actually patronized by the social order as a means of stabilizing and perpetuating the existing system.

C. C. MORRISON

In the relationship between man and religion, the state is firmly committed to a position of neutrality.

THOMAS CAMPBELL CLARK

The church is the only place where someone speaks to me and I do not have to answer back.

CHARLES DEGAULLE

No religion can long continue to maintain its purity when the church becomes the subservient vassal of the state.

FELIX ADLER

CITIZENSHIP *Also see:* AMERICA, COUNTRY, DUTY, HEROISM, PATRIOTISM, RIGHTS.

Citizenship consists in the service of the country.

JAWAHARLAL NEHRU

Voting is the least arduous of a citizen's duties. He has the prior and harder duty of making up his mind.

RALPH BARTON PERRY

The first requisite of a good citizen in this republic of ours is that he should be able and willing to pull his weight.

THEODORE ROOSEVELT

Citizenship comes first today in our crowded world. . . . No man can enjoy the privileges of education and thereafter with a clear conscience break his contract with society.

ISAIAH BOWMAN

Every good citizen makes his country's honor his own, and cherishes it not only as precious but as sacred. He is willing to risk his life in its defense and is conscious that he gains protection while he gives it.

ANDREW JACKSON

Let us at all times remember that all American citizens are brothers of a common country, and should dwell together in bonds of fraternal feeling.

ABRAHAM LINCOLN

Now the trumpet summons us again—not as a call to bear arms, though arms we need—not as a call to battle, though embattled we are—but a call to bear the burden of a long twilight struggle year in and year out, "rejoicing in hope, patient in tribulation"—a struggle against the common enemies of man: tyranny, poverty, disease and war itself.

JOHN FITZGERALD KENNEDY

If you will help run our government in the American way, then there will never be danger of our government running America in the wrong way.

OMAR N. BRADLEY

CIVILIZATION Also see: ADVENTURE, BEHAVIOR, CULTURE, DOUBT, IMPROVEMENT, PROGRESS.

Anyone can be a barbarian; it requires a terrible effort to remain a civilized man.

LEONARD SIDNEY WOOLF

The true test of civilization is, not the census, nor the size of the cities, nor the crops, but the kind of man that the country turns out.

RALPH WALDO EMERSON

Civilization begins with order, grows with liberty, and dies with chaos.

WILL DURANT

You can't say civilization isn't advancing: in every war, they kill you in a new way.

WILL ROGERS

The three great elements of modern civilization, Gunpowder, Printing, and the Protestant Religion.

THOMAS CARLYLE

Civilization is the order and freedom promoting cultural activity.

WILL DURANT

In the advance of civilization, it is new knowledge which paves the way, and the pavement is eternal.

W. R. WHITNEY

Civilization ceases when we no longer respect and no longer put into their correct places the fundamental values, such as work, family and country; such as the individual, honor and religion.

R. P. LEBRET

Every advance in civilization has been denounced as unnatural while it was recent.

BERTRAND RUSSELL

The true civilization is where every man gives to every other every right that he claims for himself.

ROBERT GREEN INGERSOLL

All the things now enjoyed by civilization have been created by some man and sold by another man before anybody really enjoyed the benefits of them.

JAMES G. DALY

CLASS *Also see:* ARISTOCRACY, ORDER, SOCIETY.

All mankind is divided into three classes: those that are immovable, those that are movable, and those that move.

ARABIAN PROVERB

There is nothing to which men cling more tenaciously than the privileges of class.

LEONARD SIDNEY WOOLF

Let him who expects one class of society to prosper in the highest degree, while the other is in distress, try whether one side of the face can smile while the other is pinched.

THOMAS FULLER

The distinctions separating the social classes are false; in the last analysis they rest on force.

ALBERT EINSTEIN

The ignorant classes are the dangerous classes.

HENRY WARD BEECHER

I never would believe that Providence had sent a few men into the world, ready booted and spurred to ride, and millions ready saddled and bridled to be ridden.

RICHARD RUMBOLD

Other lands have their vitality in a few, a class, but we have it in the bulk of our people.

WALT WHITMAN

CLEVERNESS *Also see:* CYNIC, INTELLIGENCE, WIT.

Clever men are good, but they are not the best.

THOMAS CARLYLE

Cleverness is serviceable for everything, sufficient for nothing.

AMIEL

The doctrine of human equality reposes on this: that there is no man really clever who has not found that he is stupid.

GILBERT K. CHESTERTON

Cleverness is not wisdom.

EURIPIDES

The desire to seem clever often keeps us from being so.

FRANÇOIS DE LA ROCHEFOUCAULD

It is great cleverness to know how to conceal our cleverness.

FRANÇOIS DE LA ROCHEFOUCAULD

COMMITTEE

If you want to kill any idea in the world today, get a committee working on it.

CHARLES F. KETTERING

When it comes to facing up to serious problems, each candidate will pledge to appoint a committee. And what is a committee? A group of the unwilling, picked from the unfit, to do the unnecessary. But it all sounds great in a campaign speech.

RICHARD LONG HARKNESS

To get something done a committee should consist of three men, two of whom are absent.

ANONYMOUS

A committee is a group that keeps minutes and loses hours.

MILTON BERLE

A cul-de-sac to which ideas are lured and then quietly strangled.

JOHN A. LINCOLN

COMMON SENSE Also see: CANDOR, INTELLIGENCE, PRUD-
ENCE, REASON, UNDERSTAND-
ING.

Common sense is very uncommon.

HORACE GREELEY

Common sense is in spite of, not as a result of education.

VICTOR HUGO

He was one of those men who possess almost every gift, except the gift of the power to use them.

CHARLES KINGSLEY

Common sense is instinct, and enough of it is genius.

JOSH BILLINGS

Common sense and nature will do a lot to make the pilgrimage of life not too difficult.

W. SOMERSET MAUGHAM

Nothing is more fairly distributed than common sense: no one thinks he needs more of it than he already has.

DESCARTES

Common sense is the knack of seeing things as they are, and doing things as they ought to be done.

JOSH BILLINGS

COMMUNICATION Also see: CONVERSATION, NEWSPAPER, TELEVISION.

A world community can exist only with world communication, which means something more than extensive shortwave facilities scattered about the globe. It means common understanding, a common tradition, common ideas, and common ideals.

ROBERT M. HUTCHINS

News is that which comes from the North, East, West and South, and if it comes from only one point on the compass, then it is a class publication and not news.

BENJAMIN DISRAELI

The fantastic advances in the field of electronic communication constitute a greater danger to the privacy of the individual.

EARL WARREN

We shall never be able to remove suspicion and fear as potential causes of war until communication is permitted to flow, free and open, across international boundaries.

HARRY S. TRUMAN

COMMUNISM Also see: ARISTOCRACY, CAPITALISM, DEMOCRACY.

Communism is a society where each one works according to his abilities and gets according to his needs.

PIERRE JOSEPH PROUDHON

The theory of Communism may be summed up in one sentence: abolish all private property.

KARL MARX

Communism possesses a language which every people can understand—its elements are hunger, envy, and death.

HEINRICH HEINE

A communist is like a crocodile: when it opens its mouth you cannot tell whether it is trying to smile or preparing to eat you up.

WINSTON CHURCHILL

Communism is the death of the soul. It is the organization of total conformity—in short, of tyranny—and it is committed to making tyranny universal.

ADLAI E. STEVENSON

Communism has nothing to do with love. Communism is an excellent hammer which we use to destroy our enemy.

MAO TSE-TUNG

I never agree with Communists or any other kind of kept men.

H. L. MENCKEN

Communism means barbarism.

JAMES RUSSELL LOWELL

COMPASSION *Also see:* KINDNESS, MERCY, PITY, SYMPATHY.

The dew of compassion is a tear.

LORD BYRON

The mind is no match with the heart in persuasion; constitutionality is no match with compassion.

EVERETT M. DIRKSEN

The value of compassion cannot be over-emphasized. Anyone can criticize. It takes a true believer to be compassionate. No greater burden can be borne by an individual than to know no one cares or understands.

ARTHUR H. STAINBACK

Man may dismiss compassion from his heart, but God never will.

WILLIAM COWPER

COMPETITION . . . *See* RIVALRY.

COMPLAINT *Also see:* DISCONTENT.

Had we not faults of our own, we should take less pleasure in complaining of others.

FÉNELON

Constant complaint is the poorest sort of pay for all the comforts we enjoy.

BENJAMIN FRANKLIN

I will not be as those who spend the day in complaining of headache, and the night in drinking the wine that gives it.

JOHANN WOLFGANG VON GOETHE

The usual fortune of complaint is to excite contempt more than pity.

SAMUEL JOHNSON

We have no more right to put our discordant states of mind into the lives of those around us and rob them of their sunshine and brightness than we have to enter their houses and steal their silverware.

JULIA MOSS SETON

The wheel that squeaks the loudest is the one that gets the grease.

JOSH BILLINGS

The wheel that squeaks the loudest is the first to be replaced.

ANONYMOUS

COMPLIMENT *Also see:* FLATTERY, PRAISE.

If you can't get a compliment any other way, pay yourself one.

MARK TWAIN

When a man makes a woman his wife, it's the highest compliment he can pay her, and it's usually the last.

HELEN ROWLAND

I have been complimented many times and they always embarrass me; I always feel that they have not said enough.

MARK TWAIN

Don't tell a woman she's pretty; tell her there's no other woman like her, and all roads will open to you.

JULES RENARD

COMPROMISE *Also see:* AGREEMENT, EXPEDIENCY.

Better bend than break.

SCOTTISH PROVERB

Compromise is never anything but an ignoble truce between the duty of a man and the terror of a coward.

REGINALD WRIGHT KAUFFMAN

Compromise makes a good umbrella, but a poor roof; it is temporary expedient, often wise in party politics, almost sure to be unwise in statesmanship.

JAMES RUSSELL LOWELL

It is the weak man who urges compromise—never the strong man.

ELBERT HUBBARD

People talk about the middle of the road as though it were unacceptable. Actually, all human problems, excepting morals, come into the gray areas. Things are not all black and white. There have to be compromises. The middle of the road is all of the usable surface. The extremes, right and left, are in the gutters.

DWIGHT D. EISENHOWER

Life cannot subsist in society but by reciprocal concessions.

SAMUEL JOHNSON

Real life is, to most men, a long second-best, a perpetual compromise between the ideal and the possible; but the world of pure reason knows no compromise, no practical limitations, no barrier to the creative activity.

BERTRAND RUSSELL

From the beginning of our history the country has been afflicted with compromise. It is by compromise that human rights have been abandoned.

CHARLES SUMNER

All government, indeed every human benefit and enjoyment, every virtue, and every prudent act, is founded on compromise and barter.

EDMUND BURKE

CONCEIT . . . *See* VANITY.

CONDUCT . . . *See* BEHAVIOR.

CONFESSION *Also see:* CONSCIENCE, GUILT, SIN.

To confess a fault freely is the next thing to being innocent of it.

PUBLILIUS SYRUS

Nothing spoils a confession like repentance.

ANATOLE FRANCE

It is the confession, not the priest, that gives us absolution.

OSCAR WILDE

Open confession is good for the soul.

SCOTTISH PROVERB

The confession of evil works is the first beginning of good works.

ST. AUGUSTINE

CONFIDENCE *Also see:* BELIEF, BOLDNESS, CENSORSHIP, DOUBT, FAITH, SECURITY, SELF-CONFIDENCE, TRUST.

I have great faith in fools—self-confidence my friends call it.

EDGAR ALLAN POE

For they conquer who believe they can.

JOHN DRYDEN

Have confidence that if you have done a little thing well, you can do a bigger thing well too.

STOREY

If once you forfeit the confidence of your fellow-citizens, you can never regain their respect and esteem.

ABRAHAM LINCOLN

Only trust thyself, and another shall not betray thee.

WILLIAM PENN

True prosperity is the result of well-placed confidence in ourselves and our fellow man.

BURT

CONFORMITY *Also see:* ADAPTABILITY, AGREEMENT, CUSTOM, TRADITION.

Conform and be dull.

J. FRANK DOBIE

Our wretched species is so made that those who walk on the well-trodden path always throw stones at those who are showing a new road.

VOLTAIRE

The surest way to corrupt a youth is to instruct him to hold in higher esteem those who think alike than those who think differently.

NIETZSCHE

If a man does not keep pace with his companions, perhaps it is because he hears a different drummer. Let him step to the music which he hears, however measured or far away.

HENRY DAVID THOREAU

Singularity in the right hath ruined many; happy those who are convinced of the general opinion.

BENJAMIN FRANKLIN

We are discreet sheep; we wait to see how the drove is going, and then go with the drove.

MARK TWAIN

CONSCIENCE *Also see:* HONOR, MORALITY, VIRTUE.

Conscience—the only incorruptible thing about us.

HENRY FIELDING

The only tyrant I accept in this world is the still voice within.

MAHATMA GANDHI

No ear can hear nor tongue can tell the tortures of the inward hell!

LORD BYRON

Conscience is a mother-in-law whose visit never ends.

H. L. MENCKEN

Conscience is the mirror of our souls, which represents the errors of our lives in their full shape.

GEORGE BANCROFT

He who sacrifices his conscience to ambition burns a picture to obtain the ashes.

CHINESE PROVERB

'Tis the business of little minds to shrink; but he whose heart is firm, and whose conscience approves his conduct, will pursue his principles unto death.

THOMAS PAINE

CONSCIENTIOUS OBJECTION . . . *See* DRAFT.

CONSERVATION *Also see:* NATURE, POLLUTION.

Conservation is ethically sound. It is rooted in our love of the land, our respect for the rights of others, our devotion to the rule of law.

LYNDON BAINES JOHNSON

As soils are depleted, human health, vitality and intelligence go with them.

LOUIS BROMFIELD

Conservation means the wise use of the earth and its resources for the lasting good of men.

GIFFORD PINCHOT

World-wide practice of Conservation and the fair and continued access by all nations to the resources they need are the two indispensable foundations of continuous plenty and of permanent peace.

GIFFORD PINCHOT

CONTEMPT . . . *See* HATE.

CONTENTMENT *Also see:* AMUSEMENT, ENJOYMENT, HAPPINESS, JOY, PEACE.

The secret of contentment is knowing how to enjoy what you have, and to be able to lose all desire for things beyond your reach.

LIN YUTANG

Nothing contributes more to a persons's peace of mind than having no opinions at all.

G. C. LICHTENBERG

It is right to be contented with what we have, never with what we are.

JAMES MACKINTOSH

One who is contented with what he has done will never become famous for what he will do.

CHRISTIAN NESTELL BOVEE

Since we cannot get what we like, let us like what we can get.

SPANISH PROVERB

My motto is: Contented with little, yet wishing for more.

CHARLES LAMB

If you are content, you have enough to live comfortably.

PLAUTUS

CONTRAST *Also see:* DIFFERENCE.

The superiority of some men is merely local. They are great because their associates are little.

SAMUEL JOHNSON

Where there is much light, the shadow is deep.

JOHANN WOLFGANG VON GOETHE

Joy and grief are never far apart.

ROBERT ELDRIDGE WILLMOTT

The rose and the thorn, and sorrow and gladness are linked together.

SAADI

The lustre of diamonds is invigorated by the interposition of darker bodies; the lights of a picture are created by the shades; the highest pleasure which nature has indulged to sensitive perception is that of rest after fatigue.

SAMUEL JOHNSON

CONVERSATION *Also see:* ARGUMENT, GOSSIP, LOQUACITY.

Conversation is an art in which man has all mankind for competitors.

RALPH WALDO EMERSON

Silence is one great art of conversation.

WILLIAM HAZLITT

Not only to say the right thing in the right place, but far more difficult, to leave unsaid the wrong thing at the tempting moment.

GEORGE SALA

Conceit causes more conversation than wit.

FRANÇOIS DE LA ROCHEFOUCAULD

Conversation would be vastly improved by the constant use of four simple words: I do not know.

ANDRÉ MAUROIS

Never hold anyone by the button or the hand in order to be heard out; for if people are unwilling to hear you, you had better hold your tongue than them.

LORD CHESTERFIELD

Conversation should be pleasant without scurrility, witty without affectation, free without indecency, learned without conceitedness, novel without falsehood.

WILLIAM SHAKESPEARE

COUNTRY *Also see:* AMERICA, CITIZENSHIP, DEMOCRACY, NATION, PATRIOTISM.

So long as you are ready to die for humanity, the life of your country is immortal.

GUISEPPE MAZZINI

I have no country to fight for: my country is the earth, and I am a citizen of the world.

EUGENE V. DEBS

Our country. In her intercourse with foreign nations may she always be in the right; but our country right or wrong!

STEPHEN DECATUR

The world is my country, all mankind are my brethren, and to do good is my religion.

THOMAS PAINE

There is no such thing as a little country. The greatness of a people is no more determined by their number than the greatness of a man is determined by his height.

VICTOR HUGO

The most certain test by which we judge whether a country is really free is the amount of security enjoyed by minorities.

LORD ACTON

Let it be borne on the flag under which we rally in every exigency, that we have one country, one constitution, one destiny.

DANIEL WEBSTER

Our country is the world—our countrymen are mankind.

WILLIAM LLOYD GARRISON

There is no greater sign of a general decay of virtue in a nation, than a want of zeal in its inhabitants for the good of their country.

JOSEPH ADDISON

My kind of loyalty was loyalty to one's country, not to its institutions or its officeholders. The country is the real thing, the substantial thing, the eternal thing; it is the thing to watch over, and care for, and be loyal to.

MARK TWAIN

COURAGE *Also see:* BOLDNESS, COWARDICE, DANGER, DEFEAT, FIRMNESS, HEROISM, SPIRIT.

Courage is almost a contradiction in terms: it means a strong desire to live taking the form of readiness to die.

GILBERT K. CHESTERTON

The greatest test of courage on earth is to bear defeat without losing heart.

ROBERT GREEN INGERSOLL

It takes vision and courage to create—it takes faith and courage to prove.

OWEN D. YOUNG

I'd rather give my life than be afraid to give it.

LYNDON BAINES JOHNSON

Courage is resistance to fear, mastery of fear—not absence of fear.

MARK TWAIN

This is no time for ease and comfort. It is the time to dare and endure.

WINSTON CHURCHILL

Far better it is to dare mighty things, to win glorious triumphs, even though checkered by failure, than to take rank with those poor spirits who neither enjoy much nor suffer much, because they live in the grey twilight that knows not victory nor defeat.

THEODORE ROOSEVELT

Last, but by no means least, courage—moral courage, the courage of one's convictions, the courage to see things through. The world is in a constant conspiracy against the brave. It's the age-old struggle—the roar of the crowd on one side and the voice of your conscience on the other.

DOUGLAS MACARTHUR

Give us the fortitude to endure the things which cannot be changed, and the courage to change the things which should be changed, and the wisdom to know one from the other.

OLIVER J. HART

No man in the world has more courage than the man who can stop after eating one peanut.

CHANNING POLLOCK

COURT *Also see:* JUSTICE, LAW.

A court is a place where what was confused before becomes more unsettled than ever.

HENRY WALDORF FRANCIS

Dictum is what a court thinks but is afraid to decide.

HENRY WALDORF FRANCIS

The place of justice is a hallowed place.

FRANCIS BACON

The penalty for laughing in a courtroom is six months in jail; if it were not for this penalty, the jury would never hear the evidence.

H. L. MENCKEN

COURTESY *Also see:* CHARM, CULTURE, GALLANTRY, MANNERS.

Life is not so short but that there is always time for courtesy.

RALPH WALDO EMERSON

It is better to have too much courtesy than too little, provided you are not equally courteous to all, for that would be injustice.

BALTASAR GRACIÁN

Courtesies of a small and trivial character are the ones which strike deepest in the grateful and appreciating heart.

HENRY CLAY

Nothing is ever lost by courtesy. It is the cheapest of the pleasures; costs nothing and conveys much. It pleases him who gives and him who receives, and thus, like mercy, it is twice blessed.

ERASTUS WIMAN

If a man be gracious and courteous to strangers, it shows he is a citizen of the world.

FRANCIS BACON

Politeness is the art of choosing among one's real thoughts.

ABEL STEVENS

True politeness consists in being easy one's self, and in making every one about one as easy as one can.

ALEXANDER POPE

COWARDICE *Also see:* FEAR, SILENCE.

The cowards never started—and the weak died along the way.

ANONYMOUS

Great occasions do not make heroes or cowards; they simply unveil them to the eyes of men.

BISHOP WESTCOTT

A coward is much more exposed to quarrels than a man of spirit.

THOMAS JEFFERSON

At the bottom of a good deal of the bravery that appears in the world there lurks a miserable cowardice. Men will face powder and steel because they cannot face public opinion.

EDWIN HUBBEL CHAPIN

It is better to be the widow of a hero than the wife of a coward.

DOLORES IBARRURI

Fear has its use but cowardice has none.

MAHATMA GANDHI

To know what is right and not to do it is the worst cowardice.

CONFUCIUS

The people to fear are not those who disagree with you, but those who disagree with you and are too cowardly to let you know.

NAPOLEON BONAPARTE

Faint heart ne'er won fair lady.

MIGUEL DE CERVANTES

It is the coward who fawns upon those above him. It is the coward who is insolent whenever he dares be so.

JUNIUS

How many feasible projects have miscarried through despondency, and been strangled in their birth by a cowardly imagination.

JEREMY COLLIER

Dishonesty, cowardice and duplicity are never impulsive.

GEORGE A. KNIGHT

A cowardly cur barks more fiercely than it bites.

QUINTUS CURTIUS RUFUS

CREATIVITY Also see: ACTION, ART, GOD, INVENTION, LITERATURE.

Ideas are the root of creation.

ERNEST DIMNET

Man was made at the end of the week's work when God was tired.

MARK TWAIN

It is wise to learn; it is God-like to create.

JOHN SAXE

Had I been present at the creation of the world I would have proposed some improvements.

ALFONSO X

Creation is a drug I can't do without.

CECIL B. DEMILLE

The merit of originality is not novelty; it is sincerity.

THOMAS CARLYLE

CREDIT Also see: BORROWING, DEBT, REPUTATION.

The surest way to establish your credit is to work yourself into the position of not needing any.

MAURICE SWITZER

The private control of credit is the modern form of slavery.

UPTON SINCLAIR

No man's credit is as good as his money.

ED HOWE

Remember that credit is money.

BENJAMIN FRANKLIN

Nothing so cements and holds together all the parts of a society as faith or credit, which can never be kept up unless men are under some force or necessity of honestly paying what they owe to one another.

CICERO

Men . . . are sent into the world with bills of credit, and seldom draw to their full extent.

HORACE WALPOLE

Credit is like a looking-glass, which when once sullied by a breath, may be wiped clear again; but if once cracked can never be repaired.

WALTER SCOTT

Buying on trust is the way to pay double.

ANONYMOUS

Acquaintance: a person whom we know well enough to borrow from, but not well enough to lend to.

AMBROSE BIERCE

CREDULITY Also see: BELIEF, DOUBT, FAITH, INNOCENCE, LYING.

Credulity is belief in slight evidence, with no evidence, or against evidence.

TRYON EDWARDS

The only disadvantage of an honest heart is credulity.

PHILIP SIDNEY

The great masses of the people . . . will more easily fall victims to a great lie than to a small one.

ADOLF HITLER

I prefer credulity to skepticism and cynicism for there is more promise in almost anything than in nothing at all.

RALPH BARTON PERRY

I cannot spare the luxury of believing that all things beautiful are what they seem.

FITZ-GREENE HALLECK

Let us believe neither half of the good people tell us of ourselves, nor half the evil they say of others.

JOHN PETIT-SENN

The more gross the fraud, the more glibly will it go down and the more greedily will it be swallowed, since folly will always find faith wherever imposters will find impudence.

CHRISTIAN NESTELL BOVEE

CRIME Also see: DISHONESTY, FRAUD, GUILT, MURDER, RIOT, SIN, VICE, WICKEDNESS, WRONG.

All crime is a kind of disease and should be treated as such.

MAHATMA GANDHI

Society prepares the crime; the criminal commits it.

HENRY THOMAS BUCKLE

We enact many laws that manufacture criminals, and then a few that punish them.

ALLEN TUCKER

And who are the greater criminals—those who sell the instruments of death, or those who buy them and use them?

ROBERT EMMET SHERWOOD

Providence sees to it that no man gets happiness out of crime.

VITTORIO ALTIERI

The real significance of crime is in its being a breach of faith with the community of mankind.

JOSEPH CONRAD

Purposelessness is the fruitful mother of crime.

CHARLES H. PARKHURST

Whoever profits by the crime is guilty of it.

ANONYMOUS

What is crime amongst the multitude, is only vice among the few.

BENJAMIN DISRAELI

Capital punishment is as fundamentally wrong as a cure for crime as charity is wrong as a cure for poverty.

HENRY FORD

Crime is a product of social excess.

LENIN

If poverty is the mother of crimes, want of sense is the father.

JEAN DE LA BRUYÈRE

Few men have virtue to withstand the highest bidder.

GEORGE WASHINGTON

Small crimes always precede great ones. Never have we seen timid innocence pass suddenly to extreme licentiousness.

JEAN BAPTISTE RACINE

Organized crime constitutes nothing less than a guerilla war against society.

LYNDON BAINES JOHNSON

Fear follows crime, and is its punishment.   VOLTAIRE

We easily forget crimes that are known only to ourselves.

FRANÇOIS DE LA ROCHEFOUCAULD

CRISIS *Also see:* CALAMITY, CHARACTER.

Every little thing counts in a crisis.

JAWAHARLAL NEHRU

These are the times that try men's souls.

THOMAS PAINE

Crises and deadlocks when they occur have at least this advantage, that they force us to think.

JAWAHARLAL NEHRU

Crises refine life. In them you discover what you are.

ALLAN K. CHALMERS

The wise man does not expose himself needlessly to danger, since there are few things for which he cares sufficiently; but he is willing, in great crises, to give even his life—knowing that under certain conditions it is not worth-while to live.

ARISTOTLE

. . . as we wake or sleep, we grow strong or we grow weak, and at last some crisis shows us what we have become.

BISHOP WESTCOTT

CRITICISM *Also see:* ADVICE, CENSURE, JUDGMENT, PRAISE.

I never give them hell; I just tell them the truth and they think it is hell.

HARRY S. TRUMAN

Blame is safer than praise.

RALPH WALDO EMERSON

To avoid criticism do nothing, say nothing, be nothing.

ELBERT HUBBARD

Remember that nobody will ever get ahead of you as long as he is kicking you in the seat of the pants.

WALTER WINCHELL

Each generation produces its squad of "moderns" with pea-shooters to attach Gibralter.

CHANNING POLLOCK

Criticism, as it was first instituted by Aristotle, was meant as a standard of judging well.

SAMUEL JOHNSON

It is much easier to be critical than to be correct.

BENJAMIN DISRAELI

The public is the only critic whose opinion is worth anything at all.

MARK TWAIN

CRUELTY *Also see:* ABUSE, EVIL, INJURY, PUNISHMENT, VIOLENCE, WAR.

If it were absolutely necessary to choose, I would rather be guilty of an immoral act than of a cruel one.

ANATOLE FRANCE

One of the ill effects of cruelty is that it makes the bystanders cruel.

THOMAS FOWELL BUXTON

All cruelty springs from hard-heartedness and weakness.

SENECA

Cruelty and fear shake hands together.

HONORÉ DE BALZAC

Cruelty, like every other vice, requires no motive outside of itself; it only requires opportunity.

GEORGE ELIOT

Cruelty is a part of nature, at least of human nature, but it is the one thing that seems unnatural to us.

ROBINSON JEFFERS

CULTURE *Also see:* ART, CIVILIZATION, COURTESY, LITERATURE, MANNERS.

Culture is the habit of being pleased with the best and knowing why.

HENRY VAN DYKE

Every man's ability may be strengthened or increased by culture.

JOHN ABBOTT

The acquiring of culture is the development of an avid hunger for knowledge and beauty.

JESSE BENNETT

No culture can live, if it attempts to be exclusive.

MAHATMA GANDHI

Culture is the widening of the mind and of the spirit.

JAWAHARLAL NEHRU

That is true culture which helps us to work for the social betterment of all.

HENRY WARD BEECHER

The end of culture is right living.

W. SOMERSET MAUGHAM

CUNNING . . . *See* DECEIT

CURIOSITY *Also see:* INTEREST, QUESTION, SCIENCE, SPEC-
ULATION, WONDER.

The first and simplest emotion which we discover in the human mind, is curiosity.

EDMUND BURKE

One of the secrets of life is to keep our intellectual curiosity acute.

WILLIAM LYON PHELPS

Creatures whose mainspring is curiosity enjoy the accumulating of facts far more than the pausing at times to reflect on those facts.

CLARENCE DAY

It is a shameful thing to be weary of inquiry when what we search for is excellent.

CICERO

The important thing is not to stop questioning. Curiosity has its own reason for existing. One cannot help but be in awe when he contemplates the mysteries of eternity, of life, of the marvelous structure of reality. It is enough if one tries merely to comprehend a little of this mystery every day. Never lose a holy curiosity.

ALBERT EINSTEIN

Curiosity is as much the parent of attention, as attention is of memory.

RICHARD WHATELY

CUSTOM *Also see:* CONFORMITY, FASHION, HABIT, TRADI-
TION.

Custom meets us at the cradle and leaves us only at the tomb.

ROBERT GREEN INGERSOLL

The old ways are the safest and surest ways.

CHARLES CALEB COLTON

The custom and fashion of today will be the awkwardness and outrage of tomorrow—so arbitrary are these transient laws.

ALEXANDRE DUMAS

Take the course opposite to custom and you will almost always do well.
JEAN-JACQUES ROUSSEAU

Men will sooner surrender their rights than their customs.
MORITZ GUEDMANN

Custom governs the world; it is the tyrant of our feelings and our manners and rules the world with the hand of a despot.
J. BARTLETT

There is nothing that strengthens a nation like reading of a nation's own history, whether that history is recorded in books or embodied in customs, institutions and monuments.
JOSEPH ANDERSON

Men commonly think according to their inclinations, speak according to their learning and imbibed opinions, but generally act according to custom.
FRANCIS BACON

There is no tyrant like custom, and no freedom where its edicts are not resisted.
CHRISTIAN NESTELL BOVEE

Ancient custom has the force of law.
LEGAL MAXIM

CYNIC Also see: CREDULITY, DOUBT, PESSIMISM, PREJUDICE, SARCASM, SKEPTICISM.

It takes a clever man to turn cynic and a wise man to be clever enough not to.
FANNIE HURST

A cynic is a man who knows the price of everything, and the value of nothing.
OSCAR WILDE

A cynic is just a man who found out when he was ten that there wasn't any Santa Claus, and he's still upset.
J. G. COZZENS

A cynic is a man who, when he smells flowers, looks around for a coffin.
H. L. MENCKEN

A cynic can chill and dishearten with a single word.
RALPH WALDO EMERSON

The only deadly sin I know is cynicism.
HENRY L. STIMSON

The cynic is one who never sees a good quality in a man, and never fails to see a bad one.

HENRY WARD BEECHER

DANGER Also see: ADVENTURE, BOLDNESS, CALAMITY, CAUTION, CENSORSHIP, COURAGE, FEAR.

As soon as there is life there is danger.

RALPH WALDO EMERSON

In this world there is always danger for those who are afraid of it.

GEORGE BERNARD SHAW

The most dangerous thing in the world is to try to leap a chasm in two jumps.

WILLIAM LLOYD GEORGE

If we survive danger it steels our courage more than anything else.

REINHOLD NIEBUHR

A timid person is frightened before a danger, a coward during the time, and a courageous person afterwards.

JEAN PAUL RICHTER

This country has come to feel the same when Congress is in session as when the baby gets hold of a hammer.

WILL ROGERS

We cannot banish dangers, but we can banish fears. We must not demean life by standing in awe of death.

DAVID SARNOFF

The mere apprehension of a coming evil has put many into a situation of the utmost danger.

LUCAN

There is danger when a man throws his tongue into high gear before he gets his brain a-going.

C. C. PHELPS

The person who runs away exposes himself to that very danger more than a person who sits quietly.

JAWAHARLAL NEHRU

We are confronted by a first danger, the destructiveness of applied atomic energy. And then we are confronted by a second danger, that we do not enough appreciate the first danger.

RAYMOND G. SWING

DEATH Also see: ABSENCE, BIRTH, CIVILIZATION, COMMU-

NISM, COWARDICE, DANGER, DEFEAT, DE-
SPAIR, DESTINY, DISEASE, LIFE,
IMMORTALITY.

Nothing in this life became him like leaving it.

WILLIAM SHAKESPEARE

I never think he is quite ready for another world who is altogether weary
of this.

HUGH HAMILTON

All say, ''How hard it is that we have to die''—a strange complaint to
come from the mouths of people who have had to live.

MARK TWAIN

Some people are so afraid to die that they never begin to live.

HENRY VAN DYKE

Most people would rather die than think: many do.

BERTRAND RUSSELL

God's finger touched him, and he slept.

ALFRED, LORD TENNYSON

The gods conceal from men the happiness of death, that they may endure
life.

LUCAN

Men fear death, as if unquestionably the greatest evil, and yet no man
knows that it may not be the greatest good.

WILLIAM MITFORD

Death—the last sleep? No, it is the final awakening.

WALTER SCOTT

I look upon life as a gift from God. I did nothing to earn it. Now that
the time is coming to give it back, I have no right to complain.

JOYCE CARY

Good men must die, but death cannot kill their names.

PROVERB

I am ready to meet my maker, but whether my maker is prepared for
the great ordeal of meeting me is another matter.

WINSTON CHURCHILL

Death is a very dull, dreary affair, and my advice to you is to have
nothing whatever to do with it.

W. SOMERSET MAUGHAM

DEBT *Also see:* BORROWING, CREDIT, MONEY.

Some debts are fun when you are acquiring them, but none are fun when you set about retiring them.

OGDEN NASH

Debt is a prolific mother of folly and of crime.

BENJAMIN DISRAELI

A small debt produces a debtor; a large one, an enemy.

PUBLILIUS SYRUS

A habit of debt is very injurious to the memory.

AUSTIN O'MALLEY

Some people use one half their ingenuity to get into debt, and the other half to avoid paying it.

GEORGE D. PRENTICE

We often pay our debts not because it is only fair that we should, but to make future loans easier.

FRANÇOIS DE LA ROCHEFOUCAULD

Debt is the fatal disease of republics, the first thing and the mightiest to undermine governments and corrupt the people.

WENDELL PHILLIPS

Debt is the worst poverty.

THOMAS FULLER

Our national debt, after all, is an internal debt, owed not only by the nation but to the nation. If our children have to pay the interest they will pay that interest to themselves.

FRANKLIN DELANO ROOSEVELT

Do not accustom yourself to consider debt only as an inconvenience; you will find it a calamity.

SAMUEL JOHNSON

A man in debt is so far a slave.

RALPH WALDO EMERSON

Never spend your money before you have it.

THOMAS JEFFERSON

Debt is the slavery of the free.

PUBLILIUS SYRUS

DECEIT Also see: FRAUD, SKEPTICISM.

You can fool some of the people all the time, and all of the people some of the time, but you cannot fool all of the people all the time.

ABRAHAM LINCOLN

The sure way to be cheated is to think one's self more cunning than others.

FRANÇOIS DE LA ROCHEFOUCAULD

It is double the pleasure to deceive the deceiver.

JEAN DE LA FONTAINE

All deception in the course of life is indeed nothing else but a lie reduced to practice, and falsehood passing from words into things.

ROBERT SOUTH

Hateful to me as the gates of Hades is that man who hides one thing in his heart and speaks another.

HOMER

DECENCY Also see: CENSORSHIP, MODESTY, MORALITY, VIRTUE.

Decency is the least of all laws, but yet it is the law which is most strictly observed.

FRANÇOIS DE LA ROCHEFOUCAULD

Don't overestimate the decency of the human race.

H. L. MENCKEN

We are decent 99 percent of the time, when we could easily be vile.

R. W. RILS

No law reaches it, but all right-minded people observe it.

CHAMFORT

DECISION Also see: CHOICE.

It does not take much strength to do things, but it requires great strength to decide on what to do.

ELBERT HUBBARD

I hate to see things done by halves. If it be right, do it boldly,—if it be wrong leave it undone.

BERNARD GILPIN

When possible make the decisions now, even if action is in the future. A reviewed decision usually is better than one reached at the last moment.

WILLIAM B. GIVEN, JR.

All our final decisions are made in a state of mind that is not going to last.

MARCEL PROUST

DEFEAT *Also see:* COURAGE, FAILURE, VICTORY.

What is defeat? Nothing but education, nothing but the first step to something better.

WENDELL PHILLIPS

There are some defeats more triumphant than victories.

MICHEL DE MONTAIGNE

It is defeat that turns bone to flint; it is defeat that turns gristle to muscle; it is defeat that makes men invincible.

HENRY WARD BEECHER

Politics has become so expensive that it takes a lot of money even to be defeated.

WILL ROGERS

Defeat is not the worst of failures. Not to have tried is the true failure.

GEORGE EDWARD WOODBERRY

Believe you are defeated, believe it long enough, and it is likely to become a fact.

NORMAN VINCENT PEALE

I would rather lose in a cause that I know some day will triumph than to triumph in a cause that I know some day will fail.

WENDELL L. WILLKIE

Defeat never comes to any man until he admits it.

JOSEPHUS DANIELS

Those who are prepared to die for any cause are seldom defeated.

JAWAHARLAL NEHRU

The problems of victory are more agreeable than those of defeat, but they are no less difficult.

WINSTON CHURCHILL

Defeat should never be a source of courage, but rather a fresh stimulant.

ROBERT SOUTH

DELIGHT . . . *See* JOY.

DELUSION *Also see:* REALITY, SELF-KNOWLEDGE.

No man is happy without a delusion of some kind. Delusions are as necessary to our happiness as realities.

CHRISTIAN NESTELL BOVEE

The worst deluded are the self-deluded.

CHRISTIAN NESTELL BOVEE

Love is the delusion that one woman differs from another.

H. L. MENCKEN

DEMOCRACY *Also see:* AMERICA, EQUALITY, FREEDOM, LIBERTY.

Democracy is good. I say this because other systems are worse.

JAWAHARLAL NEHRU

Democracy is based upon the conviction that there are extraordinary possibilities in ordinary people.

HARRY EMERSON FOSDICK

In a democracy, the individual enjoys not only the ultimate power but carries the ultimate responsibility.

NORMAN COUSINS

Democracy . . . is a system of self-determination. It's the right to make the wrong choice.

JOHN PATRICK

Too many people expect wonders from democracy, when the most wonderful thing of all is just having it.

WALTER WINCHELL

Democracy is the government of the people, by the people, for the people.

ABRAHAM LINCOLN

As I would not be a slave, so I would not be a master. This expresses my idea of democracy.

ABRAHAM LINCOLN

Man's capacity for justice makes democracy possible, but man's inclination to injustice makes democracy necessary.

REINHOLD NIEBUHR

In free countries, every man is entitled to express his opinions—and every other man is entitled not to listen.

G. NORMAN COLLIE

DEPENDENCE *Also see:* FREEDOM, INDEPENDENCE.

There is no dependence that can be sure but a dependence upon one's self.

JOHN GAY

He who imagines he can do without the world deceives himself much; but he who fancies the world cannot do without him is still more mistaken.

FRANÇOIS DE LA ROCHEFOUCAULD

No degree of knowledge attainable by man is able to set him above the want of hourly assistance.

SAMUEL JOHNSON

Depend on no man, on no friend but him who can depend on himself. He only who acts conscientiously toward himself, will act so toward others.

JOHANN KASPAR LAVATER

There is no one subsists by himself alone.

OWEN FELLTHAM

DESIRE *Also see:* AMBITION, LOVE, PASSION, WANT.

Desire is the essence of a man.

BENEDICT SPINOZA

It is much easier to suppress a first desire than to satisfy those that follow.

FRANÇOIS DE LA ROCHEFOUCAULD

There are two tragedies in life. One is not get your heart's desire. The other is to get it.

GEORGE BERNARD SHAW

By annihilating the desires, you annihilate the mind. Every man without passions has within him no principle of action, nor motive to act.

CLAUDE ADRIEN HELVÉTIUS

All human activity is prompted by desire.

BERTRAND RUSSELL

We trifle when we assign limits to our desires, since nature hath set none.

CHRISTIAN NESTELL BOVEE

Every human mind is a great slumbering power until awakened by a keen desire and by definite resolution to do.

EDGAR F. ROBERTS

You will become as small as your controlling desire; as great as your dominant aspiration.

JAMES ALLEN

DESPAIR *Also see:* DISAPPOINTMENT, HOPE, PAIN, POVERTY, SORROW.

The man who lives only by hope will die with despair.

ITALIAN PROVERB

When we are flat on our backs there is no way to look but up.

ROGER W. BABSON

Despair is like forward children, who, when you take away one of their playthings, throw the rest into the fire for madness. It grows angry with itself, turns its own executioner, and revenges its misfortunes on its own head.

PIERRE CHARRON

It becomes no man to nurse despair, but, in the teeth of clenched antagonisms, to follow up the worthiest till he die.

ALFRED, LORD TENNYSON

It is a miserable state of mind to have few things to desire, and many things to fear.

FRANCIS BACON

The fact that God has prohibited despair gives misfortune the right to hope all things, and leaves hope free to dare all things.

ANNE SOPHIE SWETCHINE

DESTINY Also see: FATE, FORTUNE, FUTURE, GOD.

Destiny is no matter of chance. It is a matter of choice: It is not a thing to be waited for, it is a thing to be achieved.

WILLIAM JENNINGS BRYAN

Lots of folks confuse bad management with destiny.

KIN HUBBARD

Destiny: A tyrant's authority for crime and a fool's excuse for failure.

AMBROSE BIERCE

Men heap together the mistakes of their lives, and create a monster they call Destiny.

JOHN OLIVER HOBBES

Our destiny changes with our thought; we shall become what we wish to become, do what we wish to do, when our habitual thought corresponds with our desire.

ORISON S. MARDEN

DIFFERENCE Also see: ARGUMENT, CONTRAST, QUARREL, VARIETY.

The difference is no less real because it is of degree.

BENJAMIN NATHAN CARDOZO

The difference between the right word and the almost right word is the difference between lightning and the lightning bug.

MARK TWAIN

If men would consider not so much wherein they differ, as wherein they agree, there would be far less of uncharitableness and angry feeling in the world.

JOSEPH ADDISON

Honest differences are often a healthy sign of progress.

MAHATMA GANDHI

If by saying that all men are born equal, you mean that they are equally born, it is true, but true in no other sense; birth, talent, labor, virtue, and providence, are forever making differences.

EUGENE EDWARDS

Where there is no difference, there is only indifference.

LOUIS NIZER

DIFFICULTY *Also see:* ADVERSITY, ANXIETY, LABOR.

Difficulties are meant to rouse, not discourage. The human spirit is to grow strong by conflict.

WILLIAM ELLERY CHANNING

No man who is occupied in doing a very difficult thing, and doing it very well, ever loses his self-respect.

GEORGE BERNARD SHAW

There are two ways of meeting difficulties: you alter the difficulties or you alter yourself meeting them.

PHYLLIS BOTTOME

Difficulties strengthen the mind, as labor does the body.

SENECA

Undertake something that is difficult; it will do you good. Unless you try to do something beyond what you have already mastered, you will never grow.

RONALD E. OSBORN

DIGNITY *Also see:* HONOR, PRIDE, RIGHTS, WORK.

True dignity is never gained by place, and never lost when honors are withdrawn.

PHILIP MASSINGER

There is a healthful hardiness about real dignity that never dreads contact and communion with others however humble.

WASHINGTON IRVING

No race can prosper till it learns that there is as much dignity in tilling a field as in writing a poem.

BOOKER T. WASHINGTON

When boasting ends, there dignity begins.

OWEN D. YOUNG

Our dignity is not in what we do, but what we understand.

GEORGE SANTAYANA

Human rights rest on human dignity. The dignity of man is an ideal worth fighting for and worth dying for.

ROBERT MAYNARD

The ultimate end of all revolutionary social change is to establish the sanctity of human life, the dignity of man, the right of every human being to liberty and well-being.

EMMA GOLDMAN

DILIGENCE *Also see:* BUSY, EFFORT, INDUSTRY, LABOR, PER-
SEVERANCE, WORK.

The expectations of life depend upon diligence; the mechanic that would perfect his work must first sharpen his tools.

CONFUCIUS

Diligence is the mother of good luck.

BENJAMIN FRANKLIN

He who labors diligently need never despair; for all things are accomplished by diligence and labor.

MENANDER OF ATHENS

What we hope ever to do with ease, we must learn first to do with diligence.

SAMUEL JOHNSON

Few things are impossible to diligence and skill . . .   Great works are performed, not by strength, but perseverance.

SAMUEL JOHNSON

DIPLOMACY *Also see:* DISCRETION, JUDGMENT, POLITICS,
TACT.

I have discovered the art of deceiving diplomats. I speak the truth, and they never believe me.

CAMILLO DI CAVOUR

Diplomacy is to do and say the nastiest things in the nicest way.

ISAAC GOLDBERG

To say nothing, especially when speaking, is half the art of diplomacy.

WILL DURANT

A diplomat is a person who can tell you to go to Hell in such a way that you actually look forward to the trip.

ANONYMOUS

The principle of give and take is the principle of diplomacy—give one and take ten.

MARK TWAIN

Diplomacy is the art of letting someone have your way.

DANIELE VARE

Diplomacy is a disguised war, in which states seek to gain by barter and intrigue, by the cleverness of arts, the objectives which they would have to gain more clumsily by means of war.

RANDOLPH BOURNE

Let us never negotiate out of fear. But let us never fear to negotiate.

JOHN FITZGERALD KENNEDY

This is the devilish thing about foreign affairs: they are foreign and will not always conform to our whims.

JAMES RESTON

DISAPPOINTMENT Also see: DEFEAT, FAILURE, HOPE.

Man must be disappointed with the lesser things of life before he can comprehend the full value of the greater.

EDWARD G. BULWER-LYTTON

Disappointment is the nurse of wisdom.

BOYLE ROCHE

Too many people miss the silver lining because they're expecting gold.

MAURICE SEITTER

Disappointment to a noble soul is what cold water is to burning metal; it strengthens, tempers, intensifies, but never destroys it.

ELIZA TABOR

The disappointment of manhood succeeds the delusion of youth.

BENJAMIN DISRAELI

If you expect perfection from people your whole life is a series of disappointments, grumblings and complaints. If, on the contrary, you pitch your expectations low, taking folks as the inefficient creatures which they are, you are frequently surprised by having them perform better than you had hoped.

BRUCE BARTON

DISARMAMENT Also see: NUCLEAR WARFARE, WAR.

The notion that disarmament can put a stop to war is contradicted by the nearest dogfight.

GEORGE BERNARD SHAW

Today, every inhabitant of this planet must contemplate the day when it may no longer be habitable. Every man, woman and child lives under a nuclear sword of Damocles, hanging by the slenderest of threads, capable of being cut at any moment by accident, miscalculation or madness. The weapons of war must be abolished before they abolish us.

JOHN FITZGERALD KENNEDY

The best way to begin disarming is to begin—and the United States is ready to conclude firm agreements in these areas and to consider any other reasonable proposal.

LYNDON BAINES JOHNSON

There is no more dangerous misconception than this which misconstrues the arms race as the cause rather than a symptom of the tensions and divisions which threaten nuclear war. If the history of the past fifty years teaches us anything, it is that peace does not follow disarmament—disarmament follows peace.

BERNARD M. BARUCH

DISCIPLINE *Also see:* CHEERFULNESS, ORDER, PARENTS.

To be in good moral condition requires at least as much training as to be in good physical condition.

JAWAHARLAL NEHRU

A stern discipline pervades all nature, which is a little cruel that it may be very kind.

EDMUND SPENSER

You never will be the person you can be if pressure, tension, and discipline are taken out of your life.

JAMES G. BILKEY

What we do on some great occasion will probably depend on what we already are; and what we are will be the result of previous years of self-discipline.

H. P. LIDDON

Man is still responsible. He must turn the alloy of modern experience into the steel of mastery and character. His success lies not with the stars but with himself. He must carry on the fight of self-correction and discipline.

FRANK CURTIS WILLIAMS

He that has learned to obey will know how to command.

SOLON

If the self-discipline of the free cannot match the iron discipline of the mailed fist, in economic, scientific, and all other kinds of struggles as well as the military, then the peril of freedom will continue to rise.

JOHN FITZGERALD KENNEDY

DISCONTENT Also see: ANXIETY, COMPLAINT, CONTENT-MENT, DISSENT, REBELLION.

One thing only has been lent to youth and age in common—discontent.

MATTHEW ARNOLD

Restlessness and discontent are the necessities of progress.

THOMAS EDISON

Discontent is the first step in the progress of a man or a nation.

OSCAR WILDE

Discontent is something that follows ambition like a shadow.

HENRY H. HASKINS

Who is not satisfied with himself will grow; who is not sure of his own correctness will learn many things.

CHINESE PROVERB

The discontented man finds no easy chair.

BENJAMIN FRANKLIN

Who with a little cannot be content, endures an everlasting punishment.

ROBERT HERRICK

DISCOVERY Also see: INVENTION, ORIGINALITY.

What is wanted is not the will to believe but the wish to find out, which is the exact opposite.

BERTRAND RUSSELL

If I have ever made any valuable discoveries, it has been owing more to patient attention, than to any other talent.

ISAAC NEWTON

Great discoveries and improvements invariably involve the cooperation of many minds. I may be given credit for having blazed the trail but when I look at the subsequent developments I feel the credit is due to others rather than to myself.

ALEXANDER GRAHAM BELL

Through every rift of discovery some seeming anomaly drops out of the darkness, and falls, as a golden link, into the great chain of order.

EDWIN HUBBEL CHAPIN

DISCRETION *Also see:* CAUTION, COMMON SENSE, JUDG-
MENT, PRUDENCE.

Be discreet in all things, and so render it unnecessary to be mysterious
about any.

FIRST DUKE OF WELLINGTON

I have never been hurt by anything I didn't say.

CALVIN COOLIDGE

If thou art a master, be sometimes blind; if a servant, sometimes deaf.

THOMAS FULLER

Discretion in speech is more than eloquence.

FRANCIS BACON

Great ability without discretion comes almost invariably to a tragic end.

GAMBETTA

An ounce of discretion is worth a pound of learning.

PROVERB

Philosophy is nothing but discretion.

JOHN SELDEN

DISCUSSION . . . *See* CONVERSATION.

DISEASE *Also see:* AFFLICTION, CRIME, DEATH, DEBT, HEALTH,
MEDICINE, PAIN.

Some remedies are worse than the diseases.

PUBLILIUS SYRUS

Disease is a physical process that generally begins that equality which
death completes.

SAMUEL JOHNSON

We classify disease as error, which nothing but Truth or Mind can heal.

MARY BAKER EDDY

Disease is the retribution of outraged Nature.

HOSEA BALLOU

A bodily disease may be but a symptom of some ailment in the spiritual
past.

NATHANIEL HAWTHORNE

We are the carriers of health and disease—either the divine health of
courage and nobility or the demonic diseases of hate and anxiety.

JOSHUA LOTH LIEBMAN

There are no such things as incurables; there are only things for which man has not found a cure.

- BERNARD M. BARUCH

Sickness and disease are in weak minds the sources of melancholy; but that which is painful to the body, may be profitable to the soul. Sickness puts us in mind of our mortality, and, while we drive on heedlessly in the full career of worldly pomp and jollity, kindly pulls us by the ear, and brings us to a proper sense of our duty.

RICHARD E. BURTON

It is with disease of the mind, as with those of the body; we are half dead before we understand our disorder, and half cured when we do.

CHARLES CALEB COLTON

DISHONESTY *Also see:* CRIME, DECEIT, FRAUD, HYPOCRISY, INJUSTICE, LYING.

If all mankind were suddenly to practice honesty, many thousands of people would be sure to starve.

G. C. LICHTENBERG

Honesty pays, but it doesn't seem to pay enough to suit some people.
KIN HUBBARD

Don't place too much confidence in the man who boasts of being as honest as the day is long. Wait until you meet him at night.

ROBERT C. EDWARDS

False words are not only evil in themselves, but they infect the soul with evil.

SOCRATES

Hope of ill gain is the beginning of loss.

DEMOCRITUS

Dishonesty, cowardice and duplicity are never impulsive.

GEORGE A. KNIGHT

DISSENT *Also see:* ARGUMENT, DIFFERENCE, DIFFICULTY, QUARREL.

Dissent does not include the freedom to destroy the system of law which guarantees freedom to speak, assemble and march in protest. Dissent is not anarchy.

SEYMOUR F. SIMON

The United States can . . . be proud that it has institutions and a structure that permit its citizens to express honest dissent, even though those who do so may be maligned by the highest official in the land.

NEW YORK TIMES

In a number of cases dissenting opinions have in time become the law.

CHARLES EVANS HUGHES

Those who begin coercive elimination of dissent soon find themselves exterminating dissenters. Compulsory unification of opinion achieves only the unanimity of the graveyard.

FELIX FRANKFURTER

Mere unorthodoxy or dissent from the prevailing mores is not to be condemned. The absence of such voices would be a symptom of grave illness in our society.

EARL WARREN

Thought that is silenced is always rebellious. . . . Majorities, of course, are often mistaken. This is why the silencing of minorities is always dangerous. Criticism and dissent are the indispensable antidote to major delusions.

ALAN BARTH

DISTRUST *Also see:* DOUBT, FAITH, FEAR, SUSPICION.

The disease of mutual distrust among nations is the bane of modern civilization.

FRANZ BOAS

However much we may distrust men's sincerity, we always believe they speak to us more sincerely than to others.

FRANÇOIS DE LA ROCHEFOUCAULD

What loneliness is more lonely than distrust?

GEORGE ELIOT

The man who trusts men will make fewer mistakes than he who distrusts them.

CAMILLO DI CAVOUR

DOUBT *Also see:* AGNOSTICISM, DISTRUST, FAITH, INCREDUL-
ITY, SKEPTICISM, SUSPICION, WISDOM.

We know accurately only when we know little; with knowledge doubt enters.

JOHANN WOLFGANG VON GOETHE

I respect faith, but doubt is what gets you an education.

WILSON MIZNER

Men become civilized, not in proportion to their willingness to believe, but in proportion to their readiness to doubt.

H. L. MENCKEN

Doubt is the beginning, not the end, of wisdom.

GEORGE ILES

Just think of the tragedy of teaching children not to doubt.

CLARENCE DARROW

Faith keeps many doubts in her pay. If I could not doubt, I should not believe.

HENRY DAVID THOREAU

In all affairs it's a healthy thing now and then to hang a question mark on the things you have long taken for granted.

BERTRAND RUSSELL

DRAFT *Also see:* SOLDIER, WAR.

Peacetime conscription is the greatest step toward regimentation and militarism ever undertaken by the Congress of the United States.

BURTON KENDALL WHEELER

A young man who does not have what it takes to perform military service is not likely to have what it takes to make a living.

JOHN FITZGERALD KENNEDY

Pressed into service means pressed out of shape.

ROBERT FROST

People have not been horrified by war to a sufficient extent . . . War will exist until that distant day when the conscientious objector enjoys the same reputation and prestige as the warrior does today.

JOHN FITZGERALD KENNEDY

DREAM *Also see:* AMERICA, DEMOCRACY, ILLUSION, IMAGI-
NATION, REVERIE.

Keep true to the dreams of thy youth.

JOHANN VON SCHILLER

Dreaming permits each and every one of us to be quietly and safely insane every night of our lives.

CHARLES WILLIAM DEMENT

The smaller the head, the bigger the dream.

AUSTIN O'MALLEY

Dreaming is an act of pure imagination, attesting in all men a creative power, which, if it were available in waking, would make every man a Dante or Shakespeare.

H. F. HEDGE

If one advances confidently in the directions of his dreams, and endeavors to live the life which he has imagined, he will meet with a success unexpected in common hours.

HENRY DAVID THOREAU

Dreams are nothing but incoherent ideas, occasioned by partial or imperfect sleep.

BENJAMIN RUSH

All men of action are dreamers.

JAMES G. HUNEKER

The more a man dreams, the less he believes.

H. L. MENCKEN

People who insist on telling their dreams are among the terrors of the breakfast table.

MAX BEERBOHM

The end of wisdom is to dream high enough to lose the dream in the seeking of it.

WILLIAM FAULKNER

Toil, feel, think, hope; you will be sure to dream enough before you die, without arranging it.

JOHN STERLING

It is difficult to say what is impossible, for the dream of yesterday is the hope of today and the reality of tomorrow.

ROBERT H. GODDARD

A lost but happy dream may shed its light upon our waking hours, and the whole day may be infected with the gloom of a dreary or sorrowful one; yet of neither may we be able to recover a trace.

WALTER DE LA MARE

DRESS *Also see:* APPEARANCE, FASHION, TASTE.

Be careless in your dress if you must, but keep a tidy soul.

MARK TWAIN

The body is the shell of the soul, and dress the husk of that shell; but the husk often tells what the kernel is.

ANONYMOUS

Eat to please thyself, but dress to please others.

BENJAMIN FRANKLIN

Clothes don't make the man, but clothes have got many a man a good job.

HERBERT HAROLD VREELAND

There is new strength, repose of mind, and inspiration in fresh apparel.

ELLA WHEELER WILCOX

The well-dressed man is he whose clothes you never notice.

W. SOMERSET MAUGHAM

No man is esteemed for gay garments but by fools and women.

SIR WALTER RALEIGH

If a woman rebels against high-heeled shoes, she should take care to do it in a very smart hat.

GEORGE BERNARD SHAW

Good clothes open all doors.

THOMAS FULLER

Clothes make the man.

LATIN PROVERB

Do not conceive that fine clothes make fine men, any more than fine feathers make fine birds. A plain, genteel dress is more admired, obtains more credit in the eyes of the judicious and sensible.

GEORGE WASHINGTON

Keeping your clothes well pressed will keep you from looking hard pressed.

COLEMAN COX

DRUGS Also see: CRIME.

The time has come to stop the sale of slavery to the young.

LYNDON BAINES JOHNSON

We have drugs to make women speak, but none to keep them silent.

ANATOLE FRANCE

The young physician starts life with 20 drugs for each disease, and the old physician ends life with one drug for 20 diseases.

WILLIAM OSLER

DRUNKENNESS Also see: ABSTINENCE, VICE.

The sight of a drunkard is a better sermon against that vice than the best that was ever preached on the subject.

JOHN FAUCIT SAVILLE

Drunkenness is the ruin of a person. It is premature old age. It is temporary death.

ST. BASIL

Alcoholism is tragically high on the list of our nation's health problems. Five million Americans are alcoholics. They bring incalculable grief to millions of families. They cost their families, their employers and society billions of dollars.

LYNDON BAINES JOHNSON

Extensive interviews show that not one alcoholic has ever actually seen a pink elephant.

YALE UNIVERSITY, CENTER OF ALCOHOL STUDIES

Always remember, that I have taken more out of alcohol than alcohol has taken out of me.

WINSTON CHURCHILL

Drunkenness is temporary suicide: the happiness that it brings is merely negative, a momentary cessation of unhappiness.

BERTRAND RUSSELL

Drunkenness is not a mere matter of intoxicating liquors; it goes deeper—far deeper. Drunkenness is the failure of a man to control his thoughts.

DAVID GRAYSON

Drunkenness is nothing else but a voluntary madness.

SENECA

DUTY *Also see:* AFFECTION, AUTHORITY, BOLDNESS, BUSY, RESPONSIBILITY, RIGHTS.

Only aim to do your duty, and mankind will give you credit where you fail.

THOMAS JEFFERSON

Men do less than they ought, unless they do all that they can.

THOMAS CARLYLE

The reward of one duty is the power to fulfill another.

GEORGE ELIOT

. . . it is just as hard to do your duty when men are sneering at you as when they are shooting at you.

WOODROW WILSON

A duty dodged is like a debt unpaid; it is only deferred, and we must come back and settle the account at last.

JOSEPH F. NEWTON

Let us do our duty in our shop or our kitchen, in the market, the street, the office, the school, the home, just as faithfully as if we stood in the front rank of some great battle, and knew that victory for mankind depended on our bravery, strength and skill. When we do that, the humblest of us will be serving in that great army which achieves the welfare of the world.

THEODORE PARKER

Never mind your happiness; do your duty.

WILL DURANT

It is the duty of the government to make it difficult for people to do wrong, easy to do right.

WILLIAM E. GLADSTONE

A man who neglects his duty as a citizen is not entitled to his rights as a citizen.

TIORIO

Knowledge of our duties is the most essential part of the philosophy of life. If you escape duty you avoid action. The world demands results.

GEORGE W. GOETHALS

Who escapes a duty, avoids a gain.

THEODORE PARKER

EARTH *Also see:* NATURE, WORLD, UNIVERSE.

The earth is given as a common for men to labor and live in.

THOMAS JEFFERSON

How far must suffering and misery go before we see that even in the day of vast cities and powerful machines, the good earth is our mother and that if we destroy her, we destroy ourselves?

PAUL BIGELOW SEARS

The earth and its resources belong of right to its people.

GIFFORD PINCHOT

There is enough for all. The earth is a generous mother; she will provide in plentiful abundance food for all her children if they will but cultivate her soil in justice and in peace.

BOURKE COCKRAN

Our earth is but a small star in a great universe. Yet of it we can make, if we choose, a planet unvexed by war, untroubled by hunger or fear, undivided by senseless distinctions of race, color or theory.

STEPHEN VINCENT BENÉT

Earth, thou great footstool of our God, who reigns on high; thou fruitful source of all our raiment, life, and food; our house, our parent, and our nurse.

ISAAC WATTS

The pagans do not know God, and love only the earth. The Jews know the true God, and love only the earth. The Christians know the true God, and do not love the earth.

BLAISE PASCAL

''The earth is the Lord's fullness thereof'': this is no longer a hollow dictum of religion, but a directive for economic action toward human brotherhood.

LEWIS MUMFORD

EATING *Also see:* GLUTTON.

Eat, drink, and be merry, for tomorrow ye diet.

WILLIAM GILMORE BEYMER

To eat is human; to digest, divine.

C. T. COPELAND

The way to a man's heart is through his stomach.

FANNY FERN

He who does not mind his belly will hardly mind anything else.

SAMUEL JOHNSON

There is no love sincerer than the love of food.

GEORGE BERNARD SHAW

When it comes to eating, you can sometimes help yourself more by helping yourself less.

RICHARD ARMOUR

Tell me what you eat, and I will tell you what you are.

ANTHELME BRILLAT-SAVARIN

A saw few die of hunger; of eating, a hundred thousand.

BENJAMIN FRANKLIN

The proof of the pudding is in the eating.

MIGUEL DE CERVANTES

Part of the secret of success in life is to eat what you like and let the food fight it out inside.

MARK TWAIN

The difference between a rich man and a poor man is this—the former eats when he pleases, and the latter when he can get it.

SIR WALTER RALEIGH

ECONOMY *Also see:* BARGAIN, MONEY, PRUDENCE.

There can be no economy where there is no efficiency.

BEACONSFIELD

Without economy none can be rich, and with it few will be poor.

SAMUEL JOHNSON

Nothing is cheap which is superfluous, for what one does not need, is dear at a penny.

PLUTARCH

Beware of little expenses; a small leak will sink a great ship.

BENJAMIN FRANKLIN

Ere you consult your fancy, consult your purse.

BENJAMIN FRANKLIN

He who will not economize will have to agonize.

CONFUCIUS

The world abhors closeness, and all but admires extravagance; yet a slack hand shows weakness, and a tight hand strength.

THOMAS FOWELL BUXTON

I place economy among the first and most important virtues, and public debt as the greatest of dangers. . . . We must make our choice between economy and liberty, or profusion and servitude. If we can prevent the government from wasting the labors of the people under the pretense of caring for them, they will be happy.

THOMAS JEFFERSON

Economy is a way of spending money without getting any pleasure out of it.

ARMAND SALACROU

Economy is for the poor; the rich may dispense with it.

CHRISTIAN NESTELL BOVEE

Let honesty and industry be thy constant companions, and spend one penny less than thy clear gains; then shall thy pocket begin to thrive; creditors will not insult, nor want oppress, nor hungerness bite, nor nakedness freeze thee.

BENJAMIN FRANKLIN

EDUCATION *Also see:* CULTURE, DEFEAT, DOUBT, READING, STUDY.

Only the educated are free.

EPICTETUS

Education is a better safeguard of liberty than a standing army.

EDWARD EVERET

Education is a progressive discovery of our ignorance.

WILL DURANT

I have never let my schooling interfere with my education.

MARK TWAIN

Education makes people easy to lead, but difficult to drive; easy to govern, but impossible to enslave.

HENRY PETER BROUGHAM

If a man empties his purse into his head, no man can take it away from him. An investment in knowledge always pays the best interest.

BENJAMIN FRANKLIN

Education is a social process . . . Education is growth. . . . Education is, not a preparation for life; education is life itself.

JOHN DEWEY

Education is that which discloses to the wise and disguises from the foolish their lack of understanding.

AMBROSE BIERCE

Education is too important to be left solely to the educators.

FRANCIS KEPPEL

He who opens a school door, closes a prison.

VICTOR HUGO

The best education in the world is that by struggling to get a living.

WENDELL PHILLIPS

My father must have had some elementary education for he could read and write and keep accounts inaccurately.

GEORGE BERNARD SHAW

Our progress as a nation can be no swifter than our progress in education.

JOHN FITZGERALD KENNEDY

EFFICIENCY *Also see:* ABILITY, DILIGENCE, GENIUS, INDUSTRY, ORDER, TECHNOLOGY.

It is more than probable that the average man could, with no injury to his health, increase his efficiency fifty percent.

WALTER SCOTT

A sense of the value of time—that is, of the best way to divide one's time into one's various activities—is an essential preliminary to efficient work; it is the only method of avoiding hurry.

ARNOLD BENNETT

In the old world that is passing, in the new world that is coming, national efficiency has been and will be a controlling factor in national safety and welfare.

GIFFORD PINCHOT

Loyal and efficient work in a great cause, even though it may not be immediately recognized, ultimately bears fruit.

JAWAHARLAL NEHRU

We want the spirit of America to be efficient; we want American character to be efficient; we want American character to display itself in what I may, perhaps, be allowed to call spiritual efficiency—clear disinterested thinking and fearless action along the right lines of thought.

WOODROW WILSON

Obviously, the highest type of efficiency is that which can utilize existing material to the best advantage.

JAWAHARLAL NEHRU

EFFORT *Also see:* ACHIEVEMENT, ACTION, DILIGENCE, EN-
ERGY, INDUSTRY, LABOR, PERSEVER-
ANCE, WORK.

It is hard to fail, but it is worse never to have tried to succeed. In this life we get nothing save by effort.

THEODORE ROOSEVELT

The only method by which people can be supported is out of the effort of those who are earning their own way. We must not create a deterrent to hard work.

ROBERT A. TAFT

A law of nature rules that energy cannot be destroyed. You change its form from coal to steam, from steam to power in the turbine, but you do not destroy energy. In the same way, another law governs human activity and rules that honest effort cannot be lost, but that some day the proper benefits will be forthcoming.

PAUL SPEICHER

Things don't turn up in this world until somebody turns them up.

JAMES A. GARFIELD

Many a man never fails because he never tries.

NORMAN MACEWAN

EGOTISM . . . *See* VANITY.

ELOQUENCE *Also see:* LOQUACITY.

True eloquence consists in saying all that is proper, and nothing more.

FRANÇOIS DE LA ROCHEFOUCAULD

Eloquence is logic on fire.

LYMAN BEECHER

Eloquence is the child of knowledge.

BENJAMIN DISRAELI

Noise proves nothing. Often a hen who has merely laid an egg cackles as if she had laid an asteroid.

MARK TWAIN

There is no eloquence without a man behind it.

RALPH WALDO EMERSON

True eloquence does not consist in speech. Words and phrases may be marshalled in every way, but they cannot compass it. It must consist in the man, in the subject, and in the occasion. It comes, if at all, like the outbreaking of a fountain from the earth, or the bursting forth of volcanic fires, with spontaneous, original native force.

DANIEL WEBSTER

EMINENCE . . . *See* ESTEEM.

EMOTION *Also see:* CURIOSITY, PASSION, REASON, SENTIMENT.

When dealing with people remember you are not dealing with creatures of logic, but with creatures of emotion, creatures bristling with prejudice, and motivated by pride and vanity.

DALE CARNEGIE

Emotion is not something shameful, subordinate, second-rate; it is a supremely valid phase of humanity at its noblest and most mature.

JOSHUA LOTH LIEBMAN

The young man who has not wept is a savage, and the old man who will not laugh is a fool.

GEORGE SANTAYANA

By starving emotions we become humorless, rigid and stereotyped; by repressing them we become literal, reformatory and holier-than-thou; encouraged, they perfume life; discouraged, they poison it.

JOSEPH COLLINS

EMPLOYMENT *Also see:* BUSINESS, BUSY, EFFORT, WORK.

Not to enjoy life, but to employ life, ought to be our aim and inspiration.

JOHN ROSS MACDUFF

Each man's task is his life preserver.

GEORGE B. EMERSON

When you hire people that are smarter than you are, you prove you are smarter than they are.

R. H. GRANT

Early to bed and early to rise probably indicates unskilled labor.

JOHN CIARDI

Employment, which Galen calls "nature's physician," is so essential to human happiness that indolence is justly considered as the mother of misery.

RICHARD E. BURTON

The employer generally gets the employees he deserves.

WALTER GILBEY

END and MEANS *Also see:* AIM, DEATH, PURPOSE, RESULT.

The end must justify the means.

MATTHEW PRIOR

Knowledge of means without knowledge of ends is animal training.

EVERETT DEAN MARTIN

If well thou hast begun, go on; it is the end that crowns us, not the fight.

ROBERT HERRICK

Freedom is only good as a means; it is no end in itself.

HERMAN MELVILLE

The end justifies the means only when the means used are such as actually bring about the desired and desirable end.

JOHN DEWEY

In everything we ought to look to the end.

JEAN DE LA FONTAINE

ENDURANCE *Also see:* PATIENCE, STRENGTH, TOLERANCE, WILL.

To endure is the first thing that a child ought to learn, and that which he will have the most need to know.

JEAN JACQUES ROUSSEAU

Whatever necessity lays upon thee, endure; whatever she commands, do.

JOHANN WOLFGANG VON GOETHE

Endurance is patience concentrated.

THOMAS CARLYLE

Still achieving, still pursuing, learn to labor and to wait.

HENRY WADSWORTH LONGFELLOW

There is a strength of quiet endurance as significant of courage as the most daring feats of prowess.

HENRY THEODORE TUCKERMAN

ENEMY *Also see:* CITIZENSHIP, DEBT, FORGIVENESS, FRIEND-
SHIP, QUARREL.

There is no little enemy.

BENJAMIN FRANKLIN

A man's greatness can be measured by his enemies.

DON PLATT

Observe your enemies, for they first find out your faults.

ANTISTHENES

If you have no enemies, you are apt to be in the same predicament in regard to friends.

ELBERT HUBBARD

Our real enemies are the people who make us feel so good that we are slowly, but inexorably, pulled down into the quicksand of smugness and self-satisfaction.

SYDNEY HARRIS

Man is his own worst enemy.

CICERO

In order to have an enemy, one must be somebody. One must be a force before he can be resisted by another force. A malicious enemy is better than a clumsy friend.

ANNE SOPHIE SWETCHINE

Nothing would more contribute to make a man wise than to have always an enemy in his view.

LORD HALIFAX

An enemy is anyone who tells the truth about you.

ELBERT HUBBARD

ENERGY *Also see:* AVERAGE, EFFICIENCY, EFFORT, FORCE,

INDUSTRY, POWER, SPIRIT, STRENGTH, ZEAL.

The world belongs to the energetic.

RALPH WALDO EMERSON

Energy and persistence conquer all things.

BENJAMIN FRANKLIN

There is no genius in life like the genius of energy and industry.

DONALD GRANT MITCHELL

Energy will do anything than can be done in the world; and no talents, no circumstances, no opportunities will make a two-legged animal a man without it.

JOHANN WOLFGANG VON GOETHE

The real difference between men is energy. A strong will, a settled purpose, an invincible determination, can accomplish almost anything; and in this lies the distinction between great men and little men.

THOMAS FULLER

ENJOYMENT *Also see:* AMUSEMENT, CHEERFULNESS, CONTENTMENT, JOY, LEISURE, PLEASURE.

The first half of life consists of the capacity to enjoy without the chance; the last half consists of the chance without the capacity.

MARK TWAIN

True enjoyment comes from activity of the mind and exercise of the body; the two are ever united.

HUMBOLDT

If your capacity to acquire has outstripped your capacity to enjoy, you are on the way to the scrap-heap.

GLEN BUCK

May we never let the things we can't have, or don't have, or shouldn't have, spoil our enjoyment of the things we do have and can have. As we value our happiness let us not forget it, for one of the greatest lessons in life is learning to be happy without the things we cannot or should not have.

RICHARD L. EVANS

ENTHUSIASM *Also see:* OPTIMISM, PASSION, ZEAL.

The enthusiasm of old men is singularly like that of infancy.

GÉRARD DE NERVAL

The worst bankrupt in the world is the man who has lost his enthusiasm.

H. W. ARNOLD

Every great and commanding movement in the annals of the world is the triumph of enthusiasm. Nothing great was ever achieved without it.

RALPH WALDO EMERSON

No person who is enthusiastic about his work has anything to fear from life.

SAMUEL GOLDWYN

EQUALITY *Also see:* ARISTOCRACY, CLEVERNESS, DEMOC-
RACY, DIFFERENCE, RACE, RIGHTS.

All human beings are born free and equal in dignity and rights.

U.N., DECLARATION OF HUMAN RIGHTS, ART. 1.

Men are equal; it is not birth but virtue that makes the difference.

VOLTAIRE

There are many humorous things in the world: among them the white man's notion that he is less savage than the other savages.

MARK TWAIN

We hold these truths to be self-evident, that all men are created equal.

THOMAS JEFFERSON

Complete equality means universal irresponsibility.

T. S. ELIOT

If there be a human being who is freer than I, then I shall necessarily become his slave. If I am freer than any other, then he will become my slave. Therefore equality is an absolutely necessary condition of freedom.

MIKHAIL A. BAKUNIN

ERROR *Also see:* CAUSE, TRUTH, WRONG.

It takes less time to do a thing right than it does to explain why you did it wrong.

HENRY WADSWORTH LONGFELLOW

The man who makes no mistakes does not usually make anything.

EDWARD PHELPS

An error doesn't become a mistake until you refuse to correct it.

ORLANDO A. BATTISTA

If I have erred, I err in company with Abraham Lincoln.

THEODORE ROOSEVELT

Error is discipline through which we advance.

WILLIAM ELLERY CHANNING

Sometimes we may learn more from a man's errors, than from his virtues.
HENRY WADSWORTH LONGFELLOW

A man whose errors take ten years to correct is quite a man.
J. ROBERT OPPENHEIMER

ESTEEM *Also see:* ADMIRATION, HONOR.

The chief ingredients in the composition of those qualities that gain esteem and praise, are good nature, truth, good sense, and good breeding.
JOSEPH ADDISON

Oftentimes nothing profits more than self-esteem, grounded on what is just and right.
JOHN MILTON

Esteem has more engaging charms than friendship and even love. It captivates hearts better, and never makes ingrates.
FRANÇOIS DE LA ROCHEFOUCAULD

ETERNITY *Also see:* BIBLE, FUTURE, GOD, HEAVEN, HELL, IMMORTALITY, TIME.

Eternity is not an everlasting flux of time, but time is a short parenthesis in a long period.
JOHN DONNE

Eternity is in love with the productions of time.
WILLIAM BLAKE

All great natures delight in stability; all great men find eternity affirmed in the very promise of their faculties.
RALPH WALDO EMERSON

Eternity has no gray hairs! The flowers fade, the heart withers, man grows old and dies, the world lies down in the sepulchre of ages, but time writes no wrinkles on the brow of eternity.
REGINALD HEBER

The sum of all sums is eternity.
LUCRETIUS

The thought of eternity consoles for the shortness of life.
LUC DE CLAPIERS

I leave eternity to Thee; for what is man that he could live the lifetime of his God?
HERMAN MELVILLE

EVIL *Also see:* CREDULITY, DANGER, VICE.

It is a sin to believe evil of others, but it is seldom a mistake.

H. L. MENCKEN

There is nothing evil save that which perverts the mind and shackles the conscience.

ST. AMBROSE

I never wonder to see men wicked, but I often wonder to see them not ashamed.

JONATHAN SWIFT

Evil often triumphs, but never conquers.

JOSEPH ROUX

A person may cause evil to others not only by his actions but by his inaction, and in either case he is justly accountable to them for the injury.

JOHN STUART MILL

There are a thousand hacking at the branches of evil to one who is striking at the root.

HENRY DAVID THOREAU

Evil events from evil causes spring.

ARISTOPHANES

It is privilege that causes evil in the world, not wickedness, and not men.

LINCOLN STEFFENS

It is the law of our humanity that man must know good through evil. No great principle ever triumphed but through much evil. No man ever progressed to greatness and goodness but through great mistakes.

FREDERICK W. ROBERTSON

All that is necessary for the triumph of evil is that good men do nothing.

EDMUND BURKE

Evil unchecked grows, evil tolerated poisons the whole system.

JAWAHARLAL NEHRU

EVOLUTION *Also see:* CHANGE.

All modern men are descended from a worm-like creature, but it shows more on some people.

WILL CUPPY

Some call it evolution and others call it God.

W. H. CARRUTH

The question is this: is man an ape or an angel? I am on the side of the angels. I repudiate with indignation and adhorrence these new-fangled theories.

BENJAMIN DISRAELI

One touch of Darwin makes the whole world kin.

GEORGE BERNARD SHAW

We must remember that there are no shortcuts in evolution.

LOUIS D. BRANDEIS

Concerning what ultimately becomes of the individual it (evolution) has added nothing and subtracted nothing.

ROBERT A. MILLIKAN

We are descended not only from monkeys, but also from monks.

ELBERT HUBBARD

EXAGGERATION Also see: ELOQUENCE, LOQUACITY.

We always weaken whatever we exaggerate.

JEAN FRANÇOIS DE LAHARPE

Exaggeration is a blood relation to falsehood and nearly as blameable.

HOSEA BALLOU

There are people so addicted to exaggeration they can't tell the truth without lying.

JOSH BILLINGS

Some so speak in exaggerations and superlatives that we need to make a large discount from their statements before we can come at their real meaning.

TRYON EDWARDS

Exaggeration is a department of lying.

BALTASAR GRACIÁN

EXAMPLE Also see: CONFORMITY, INFLUENCE.

Example is not the main thing in life—it is the only thing.

ALBERT SCHWEITZER

Other men are lenses through which we read our own minds.

FRANÇOIS DE LA ROCHEFOUCAULD

Old men are fond of giving good advice to console themselves for their inability to give bad examples.

FRANÇOIS DE LA ROCHEFOUCAULD

The first great gift we can bestow on others is a good example.

MORELL

Few things are harder to put up with than the annoyance of a good example.

MARK TWAIN

The rotten apple spoils his companion.

BENJAMIN FRANKLIN

I have ever deemed it more honorable and more profitable, too, to set a good example than to follow a bad one.

THOMAS JEFFERSON

First find the man in yourself if you will inspire manliness in others.

AMOS BRONSON ALCOTT

EXCELLENCE . . . *See* PERFECTION.

EXCUSES *Also see:* FAILURE, REGRET.

Don't make excuses, make good.

ELBERT HUBBARD

An excuse is worse and more terrible than a lie; for an excuse is a lie guarded.

ALEXANDER POPE

He that is good for making excuses is seldom good for anything else.

BENJAMIN FRANKLIN

We have forty million reasons for failure, but not a single excuse.

RUDYARD KIPLING

Uncalled-for excuses are practical confessions.

CHARLES SIMMONS

EXPECTATION . . . *See* ANTICIPATION.

EXPEDIENCY *Also see:* COMPROMISE, OPPORTUNITY.

I believe the moral losses of expediency always far outweigh the temporary gains.

WENDELL L. WILKIE

When private virtue is hazarded on the perilous cast of expediency, the pillars of the republic, however apparent their stability, are infected with decay at the very center.

EDWIN HUBBEL CHAPIN

No man is justified in doing evil on the ground of expedience.

THEODORE ROOSEVELT

Expedients are for the hour; principles for the ages.

HENRY WARD BEECHER

EXPERIENCE *Also see:* AGE, THEORY.

Men are wise in proportion, not to their experience, but to their capacity for experience.

GEORGE BERNARD SHAW

Experience is a school where a man learns what a big fool he has been.

JOSH BILLINGS

Experience is a hard teacher because she gives the test first, the lesson afterwards.

VERNON SANDERS LAW

Nothing is a waste of time if you use the experience wisely.

RODIN

Experience is something you get too late to do anything about the mistakes you made while getting it.

ANONYMOUS

When I was a boy of fourteen, my father was so ignorant I could hardly stand to have the old man around. But when I got to be twenty-one, I was astonished at how much the old man had learned in seven years.

MARK TWAIN

Experience is one thing you can't get for nothing.

OSCAR WILDE

Experience increases our wisdom but doesn't reduce our follies.

JOSH BILLINGS

EXTRAVAGANCE *Also see:* DESIRE, ECONOMY.

Extravagance is the luxury of the poor; penury is the luxury of the rich.

OSCAR WILDE

An extravagance is anything you buy that is of no earthly use to your wife.

FRANKLIN P. JONES

He who buys what he needs not, sells what he needs.

JAPANESE PROVERB

All decent people live beyond their incomes; those who aren't respectable live beyond other people's; a few gifted individuals manage to do both.
SAKI

EXTREMES *Also see:* EXTRAVAGANCE, RADICAL, REVERIE.

Mistrust the man who finds everything good; the man who finds everything evil; and still more the man who is indifferent to everything.
JOHANN KASPAR LAVATER

I would remind you that extremism in the defense of liberty is no vice. And let me also remind you that moderation in the pursuit of justice is no virtue.
BARRY M. GOLDWATER

In everything the middle course is best; all things in excess bring trouble.
PLAUTUS

Too austere a philosophy makes few wise men; too rigorous politics, few good subjects; too hard a religion, few persons whose devotion is of long continuance.
SEIGNEUR DE SAINT-EVREMOND

EYE *Also see:* ADVENTURE, BIGOTRY, ORIGINALITY, VISION.

Men are born with two eyes, but only one tongue, in order that they should see twice as much as they say.
CHARLES CALEB COLTON

One of the most wonderful things in nature is a glance of the eye; it transcends speech; it is the bodily symbol of identity.
RALPH WALDO EMERSON

The eye of the master will do more work than both his hands.
BENJAMIN FRANKLIN

An eye can threaten like a loaded and levelled gun, or it can insult like hissing or kicking; or, in its altered mood, by beams of kindness, it can make the heart dance for joy.
RALPH WALDO EMERSON

FACTS *Also see:* ACCURACY, COMPROMISE, CURIOSITY, EMOTION, THEORY.

Facts are facts and will not disappear on account of your likes.
JAWAHARLAL NEHRU

Get your facts first, and then you can distort them as much as you please.

MARK TWAIN

We should keep so close to facts that we never have to remember the second time what we said the first time.

F. MARION SMITH

A fact in itself is nothing. It is valuable only for the idea attached to it, or for the proof which it furnishes.

CLAUDE BERNARD

If you get all the facts, your judgment can be right; if you don't get all the facts, it can't be right.

BERNARD M. BARUCH

Comment is free but facts are sacred.

CHARLES P. SCOTT

FAILURE Also see: AMBITION, BOLDNESS, DEFEAT, DESPAIR, EFFORT, FATE, SUCCESS, WAR.

Show me a thoroughly satisfied man and I will show you a failure.

THOMAS A. EDISON

The only people who never fail are those who never try.

ILKA CHASE

Failures are divided into two classes—those who thought and never did, and those who did and never thought.

JOHN CHARLES SALAK

A failure is a man who has blundered but is not able to cash in the experience.

ELBERT HUBBARD

A man can fail many times, but he isn't a failure until he begins to blame somebody else.

JOHN BURROUGHS

FAITH Also see: ATHEISM, BELIEF, CONFIDENCE, COURAGE, CREDIT, CRIME, DOUBT, EFFORT, FEAR, RELIGION.

The smallest seed of faith is better than the largest fruit of happiness.

HENRY DAVID THOREAU

When faith is lost, when honor dies, the man is dead.

JOHN GREENLEAF WHITTIER

We have not lost faith, but we have transferred it from God to the medical profession.

GEORGE BERNARD SHAW

I can believe anything provided it is incredible.

OSCAR WILDE

Faith is love taking the form of aspiration.

WILLIAM ELLERY CHANNING

I always prefer to believe the best of everybody—it saves so much trouble.

RUDYARD KIPLING

FAME Also see: ADMIRATION, ESTEEM, GLORY, HONOR, NAME, REPUTATION, VANITY.

Fame is proof that people are gullible.

RALPH WALDO EMERSON

Fame usually comes to those who are thinking about something else.

HORACE GREELEY

The fame of great men ought to be judged always by the means they used to acquire it.

FRANÇOIS DE LA ROCHEFOUCAULD

The lust of fame is the last that a wise man shakes off.

TACITUS

Even the best things are not equal to their fame.

HENRY DAVID THOREAU

The highest form of vanity is love of fame.

GEORGE SANTAYANA

FAMILIARITY Also see: FRIENDSHIP.

Familiarity is a magician that is cruel to beauty but kind to ugliness.

OUIDA

All objects lose by too familiar a view.

JOHN DRYDEN

Familiarity breeds contempt—and children.

MARK TWAIN

Though familiarity may not breed contempt, it takes off the edge of admiration.

WILLIAM HAZLITT

Nothing is wonderful when you get used to it.

ED HOWE

Familiarity is the root of the closest friendships, as well as the intensest hatreds.

ANTOINE RIVAROL

FAMILY Also see: ANCESTRY, BIRTH, CHILDREN.

If you cannot get rid of the family skeleton, you may as well make it dance.

GEORGE BERNARD SHAW

A happy family is but an earlier heaven.

JOHN BOWRING

The family is one of nature's masterpieces.

GEORGE SANTAYANA

None but a mule denies his family.

ANONYMOUS

The family you come from isn't as important as the family you're going to have.

RING LARDNER

I would rather start a family than finish one.

DON MARQUIS

Family life is too intimate to be preserved by the spirit of justice. It can be sustained by a spirit of love which goes beyond justice.

REINHOLD NIEBUHR

FANATICISM Also see: ENTHUSIASM, TYRANNY, ZEAL.

Fanaticism consists in redoubling your efforts when you have forgotten your aim.

GEORGE SANTAYANA

A fanatic is one who can't change his mind and won't change the subject.

WINSTON CHURCHILL

The worst vice of the fanatic is his sincerity.

OSCAR WILDE

Fanaticism, the false fire of an overheated mind.

WILLIAM COWPER

A fanatic is a man who does what he thinks the Lord would do if only He knew the facts of the case.

FINLEY PETER DUNNE

FASHION *Also see:* APPEARANCE, DRESS.

Fashion is a form of ugliness so intolerable that we have to alter it every six months.

OSCAR WILDE

Fashion is what one wears oneself. What is unfashionable is what other people wear.

OSCAR WILDE

Every generation laughs at the old fashions, but follows religiously the new.

HENRY DAVID THOREAU

Fashion is the science of appearances, and it inspires one with the desire to seem rather than to be.

EDWIN HUBBEL CHAPIN

Ten years before its time, a fashion is indecent; ten years after, it is hideous; but a century after, it is romantic.

JAMES LAVER

Be not too early in the fashion, nor too long out of it; nor at any time in the extremes of it.

JOHANN KASPAR LAVATER

FATE *Also see:* CHARACTER, DESTINY, FORTUNE.

I do not believe in the word Fate. It is the refuge of every self-confessed failure.

ANDREW SOUTAR

What a man thinks of himself, that it is which determines, or rather indicates, his fate.

HENRY DAVID THOREAU

We make our own fortunes and we call them fate.

BENJAMIN DISRAELI

There is no good arguing with the inevitable.

JAMES RUSSELL LOWELL

Fate is the friend of the good, the guide of the wise, the tyrant of the foolish, the enemy of the bad.

WILLIAM ROUNSEVILLE ALGER

Fate often puts all the material for happiness and prosperity into a man's hands just to see how miserable he can make himself.

DON MARQUIS

FATHER *Also see:* CHILDREN, FAMILY, PARENT.

Paternity is a career imposed on you without any inquiry into your fitness.
ADLAI E. STEVENSON

The fundamental defect of fathers is that they want their children to be a credit to them.
BERTRAND RUSSELL

No man is responsible for his father. That is entirely his mother's affair.
MARGARET TURNBULL

The worst misfortune that can happen to an ordinary man is to have an extraordinary father.
AUSTIN O'MALLEY

I don't want to be a pal, I want to be a father.
CLIFTON FADIMAN

Every father expects his boy to do the things he wouldn't do when he was young.
KIN HUBBARD

FAULT *Also see:* COMPLAINT, CONFESSION, ENEMY, WEAK-NESS.

People who have no faults are terrible; there is no way of taking advantage of them.
ANATOLE FRANCE

His only fault is that he has none.
PLINY THE ELDER

A benevolent man should allow a few faults in himself, to keep his friends in countenance.
BENJAMIN FRANKLIN

If you are pleased at finding faults, you are displeased at finding perfections.
JOHANN KASPAR LAVATER

We confess small faults, in order to insinuate that we have no great ones.
FRANÇOIS DE LA ROCHEFOUCAULD

I like a friend better for having faults that one can talk about.
WILLIAM HAZLITT

The greatest of faults, I should say, is to be conscious of none.

THOMAS CARLYLE

FEAR *Also see:* BOLDNESS, COURAGE, COWARDICE, CRIME, CRUELTY, DANGER, DISEASE, SUPERSTITION.

The man who fears suffering is already suffering from what he fears.

MICHEL DE MONTAIGNE

He who fears being conquered is sure of defeat.

NAPOLEON BONAPARTE

The only thing we have to fear is fear itself.

FRANKLIN DELANO ROOSEVELT

Logic and cold reason are poor weapons to fight fear and distrust. Only faith and generosity can overcome them.

JAWAHARLAL NEHRU

If a man harbors any sort of fear, it percolates through all his thinking, damages his personality, makes him landlord to a ghost.

LLOYD DOUGLAS

FEELINGS . . . *See* EMOTION.

FIDELITY *Also see:* LOYALTY.

Another of our highly prized virtues is fidelity. We are immensely pleased with ourselves when we are faithful.

IDA ROSS WYLIE

An ideal wife is one who remains faithful to you but tries to be just as charming as if she weren't.

SACHA GUITRY

It is better to be faithful than famous.

THEODORE ROOSEVELT

Constancy is the complement of all other human virtues.

GIUSEPPE MAZZINI

Nothing is more noble, nothing more venerable than fidelity. Faithfulness and truth are the most sacred excellences and endowments of the human mind.

CICERO

FINANCE *Also see:* BUSINESS, GAIN, MONEY, SPECULATION.

High finance isn't burglary or obtaining money by false pretenses, but rather a judicious selection from the best features of those fine arts.

FINLEY PETER DUNNE

A financier is a pawn-broker with imagination.

ARTHUR WING PINERO

Alexander Hamilton originated the put and take system in our national treasury: the taxpayers put it in, and the politicians take it out.

WILL ROGERS

One-third of the people in the United States promote, while the other two-thirds provide.

WILL ROGERS

Financial sense is knowing that certain men will promise to do certain things, and fail.

ED HOWE

FIRMNESS Also see: DECISION, RESOLUTION.

The greatest firmness is the greatest mercy.

HENRY WADSWORTH LONGFELLOW

Firmness of purpose is one of the most necessary sinews of character, and one of the best instruments of success. Without it genius wastes its efforts in a maze of inconsistencies.

LORD CHESTERFIELD

The superior man is firm in the right way, and not merely firm.

CONFUCIUS

That which is called firmness in a king is called obstinacy in a donkey.

LORD ERSKINE

It is only persons of firmness that can have real gentleness.

FRANÇOIS DE LA ROCHEFOUCAULD

FLATTERY Also see: COMPLIMENT, PRAISE.

Flattery is from the teeth out. Sincere appreciation is from the heart out.

DALE CARNEGIE

None are more taken in with flattery than the proud, who wish to be the first and are not.

BENEDICT SPINOZA

It is easy to flatter: it is harder to praise.

JEAN PAUL RICHTER

Flattery is like cologne water, to be smelt of, not swallowed.

JOSH BILLINGS

FOOL Also see: ADMIRATION, BROTHERHOOD, DESPAIR, QUESTION.

The best way to convince a fool that he is wrong is to let him have his own way.

JOSH BILLINGS

Let us be thankful for the fools; but for them the rest of us could not succeed.

MARK TWAIN

What the fool does in the end, the wise man does in the beginning.

PROVERB

A fool can no more see his own folly than he can see his ears.

WILLIAM MAKEPEACE THACKERAY

FORCE Also see: CUSTOM, POWER, REVOLUTION, VIOLENCE, WAR.

When force is necessary, it must be applied boldly, decisively and completely. But one must know the limitations of force; one must know when to blend force with a maneuver, the blow with an agreement.

LEON TROTSKY

Force is not a remedy.

JOHN BRIGHT

Right reason is stronger than force.

JAMES A. GARFIELD

Force is all-conquering, but its victories are short-lived.

ABRAHAM LINCOLN

The power that is supported by force alone will have cause often to tremble.

LAJOS KOSSUTH

FORGIVENESS Also see: MERCY.

To err is human; to forgive, divine.

ALEXANDER POPE

The weak can never forgive. Forgiveness is the attribute of the strong.

MAHATMA GANDHI

Forgive many things in others; nothing in yourself.

AUSONIUS

It is easier to forgive an enemy than a friend.

MADAME DOROTHÉE DELUZY

"I can forgive, but I cannot forget," is only another way of saying, "I will not forgive.'' Forgiveness ought to be like a cancelled note—torn in two, and burned up, so that it never can be shown against one.

HENRY WARD BEECHER

Humanity is never so beautiful as when praying for forgiveness, or else forgiving another.

JEAN PAUL RICHTER

FORTUNE *Also see:* FATE, MERIT, PURSUIT, WEALTH.

Fortune is ever seen accompanying industry.

OLIVER GOLDSMITH

Fortune is the rod of the weak, and the staff of the brave.

JAMES RUSSELL LOWELL

Every man is the architect of his own fortune.

SALLUST

Fortune is a great deceiver. She sells very dear the things she seems to give us.

VINCENT VOITURE

Nature magically suits a man to his fortunes, by making them the fruit of his character.

RALPH WALDO EMERSON

FRAUD *Also see:* DECEIT, DISHONESTY.

It is fraud to accept what you cannot repay.

PUBLILIUS SYRUS

The first and worst of all frauds is to cheat oneself.

GAMALIEL BAILEY

For the most part fraud in the end secures for its companions repentance and shame.

CHARLES SIMMONS

The more gross the fraud the more glibly will it go down, and the more greedily be swallowed, since folly will always find faith where impostors will find imprudence.

CHARLES CALEB COLTON

FREEDOM *Also see:* BOOK, BORROWING, COUNTRY, DISCI-
PLINE, EDUCATION, END AND MEANS,
EQUALITY, FREEDOM OF PRESS, FREE-
DOM OF SPEECH, INDEPENDENCE, LIB-
ERTY, SECURITY.

I know but one freedom and that is the freedom of mind.

ANTOINE DE SAINT-EXUPÉRY

No man is free who is not a master of himself.

EPICTETUS

Freedom is not worth having if it does not connote freedom to err.

MAHATMA GANDHI

The unity of freedom has never relied on uniformity of opinion.

JOHN FITZGERALD KENNEDY

A hungry man is not a free man.

ADLAI E. STEVENSON

Only our individual faith in freedom can keep us free.

DWIGHT D. EISENHOWER

The cost of freedom is always high, but Americans have always paid it. And one path we shall never choose, and that is the path of surrender, or submission.

JOHN FITZGERALD KENNEDY

Freedom rings where opinions clash.

ADLAI E. STEVENSON

FREEDOM of the PRESS *Also see:* CENSORSHIP, LIBERTY.

Our liberty depends on the freedom of the press, and that cannot be limited without being lost.

THOMAS JEFFERSON

The liberty of the press is a blessing when we are inclined to write against others, and a calamity when we find ourselves overborne by the multitude of our assailants.

SAMUEL JOHNSON

The free press is the mother of all our liberties and of our progress under liberty.

ADLAI E. STEVENSON

The press is not only free, it is powerful. That power is ours. It is the proudest that man can enjoy.

BENJAMIN DISRAELI

Let it be impressed upon your minds, let it be instilled into your children, that the liberty of the press is the palladium of all the civil, political, and religious rights.

JUNIUS

FREEDOM of SPEECH *Also see:* CENSORSHIP, DISSENT,

LIBERTY, FREEDOM OF THE PRESS.

I disapprove of what you say, but will defend to the death your right to say it.

VOLTAIRE

I have always been among those who believed that the greatest freedom of speech was the greatest safety, because if a man is a fool the best thing to do is to encourage him to advertise the fact by speaking.

WOODROW WILSON

I realize that there are certain limitations placed upon the right of free speech. I may not be able to say all I think, but I am not going to say anything I do not think.

EUGENE V. DEBS

Free speech is to a great people what winds are to oceans and malarial regions, which waft away the elements of disease and bring new elements of health; and where free speech is stopped, miasma is bred, and death comes fast.

HENRY WARD BEECHER

Better a thousandfold abuse of free speech than denial of free speech. The abuse dies in a day, but the denial stays the life of the people, and entombs the hope of the race.

CHARLES BRADLAUGH

FRIENDSHIP *Also see:* AFFECTION, BROTHERHOOD, ENEMY, FAMILIARITY, LOVE, PRAISE.

The only way to have a friend is to be one.

RALPH WALDO EMERSON

Friendship is always a sweet responsibility, never an opportunity.

KAHLIL GIBRAN

If a man does not make new acquaintances as he advances through life, he will soon find himself left alone; one should keep his friendships in constant repair.

SAMUEL JOHNSON

Friendship is one mind in two bodies.

MENCIUS

Acquaintance: a degree of friendship called slight when its object is poor or obscure, and intimate when he is rich or famous.

AMBROSE BIERCE

The best way to keep your friends is not to give them away.

WILSON MIZNER

Friendship without self-interest is one of the rare and beautiful things of life.

JAMES FRANCIS BYRNES

Friendship is almost always the union of a part of one mind with a part of another: people are friends in spots.

GEORGE SANTAYANA

FRUGALITY . . . *See* ECONOMY.

FUTURE *Also see:* PAST, PRESENT.

When all else is lost, the future still remains.

CHRISTIAN NESTELL BOVEE

I never think of the future. It comes soon enough.

ALBERT EINSTEIN

I like the dreams of the future better than the history of the past.

PATRICK HENRY

My interest is in the future because I am going to spend the rest of my life there.

CHARLES F. KETTERING

The trouble with our times is that the future is not what it used to be.

PAUL VALERY

GAIN *Also see:* DUTY.

Sometimes the best gain is to lose.

GEORGE HERBERT

For everything you have missed you have gained something.

RALPH WALDO EMERSON

Gain cannot be made without some other person's loss.

PUBLILIUS SYRUS

The true way to gain much, is never to desire to gain too much.

FRANCIS BEAUMONT

No gain is so certain as that which proceeds from the economical use of what you already have.

LATIN PROVERB

GALLANTRY *Also see:* COURTESY, FLATTERY.

Gallantry of the mind is saying the most empty things in an agreeable manner.

FRANÇOIS DE LA ROCHEFOUCAULD

To give up your seat in a car to a woman, and tread on your neighbor's foot to get even.

ELBERT HUBBARD

To do a perfectly unselfish act for selfish motives.

ELBERT HUBBARD

GENEROSITY *Also see:* ARISTOCRACY, CHARITY, FEAR, KIND-NESS.

Generosity during life is a very different thing from generosity in the hour of death; one proceeds from genuine liberality and benevolence, the other from pride or fear.

HORACE MANN

Generosity is giving more than you can, and pride is taking less than you need.

KAHLIL GIBRAN

What seems to be generosity is often no more than disguised ambition, which overlooks a small interest in order to secure a great one.

FRANÇOIS DE LA ROCHEFOUCAULD

If there be any truer measure of a man than by what he does, it must be by what he gives.

ROBERT SOUTH

GENIUS *Also see:* ABILITY, ART, COMMON SENSE.

Genius does what it must, and talent does what it can.

EDWARD G. BULWER-LYTTON

When human power becomes so great and original that we can account for it only as a kind of divine imagination, we call it genius.

WILLIAM CRASHAW

Genius is entitled to respect only when it promotes the peace and improves the happiness of mankind.

LORD ESSEX

Genius begins great works; labor alone finishes them.

JOSEPH JOUBERT

Genius is one per cent inspiration and ninety-nine per cent perspiration.

THOMAS A. EDISON

To believe your own thought, to believe that what is true for you in your private heart is true for all men—that is genius.

RALPH WALDO EMERSON

Genius without education is like silver in the mine.

BENJAMIN FRANKLIN

Genius is the ability to act rightly without precedent—the power to do the right thing the first time.

ELBERT HUBBARD

When Nature has work to be done, she creates a genius to do it.

RALPH WALDO EMERSON

No great genius is without an admixture of madness.

ARISTOTLE

GENTLEMAN *Also see:* COURTESY.

. . . one who never hurts anyone's feelings unintentionally.

OLIVER HERFORD

This is the final test of a gentleman: his respect for those who can be of no possible service to him.

WILLIAM LYON PHELPS

A true man of honor feels humbled himself when he cannot help humbling others.

ROBERT E. LEE

The man who is always talking about being a gentleman, never is one.

ROBERT S. SURTEES

GIRLS *Also see:* WOMAN.

A homely girl hates mirrors.

PROVERB

I am fond of children—except boys.

LEWIS CARROLL

Some girls never know what they are going to do from one husband to another.

TOM MASSON

I never expected to see the day when girls would get sunburned in the places they do now.

WILL ROGERS

GLORY *Also see:* FAME, HONOR.

For glory gives herself only to those who have always dreamed of her.

CHARLES DE GAULLE

Glory built on selfish principles, is shame and guilt.

WILLIAM COWPER

Our greatest glory consists not in never falling, but in rising every time we fall.

OLIVER GOLDSMITH

Real glory springs from the silent conquest of ourselves.

JOSEPH P. THOMPSON

Glory paid to our ashes comes too late.

MARTIAL

GLUTTON *Also see:* ABSTINENCE, APPETITE, EATING.

Their kitchen is their shrine, the cook their priest, the table their altar, and their belly their god.

CHARLES BUCK

Glutton: one who digs his grave with his teeth.

FRENCH PROVERB

The fool that eats till he is sick must fast till he is well.

GEORGE W. THORNBURY

One meal a day is enough for a lion, and it ought to be for a man.

GEORGE FORDYCE

In general, mankind, since the improvement of cookery, eats twice as much as nature requires.

BENJAMIN FRANKLIN

One should eat to live, not live to eat.

BENJAMIN FRANKLIN

GOD *Also see:* AGNOSTICISM, ARTIST, ATHEISM, BABY, CREATIVITY, DEMOCRACY, DISHONESTY, EARTH, FAITH, FREEDOM OF THE PRESS, HEAVEN, RELIGION.

I fear God, and next to God I chiefly fear him who fears Him not.

SAADI

God enters by a private door into every individual.

RALPH WALDO EMERSON

God is not a cosmic bell-boy for whom we can press a button to get things.

HARRY EMERSON FOSDICK

God never made His work for man to mend.

JOHN DRYDEN

God is more truly imagined than expressed, and He exists more truly than He is imagined.

ST. AUGUSTINE

God is the brave man's hope, and not the coward's excuse.

PLUTARCH

When we know what God is, we shall be gods ourselves.

GEORGE BERNARD SHAW

We love the Lord, of course, but we often wonder what He finds in us.

ED HOWE

You can believe in God without believing in immortality, but it is hard to see how anyone can believe in immortality and not believe in God.

ERNEST DIMNET

The best way to know God is to love many things.

VINCENT VAN GOGH

Two men please God—who serves Him with all his heart because he knows Him; who seeks Him with all his heart because he knows Him not.

NIKITA IVANOVICH PANIN

Men talk of "finding God," but no wonder it is difficult; He is hidden in that darkest hiding-place, your heart. You yourself are a part of Him.

CHRISTOPHER MORLEY

In the faces of men and women I see God.

WALT WHITMAN

GOLD *Also see:* AVARICE, MISER.

The man who works for the gold in the job rather than for the money in the pay envelope, is the fellow who gets on.

JOSEPH FRENCH JOHNSON

Gold will be slave or master.

HORACE

A mask of gold hides all deformities.

THOMAS DEKKER

It is much better to have your gold in the hand than in the heart.

THOMAS FULLER

Curst greed of gold, what crimes thy tyrant power had caused.

VERGIL

Gold has worked down from Alexander's time . . . When something holds good for two thousand years I do not believe it can be so because of prejudice or mistaken theory.

BERNARD M. BARUCH

GOSSIP *Also see:* CONVERSATION, SLANDER.

Of every ten persons who talk about you, nine will say something bad, and the tenth will say something good in a bad way.

ANTOINE RIVAROL

Gossip is always a personal confession either of malice or imbecility.

JOSIAH GILBERT HOLLAND

The only time people dislike gossip is when you gossip about them.

WILL ROGERS

Truth is not exciting enough to those who depend on the characters and lives of their neighbors for all their amusement.

GEORGE BANCROFT

There isn't much to be seen in a little town, but what you hear makes up for it.

KIN HUBBARD

That which is everybody's business is nobody's business.

IZAAK WALTON

GOVERNMENT *Also see:* AUTHORITY, CITIZENSHIP, COMPRO-MISE, DEMOCRACY, PARTY, POLITICS.

The best of all governments is that which teaches us to govern ourselves.

JOHANN WOLFGANG VON GOETHE

Good government is no substitute for self-government.

MAHATMA GANDHI

The government is us; we are the government, you and I.

THEODORE ROOSEVELT

You can't run a government solely on a business basis . . . Government should be human. It should have a heart.

HERBERT HENRY LEHMAN

All free governments are managed by the combined wisdom and folly of the people.

JAMES A. GARFIELD

No man is good enough to govern another man without that other's consent.

ABRAHAM LINCOLN

My experience in government is that when things are noncontroversial and beautifully coordinated, there is not much going on.

JOHN FITZGERALD KENNEDY

He mocks the people who proposes that the government shall protect the rich that they in turn may care for the laboring poor.

GROVER CLEVELAND

GRACE

Beauty and grace command the world.

PARK BENJAMIN

A graceful and pleasing figure is a perpetual letter of recommendation.

FRANCIS BACON

Gracefulness had been defined to be the outward expression of the inward harmony of the soul.

WILLIAM HAZLITT

He does it with a better grace, but I do it more natural.

WILLIAM SHAKESPEARE

Grace is to the body, what good sense is to the mind.

FRANÇOIS DE LA ROCHEFOUCAULD

God appoints our graces to be nurses to other men's weaknesses.

HENRY WARD BEECHER

GRATITUDE

Gratitude is one of the least articulate of the emotions, especially when it is deep.

FELIX FRANKFURTER

Gratitude is the heart's memory.

FRENCH PROVERB

Gratitude is a duty which ought to be paid, but which none have a right to expect.

JEAN JACQUES ROUSSEAU

If you pick up a starving dog and make him prosperous, he will not bite you. This is the principal difference between a dog and a man.

MARK TWAIN

Gratitude is not only the greatest of virtues, but the parent of all the others.

CICERO

There is as much greatness of mind in acknowledging a good turn, as in doing it.

SENECA

GRAVE Also see: DEATH, MONUMENT.

The only difference between a rut and a grave is their dimensions.

ELLEN GLASGOW

A grave, wherever found, preaches a short and pithy sermon to the soul.

NATHANIEL HAWTHORNE

The grave is still the best shelter against the storms of destiny.

G. C. LICHTENBERG

There is but one easy place in this world, and that is the grave.

HENRY WARD BEECHER

We weep over the graves of infants and the little ones taken from us by death; but an early grave may be the shortest way to heaven.

TRYON EDWARDS

GRAVITY Also see: SORROW.

There is gravity in wisdom, but no particular wisdom in gravity.

JOSH BILLINGS

Too much gravity argues a shallow mind.

JOHANN KASPAR LAVATER

Those wanting wit affect gravity, and go by the name of solid men.

JOHN DRYDEN

GREED Also see: AVARICE, DESIRE, MISER, SELFISHNESS.

The greed of gain has no time or limit to its capaciousness. Its one object is to produce and consume. It has pity neither for beautiful nature nor for living human beings. It is ruthlessly ready without a moment's hesitation to crush beauty and life out of them, molding them into money.

RABINDRANATH TAGORE

The covetous man pines in plenty, like Tantalus up to the chin in water, and yet thirsty.

THOMAS ADAMS

It is economic slavery, the savage struggle for a crumb, that has converted mankind into wolves and sheep . . .

ALEXANDER BERKMAN

There is no fire like passion, there is no shark like hatred, there is no snare like folly, there is no torrent like greed.

BUDDHA

GRIEF *Also see:* AFFLICTION, MISERY, SORROW.

The only cure for grief is action.

GEORGE HENRY LEWES

Excess of grief for the dead is madness; for it is an injury to the living, and the dead know it not.

XENOPHON

Grief is the agony of an instant; the indulgence of grief the blunder of a life.

BENJAMIN DISRAELI

While grief is fresh, every attempt to divert only irritates. You must wait till it be digested, and then amusement will dissipate the remains of it.

SAMUEL JOHNSON

GUEST

Nobody can be as agreeable as an uninvited guest.

KIN HUBBARD

No one can be so welcome a guest that he will not annoy his host after three days.

PLAUTUS

Every guest hates the others, and the host hates them all.

ALBANIAN PROVERB

The first day, a guest; the second, a burden; the third, a pest.

EDOUDARD R. LABOULAYE

GUILT *Also see:* CONSCIENCE, CRIME, REPENTENCE.

Every man is guilty of all the good he didn't do.

VOLTAIRE

The guilty is he who meditates a crime; the punishment is his who lays the plot.

CONTE VITTORIO ALFIERI

The greatest incitement to guilt is the hope of sinning with impunity.

CICERO

From the body of one guilty deed a thousand ghostly fears and haunting thoughts proceed.

WILLIAM WORDSWORTH

He who flees from trial confesses his guilt.

PUBLILIUS SYRUS

It is base to filch a purse, daring to embezzle a million, but it is great beyond measure to steal a crown. The sin lessens as the guilt increases.

JOHANN VON SCHILLER

Suspicion always haunts the guilty mind.

WILLIAM SHAKESPEARE

Men's minds are too ready to excuse guilt in themselves.

LIVY

Every guilty person is his own hangman.

SENECA

HABIT *Also see:* DEBT, DUTY, TRADITION.

Each year, one viscious habit rooted out, in time ought to make the worst man good.

BENJAMIN FRANKLIN

Habit, if not resisted, soon becomes necessity.

ST. AUGSTINE

A single bad habit will mar an otherwise faultless character, as an ink-drop soileth the pure white page.

HOSEA BALLOU

The unfortunate thing about this world is that the good habits are much easier to give up than the bad ones.

W. SOMERSET MAUGHAM

The chains of habit are too weak to be felt until they are too strong to be broken.

SAMUEL JOHNSON

Habit converts luxurious enjoyments into dull and daily necessities.

ALDOUS HUXLEY

Good habits result from resisting temptation.

ANCIENT PROVERB

HAIR

By common consent gray hairs are a crown of glory; the only object of respect that can never excite envy.

GEORGE BANCROFT

Gray hair is a sign of age, not of wisdom.

GREEK PROVERB

The hair is the richest ornament of women.

MARTIN LUTHER

HAPPINESS *Also see:* APPEARANCE, BEAUTY, CHEERFULNESS, DUTY, ENJOYMENT, FAITH, FATE, PLEASURE, SECURITY, ZEST.

It is pretty hard to tell what does bring happiness; poverty and wealth have both failed.

KIN HUBBARD

Happiness is not a reward—it is a consequence. Suffering is not a punishment—it is a result.

ROBERT GREEN INGERSOLL

Be happy while you're living, for you're a long time dead.

SCOTTISH PROVERB

To fill the hour—that is happiness.

RALPH WALDO EMERSON

The grand essentials of happiness are: something to do, something to love, and something to hope for.

ALLAN K. CHALMERS

Happiness is like a sunbeam, which the least shadow intercepts, while adversity is often as the rain of spring.

CHINESE PROVERB

Happiness isn't something you experience; it's something you remember.

OSCAR LEVANT

HARDSHIP . . . *See* ADVERSITY

HASTE

No man who is in a hurry is quite civilized.

WILL DURANT

Manners require time, and nothing is more vulgar than haste.

RALPH WALDO EMERSON

Though I am always in haste, I am never in a hurry.

JOHN WESLEY

Take time for all things: great haste makes great waste.

BENJAMIN FRANKLIN

Make haste slowly.

LATIN PROVERB

Rapidity does not always mean progress, and hurry is akin to waste.

CHARLES A. STODDARD

HATE *Also see:* BLINDNESS, ENEMY.

Hatred does not cease by hatred, but only by love; this is the eternal rule.

BUDDHA

Hatred is the madness of the heart.

LORD BYRON

Heaven has no rage like love to hatred turned.

WILLIAM CONGREVE

A man who lives, not by what he loves but what he hates, is a sick man.

ARCHIBALD MACLEISH

When our hatred is violent, it sinks us even beneath those we hate.

FRANÇOIS DE LA ROCHEFOUCAULD

It is better to be hated for what you are than to be loved for what you are not.

ANDRÉ GIDE

Hatred is self-punishment.

HOSEA BALLOU

I shall never permit myself to stoop so low as to hate any man.

BOOKER T. WASHINGTON

National hatred is something peculiar. You will always find it strongest and most violent where there is the lowest degree of culture.

JOHANN WOLFGANG VON GOETHE

HEALTH *Also see:* BODY, CHEERFULNESS, DISEASE.

He who has health, has hope; and he who has hope, has everything.

ARABIAN PROVERB

To become a thoroughly good man is the best prescription for keeping a sound mind and a sound body.

FRANCIS BOWEN

It is a weariness disease to preserve health by too strict a regimen.

FRANÇOIS DE LA ROCHEFOUCAULD

The only way to keep your health is to eat what you don't want, drink what you don't like, and do what you'd rather not.

MARK TWAIN

There's a lot of people in this world who spend so much time watching their health that they haven't the time to enjoy it.

JOSH BILLINGS

HEART *Also see:* CHARITY, COMPASSION, CONFIDENCE, COURAGE, GREED, GOVERNMENT, LOVE.

The head learns new things, but the heart forever more practices old experiences.

HENRY WARD BEECHER

The heart has reasons that reason does not understand.

JACQUES BÈNIGNE BOSSUET

There is no instinct like that of the heart.

LORD BYRON

The heart of a fool is in his mouth, but the mouth of the wise man is in his heart.

BENJAMIN FRANKLIN

Nothing is less in our power than the heart, and far from commanding we are forced to obey it.

JEAN JACQUES ROUSSEAU

Two things are bad for the heart—running up stairs and running down people.

BERNARD M. BARUCH

HEAVEN *Also see:* AMBITION, DEMOCRACY, FAMILY, HELL, HOME.

Heaven will be inherited by every man who has heaven in his soul.

HENRY WARD BEECHER

The few men who have managed to reach heaven must be terribly spoiled by this time.

ED HOWE

On earth there is no heaven, but there are pieces of it.

JULES RENARD

I don't like to commit myself about heaven and hell—you see, I have friends in both places.

MARK TWAIN

To get to heaven, turn right and keep straight.

ANONYMOUS

The main objective of religion is not to get a man into heaven, but to get heaven into him.

THOMAS HARDY

HELL *Also see:* CHRISTIANITY, DECEIT, DIPLOMACY, HEAVEN.

Hell is truth seen too late.

TRYON EDWARDS

There may be some doubt about hell beyond the grave but there is no doubt about there being one on this side of it.

ED HOWE

I never given them hell; I just tell the truth and they think it's hell.

HARRY S. TRUMAN

If there is no hell, a good many preachers are obtaining money under false pretenses.

WILLIAM A. SUNDAY

The wicked work harder to reach hell than the righteous to reach heaven.

JOSH BILLINGS

To be in hell is to drift; to be in heaven is to steer.

GEORGE BERNARD SHAW

The road to Hell is paved with good intentions.

KARL MARX

HELP *Also see:* CHARITY, GENEROSITY.

God helps them that help themselves.

PROVERB

Nothing makes one feel so strong as a call for help.

GEORGE MACDONALD

Every great man is always being helped by everybody; for his gift is to get good out of all things and all persons.

JOHN RUSKIN

When a person is down in the world, an ounce of help is better than a pound of preaching.

EDWARD G. BULWAR-LYTTON

The race of mankind would perish did they cease to aid each other. We cannot exist without mutual help. All therefore that need aid have a right to ask it from their fellowmen; and no one who has the power of granting can refuse it without guilt.

WALTER SCOTT

HEROISM *Also see:* COURAGE.

Self-trust is the essence of heroism.

RALPH WALDO EMERSON

The world's battlefields have been in the heart chiefly; more heroism has been displayed in the household and the closet, than on the most memorable battlefields in history.

HENRY WARD BEECHER

Heroes are not known by the loftiness of their carriage; the greatest braggarts are generally the merest cowards.

JEAN JACQUES ROUSSEAU

A hero is no braver than an ordinary man, but he is braver five minutes longer.

RALPH WALDO EMERSON

Hero worship is strongest where there is least regard for human freedom.

HERBERT SPENCER

Hero-worship is mostly idol gossip.

ANONYMOUS

HISTORY *Also see:* CUSTOM, SPIRIT, TRADITION.

History is little more than the register of the crimes, follies and misfortunes of mankind.

EDWARD GIBBON

The men who make history have not time to write it.

METTERNICH

The main thing is to make history, not to write it.

OTTO VON VISMARCK

No historian can take part with—or against—the forces he has to study. To him even the extinction of the human race should merely be a fact to be grouped with other vital statistics.

HENRY BROOKS ADAMS

History repeats itself, and that's one of the things that's wrong with history.

CLARENCE DARROW

History is nothing but a pack of tricks that we play upon the dead.

VOLTAIRE

HOME *Also see:* FAMILY, FATHER.

A hundred men may make an encampment, but it takes a woman to make a home.

CHINESE PROVERB

Home is where the heart is.

PLINY THE ELDER

Home is the place where, when you have to go there, they have to take you in.

ROBERT FROST

Home is the most popular, and will be the most enduring of all earthly establishments.

CHANNING POLLOCK

Home interprets heaven. Home is heaven for beginners.

CHARLES H. PARKHURST

He is the happiest, be he king or peasant, who finds peace in his home.

JOHANN WOLFGANG VON GOETHE

Home life is no more natural to us than a cage is to a cockatoo.

GEORGE BERNARD SHAW

HONESTY *Also see:* ACCURACY, CANDOR, DISHONESTY, DISTRUST, TRUTH.

I would give no thought of what the world might say of me, if I could only transmit to posterity the reputation of an honest man.

SAM HOUSTON

Honesty is the rarest wealth anyone can posses, and yet all the honesty in the world ain't lawful tender for a loaf of bread.

JOSH BILLINGS

Honesty pays, but it don't seem to pay enough to suit some people.

KIN HUBBARD

We must make the world honest before we can honestly say to our children that honesty is the best policy.

GEORGE BERNARD SHAW

Make yourself an honest man, and then you may be sure there is one less rascal in the world.

THOMAS CARLYLE

Honesty is the best policy—when there is money in it.

MARK TWAIN

HONOR *Also see:* DIGNITY, DRESS, ESTEEM, GLORY, RESPECT.

It is better to deserve honors and not have them than to have them and not deserve them.

MARK TWAIN

The difference between a moral man and a man of honor is that the latter regrets a discreditable act even when it has worked.

H. L. MENCKEN

Honor lies in honest toil.

GROVER CLEVELAND

Better to die ten thousand deaths than wound my honor.

JOSEPH ADDISON

The louder he talked of his honor, the faster we counted our spoons.

RALPH WALDO EMERSON

When faith is lost, when honor dies, the man is dead!

JOHN GREENLEAF WHITTIER

HOPE *Also see:* ANTICIPATION, ATHEISM, BELIEF, BIBLE, CREDULITY, DESPAIR, DISAPPOINTMENT, FAITH, TRUST.

To the sick, while there is life there is hope.

CICERO

Hope for the best, but prepare for the worst.

ENGLISH PROVERB

A woman's hopes are woven of sunbeams; a shadow annihilates them.

GEORGE ELIOT

We should not expect something for nothing but we all do, and we call it hope.

ED HOWE

He that lives upon hope will die fasting.

BENJAMIN FRANKLIN

In all things it is better to hope than to despair.

JOHANN WOLFGANG VON GOETHE

HUMANITY *Also see:* AMERICA, BROTHERHOOD, EMOTION, FORGIVENESS, HUMILITY.

We cannot despair of humanity, since we ourselves are human beings.

ALBERT EINSTEIN

There are times when one would like to hang the whole human race, and finish the farce.

MARK TWAIN

There is nothing on earth divine except humanity.

WALTER SAVAGE LANDOR

The true grandeur of humanity is in moral elevation, sustained, enlightened and decorated by the intellect of man.

CHARLES SUMNER

Humanity to me is not a mob. A mob is a degeneration of humanity. A mob is humanity going the wrong way.

FRANK LLOYD WRIGHT

HUMAN NATURE *Also see:* BROTHERHOOD, LIFE, MAN, SOCIETY.

We have provided for the survival of man against all enemies except his fellow man.

LYMAN LLOYD BRYSON

It is human nature to think wisely and act foolishly.

ANATOLE FRANCE

It is easier to love humanity as a whole than to love one's neighbor.

ERIC HOFFER

HUMILITY *Also see:* MODESTY.

I feel coming on a strange disease—humility.

FRANK LLOYD WRIGHT

The first of all other virtues—for other people.

OLIVER WENDELL HOLMES

Without humility there can be no humanity.

JOHN BUCHAN

HUMOR *Also see:* BIBLE, JESTING, WIT.

If I had no sense of humor, I would long ago have committed suicide.

MAHATMÁ GANDHI

A man isn't poor if he can still laugh.

RAYMOND HITCHCOCK

Good humor is one of the best articles of dress one can wear in society.

WILLIAM MAKEPEACE THACKERAY

If I studied all my life, I couldn't think up half the number of funny things passed in one session of congress.

WILL ROGERS

Everything is funny as long as it is happening to somebody else.

WILL ROGERS

Whenever you find humor, you find pathos close by his side.

EDWIN PERCY WHIPPLE

HUNGER Also see: APPETITE, CULTURE, FREEDOM, GLUTTON, POPULATION.

An empty stomach is not a good political advisor.

ALBERT EINSTEIN

Hunger does not breed reform; it breeds madness, and all the ugly distempers that make an ordered life impossible.

WOODROW WILSON

A hungry man is not a free man.

ADLAI E. STEVENSON

A hungry people listens not to reason, nor cares for justice, nor is bent by any prayers.

SENECA

No one can worship God or love his neighbor on an empty stomach.

WOODROW WILSON

HUSBAND Also see: GIRLS, MARRIAGE.

All husbands are alike, but they have different faces so you can tell them apart.

ANONYMOUS

An archaeologist is the best husband any woman can have: the older she gets, the more interested he is in her.

AGATHA CHRISTIE

The husband who wants a happy marriage should learn to keep his mouth shut and his checkbook open.

GROUCHO MARX

Husbands never become good; they merely become proficient.

H. L. MENCKEN

A good husband should be deaf and a good wife should be blind.

FRENCH PROVERB

HYPOCRISY *Also see:* DECEIT, LYING, OSTENTATION.

A hypocrite is the kind of politician who would cut down a redwood tree, then mount the stump and make a speech for conservation.

ADLAI E. STEVENSON

A bad man is worse when he pretends to be a saint.

FRANCIS BACON

It is with pious fraud as with a bad action; it begets a calamitous necessity of going on.

THOMAS PAINE

Hypocrite: the man who murdered both his parents . . . pleaded for mercy on the grounds that he was an orphan.

ABRAHAM LINCOLN

Every man alone is sincere; at the entrance of a second person hypocrisy begins.

RALPH WALDO EMERSON

IDEA *Also see:* ACTION, COMMITTEE, COMMUNICATION, CREATIVITY, FACTS, THOUGHT.

Ideas are the root of creation.

ERNEST DIMNET

Ideas are the factors that lift civilization. They create revolutions. There is more dynamite in an idea than in many bombs.

JOHN H. VINCENT

There is one thing stronger than all the armies in the world, and that is an idea whose time has come.

VICTOR HUGO

The vitality of thought is in adventure. Ideas won't keep. Something must be done about them. When the idea is new, its custodians have fervor, live for it, and if need be, die for it.

ALFRED NORTH WHITEHEAD

IDEAL *Also see:* AMERICA, COMMUNICATION.

The attainment of an ideal is often the beginning of a disillusion.

STANLEY BALDWIN

Words without actions are the assassins of idealism.

HERBERT HOOVER

Some men see things as they are and say why. I dream things that never were and say, why not?

ROBERT F. KENNEDY

What we need most, is not so much to realize the ideal as to idealize the real.

H. F. HEDGE

Ideals are like the stars: we never reach them, but like the mariners of the sea, we chart our course by them.

CARL SCHURZ

IDLENESS *Also see:* ACTION, LEISURE.

Prolonged ideas paralyzes initiative.

ANONYMOUS

The way to be nothing is to do nothing.

NATHANIEL HOWE

It is impossible to enjoy idling thoroughly unless one has plenty of work to do.

JEROME K. JEROME

Idleness is the stupidity of the body, and stupidity is the idleness of the mind.

JOHANN G. SEUME

Idleness is an inlet to disorder, and makes way for licentiousness. People who have nothing to do are quickly tired of their own company.

JERMY COLLIER

An idle brain is the devil's workshop.

ENGLISH PROVERB

Purity of mind and idleness are incompatible.

MAHATMA GANDHI

IDOLATRY *Also see:* GOD.

We boast our emancipation from many superstitions; but if we have broken any idols, it is through a transfer of idolatry.

RALPH WALDO EMERSON

The idol is the measure of the worshipper.

JAMES RUSSELL LOWELL

Belief in a cruel God makes a cruel man.

THOMAS PAINE

Whatever a man seeks, honors, or exalts more than God, this is the god of his idolatry.

WILLIAM B. ULLATHORNE

When men have gone so far as to talk as though their idols have come to life, it is time that someone broke them.

RICHARD H. TAWNEY

IGNORANCE *Also see:* DIGNITY, FOOL, HAPPINESS, KNOWL-
EDGE, MYSTERY, PREJUDICE.

He knows so little and knows it so fluently.

ELLEN GLASGOW

Ignorance is a voluntary misfortune.

NICHOLAS LING

Have the courage to be ignorant of a great number of things, in order to avoid the calamity of being ignorant of everything.

SYDNEY SMITH

Everybody is ignorant, only on different subjects.

WILL ROGERS

There is nothing more frightful than ignorance in action.

JOHANN WOLFGANG VON GOETHE

Most ignorance is vincible ignorance. We don't know because we don't want to know.

ALDOUS HUXLEY

Ignorance breeds monsters to fill up the vacancies of the soul that are unoccupied by the verities of knowledge.

HORACE MANN

ILLNESS . . . *See* DISEASE

ILLUSION *Also see:* IMAGINATION, REVERIE.

Nothing is more sad than the death of an illusion.

ARTHUR KOESTLER

Better a dish of illusion and a hearty appetite for life, than a feast of reality and indigestion therewith.

HARRY A. OVERSTREET

It is respectable to have no illusions, and safe, and profitable—and dull.

JOSEPH CONRAD

The one person who has more illusions than the dreamer is the man of action.

OSCAR WILDE

IMAGINATION Also see: BUSINESS, COWARDICE, CREATIVITY, DREAM, GENIUS, MOB.

He who has imagination without learning has wings and no feet.

JOSEPH JOUBERT

Imagination rules the world.

NAPOLEON BONAPARTE

Imagination disposes of everything; it creates beauty, justice, and happiness, which are everything in this world.

BLAISE PASCAL

Imagination is a quality given a man to compensate him for what he is not, and a sense of humor was provided to console him for what he is.

OSCAR WILDE

Science does not know its debt to imagination.

RALPH WALDO EMERSON

IMITATION Also see: ADAPTABILITY, CONFORMITY, ORIGINALITY.

Imitation belittles.

CHRISTIAN NESTELL BOVEE

There is much difference between imitating a good man and counterfeiting him.

BENJAMIN FRANKLIN

To copy others is necessary, but to copy oneself is pathetic.

PABLO PICASSO

Men are so constituted that every one undertakes what he sees another successful in, whether he has aptitude for it or not.

JOHANN WOLFGANG VON GOETHE

IMMORTALITY Also see: CONVERSATION, ETERNITY, GOD, LIFE.

The average man does not know what to do with this life, yet wants another one which will last forever.

ANATOLE FRANCE

The first requisite for immortality is death.

STANISLAW J. LEC

The best argument I know for an immortal life is the existence of a man who deserves one.

WILLIAM JAMES

Immortality is the genius to move others long after you yourself have stopped moving.

FRANK ROONEY

If your contribution has been vital there will always be somebody to pick up where you left off, and that will be your claim to immortality.

WALTER GROPIUS

IMPOSSIBILITY *Also see:* PERFECTION.

The Difficult is that which can be done immediately; the Impossible that which takes a little longer.

GEORGE SANTAYANA

Most of the things worth doing in the world had been declared impossible before they were done.

LOUIS D. BRANDEIS

Nothing is impossible; there are ways that lead to everything, and if we had sufficient will we should always have sufficient means. It is often merely for an excuse that we say things are impossible.

FRANÇOIS DE LA ROCHEFOUCAULD

It is difficult to say what is impossible, for the dream of yesterday is the hope of today and the reality of tomorrow.

ROBERT H. GODDARD

IMPROVEMENT *Also see:* PROGRESS, SELF-IMPROVEMENT.

People seldom improve when they have no other model but themselves to copy after.

OLIVER GOLDSMITH

Where we cannot invent, we may at least improve.

CHARLES CALEB COLTON

As long as I can conceive something better than myself I cannot be easy unless I am striving to bring it into existence or clearing the way for it.

GEORGE BERNARD SHAW

INACTIVITY . . . *See* CHANGE.

INCREDULITY *Also see:* AGNOSTICISM, DISTRUST, DOUBT, SKEPTICISM.

Incredulity robs us of many pleasures, and gives us nothing in return.
JAMES RUSSELL LOWELL

The amplest knowledge has the largest faith. Ignorance is always incredulous.
ROBERT ELDRIDGE WILLMOTT

The curse of man, and the cause of nearly all his woe, is his stupendous capacity for believing the incredible.
H. L. MENCKEN

INDECISION

There is no more miserable human being than one in whom nothing is habitual but indecision.
WILLIAM JAMES

While the mind is in doubt it is driven this way and that by a slight impulse.
TERENCE

He is no wise man who will quit a certainty for an uncertainty.
SAMUEL JOHNSON

Indecision is debilitating; it feeds upon itself; it is, one might almost say, habit-forming. Not only that, but it is contagious; it transmits itself to others.
H. A. HOPF

Indecision has often given an advantage to the other fellow because he did his thinking beforehand.
MAURICE SWITZER

INDEPENDENCE *Also see:* DEPENDENCE, FREEDOM, INDIVIDUALITY, LIBERTY.

Without moral and intellectual independence, there is no anchor for national independence.
DAVID BEN-GURION

I would rather sit on a pumpkin and have it all to myself than be on a crowded velvet cushion.

HENRY DAVID THOREAU

So live that you can look any man in the eye and tell him to go to hell.

ANONYMOUS

There is no more independence in politics than there is in jail.

WILL ROGERS

Can anything be so elegant as to have few wants, and to serve them one's self?

RALPH WALDO EMERSON

(I am) lord of myself, accountable to none.

BENJAMIN FRANKLIN

INDIVIDUALITY *Also see:* CHARACTER, ORIGINALITY, PER-
SONALITY, PROPERTY.

The worth of the state, in the long run, is the worth of the individuals composing it.

JOHN STUART MILL

The whole theory of the universe is directed unerringly to one single individual.

WALT WHITMAN

An institution is the lengthened shadow of one man.

RALPH WALDO EMERSON

That so few now dare to be eccentric marks the chief danger of the time.

JOHN STUART MILL

Individuality is the aim of political liberty.

JAMES FENIMORE COOPER

INDOLENCE . . . *See* Idleness

INDUSTRY *Also see:* BUSINESS, BUSY, DILIGENCE, FORTUNE,
LABOR.

No thoroughly occupied man was ever yet very miserable.

LETITIA LANDON

It is better to wear out than to rust out.

RICHARD CUMBERLAND

The more we do, the more we can do.

WILLIAM HAZLITT

A man who gives his children habits of industry provides for them better than by giving them a fortune.

RICHARD WHATLEY

If you have great talents, industry will improve them; if moderate abilities, industry will supply their deficiencies. Nothing is denied to well-directed labor; nothing is ever to be attained without it.

JOSHUA REYNOLDS

In the ordinary business of life, industry can do anything which genius can do, and very many things which it cannot.

HENRY WARD BEECHER

INEQUALITY *Also see:* DIFFERENCE, EQUALITY.

One half of the world must sweat and groan that the other half may dream.

HENRY WADSWORTH LONGFELLOW

No amount of artificial reinforcement can offset the natural inequalities of human individuals.

HENRY P. FAIRCHILD

Can one preach at home inequality of races and nations and advocate abroad good-will towards all men?

DOROTHY THOMPSON

People differ in capacity, skill, health, strength; and unequal fortune is a necessary result of unequal condition. Such inequality is far from being disadvantageous either to individuals or to the community.

LEO XIII

INFERIORITY *Also see:* IGNORANCE, INEQUALITY, RACE.

The surrender of life is nothing to sinking down into acknowledgement of inferiority.

JOHN C. CALHOUN

No man likes to have his intelligence or good faith questioned, especially if he has doubts about it himself.

HENRY BROOKS ADAMS

We must interpret a bad temper as a sign of inferiority.

ALFRED ADLER

No one can make you feel inferior without your consent.

ELEANOR ROOSEVELT

Exaggerated sensitiveness is an expression of the feeling of inferiority.

ALFRED ADLER

No two men can be half an hour together but one shall acquire an evident superiority over the other.

SAMUEL JOHNSON

INFLUENCE *Also see:* AUTHORITY, POWER.

The humblest individual exerts some influence, either for good or evil, upon others.

HENRY WARD BEECHER

No man should think himself a zero, and think he can do nothing about the state of the world.

BERNARD M. BARUCH

Blessed is the influence of one true, loving human soul on another.

GEORGE ELIOT

The least movement is of importance to all nature. The entire ocean is affected by a pebble.

BLAISE PASCAL

We perceive and are affected by changes too subtle to be described.

HENRY DAVID THOREAU

I am a part of all that I have met.

ALFRED, LORD TENNYSON

INGRATITUDE *Also see:* GRATITUDE, SELFISHNESS.

Next to ingratitude the most painful thing to bear is gratitude.

HENRY WARD BEECHER

Nothing more detestable does the earth produce than an ungrateful man.

AUSONIUS

A proud man is seldom a grateful man, for he never thinks he gets as much as he deserves.

HENRY WARD BEECHER

Too great haste to repay an obligation is a kind of ingratitude.

FRANÇOIS DE LA ROCHEFOUCAULD

One ungrateful man does an injury to all who stand in need of aid.

PUBLILIUS SYRUS

INHERITANCE

We pay for the mistakes of our ancestors, and it seems only fair that they should leave us the money to pay with.

DON MARQUIS

What madness it is for a man to starve himself to enrich his heir, and so turn a friend into an enemy! For his joy at your death will be proportioned to what you leave him.

SENECA

Enjoy what thou has inherited from thy sires if thou wouldst really possess it. What we employ and use is never an oppressive burden; what the moment brings forth, that only can it profit by.

JOHANN WOLFGANG VON GOETHE

INJURY Also see: ABUSE, JUSTICE, SLANDER, VENGEANCE

No man ever did a designed injury to another, but at the same time he did a greater to himself.

LORD KAMES

If the other person injures you, you may forget the injury; but if you injure him you will always remember.

KAHLIL GIBRAN

The natural principle of war is to do the most harm to our enemy with the least harm to ourselves; and this of course is to be effected by strategem.

WASHINGTON IRVING

Never does the human soul appear so strong as when it foregoes revenge and dares to forgive an injury.

EDWIN HUBBEL CHAPIN

The injury we do and the one we suffer are not weighed in the same scale.

AESOP

INJUSTICE Also see: JUSTICE.

If thou suffer injustice, console thyself; the true unhappiness is in doing it.

DEMOCRITUS

Those who commit injustice bear the greatest burden.

HOSEA BALLOU

A book might be written on the injustice of the just.

ANTHONY HOPE

He who commits injustice is ever made more wretched than he who suffers it.

PLATO

Whatever the human law may be, neither an individual nor a nation can commit the least act of injustice against the obscurest individual without having to pay the penalty for it.

HENRY DAVID THOREAU

INNOCENCE *Also see:* GUILT, IGNORANCE, JUSTICE.

Innocence most often is a good fortune and not a virtue.

ANATOLE FRANCE

They that know no evil will suspect none.

BEN JONSON

To be innocent is to be not guilty; but to be virtuous is to overcome our evil inclinations.

WILLIAM PENN

It is better that ten guilty persons escape than that one innocent suffer.

WILLIAM BLACKSTONE

INSANITY *Also see:* ACCURACY.

Insanity is often the logic of an accurate mind overtaxed.

OLIVER WENDELL HOLMES

I teach that all men are mad.

HORACE

We do not have to visit a madhouse to find disordered minds; our planet is the mental institution of the universe.

JOHANN WOLFGANG VON GOETHE

When we remember we are all mad, the mysteries disappear and life stands explained.

MARK TWAIN

INSTINCT *Also see:* COMMON SENSE.

Instinct is the nose of the mind.

MADAME DE GIRARDIN

Instinct is the action taken in pursuance of a purpose, but without conscious perception of what the purpose is.

VAN HARTMANN

Instinct is untaught ability.

ALEXANDER BALN

The active part of man consists of powerful instincts, some of which are gentle and continuous; others violent and short; some baser, some nobler, and all necessary.

FRANCIS W. NEWMAN

It is the rooted instinct in men to admire what is better and more beautiful than themselves.

JAMES RUSSELL LOWELL

INSULT *Also see:* ABUSE, INJURY, IRONY.

A gentleman will not insult me, and no man not a gentleman can insult me.

FREDERICK DOUGLASS

He who puts up with insult invites injury.

PROVERB

The best way to procure insults is to submit to them.

WILLIAM HAZLITT

If you can't ignore an insult, top it; if you can't top it, laugh it off; and if you can't laugh it off, it's probably deserved.

RUSSELL LYNES

A graceful taunt is worth a thousand insults.

LOUIS NIZER

INTEGRITY . . . *See* HONESTY

INTELLIGENCE *Also see:* COMMON SENSE, JUDGMENT, KNOWLEDGE, PERCEPTION, PRUDENCE.

It is impossible to underrate human intelligence—beginning with one's own.

HENRY BROOKS ADAMS

When you don't have an education, you've got to use your brains.

ANONYMOUS

There is nobody so irritating as somebody with less intelligence and more sense than we have.

DON HEROLD

A weak mind is like a microscope, which magnifies trifling things but cannot receive great ones.

LORD CHESTERFIELD

There is no such thing as an underestimate of average intelligence.

HENRY BROOKS ADAMS

INTEREST *Also see:* GAIN.

There are no uninteresting things, there are only uninterested people.
GILBERT K. CHESTERTON

A man's interest in the world is only an overflow from his interest in himself.

GEORGE BERNARD SHAW

Only free peoples can hold their purpose and their honor steady to a common end and prefer the interest of mankind to any narrow interest of their own.

WOODROW WILSON

It a cursed evil to any man to become as absorbed in any subject as I am in mine.

CHARLES DARWIN

INTOLERANCE *Also see:* ANGER, BIGOTRY, PREJUDICE.

Nothing dies so hard, or rallies so often as intolerance.
HENRY WARD BEECHER

Intolerance has been the curse of every age and state.
SAMUEL DAVIES

Whoever kindles the flames of intolerance in America is lighting a fire underneath his own home.

HAROLD E. STASSEN

Bigotry and intolerance, silenced by argument, endeavors to silence by persecution, in old days by fire and sword, in modern days by the tongue.
CHARLES SIMMONS

INVENTION *Also see:* DISCOVERY.

Invention is the talent of youth, as judgment is of age.
JONATHAN SWIFT

Only an inventor knows how to borrow, and every man is or should be an inventor.

RALPH WALDO EMERSON

The march of invention has clothed mankind with powers of which a century ago the boldest imagination could not have dreamt.

HENRY GEORGE

A tool is but the extension of a man's hand, and a machine is but a complex tool. And he that invents a machine augments the power of a man and the well-being of mankind.

HENRY WARD BEECHER

JAZZ *Also see:* MUSIC.

Jazz will endure as long as people hear it through their feet instead of their brains.

JOHN PHILIP SOUSA

The chief trouble with jazz is that there is not enough of it; some of it we have to listen to twice.

DON HEROLD

Jazz may be a thrilling communion with the primitive soul; or it may be an ear-splitting bore.

WINTHROP SARGEANT

Jazz tickles your muscles, symphonies stretch your soul.

PAUL WHITEMAN

JEALOUSY *Also see:* RIVALRY, SARCASM.

There is never jealousy where there is not strong regard.

WASHINGTON IRVING

Jealousy lives upon doubts. It becomes madness or ceases entirely as soon as we pass from doubt to certainty.

FRANÇOIS DE LA ROCHEFOUCAULD

Jealousy is the injured lover's hell.

JOHN MILTON

The way to hold a husband is to keep him a little jealous; the way to lose him is to keep him a little more jealous.

H. L. MENCKEN

In jealousy there is more of self-love than of love to another.

FRANÇOIS DE LA ROCHEFOUCAULD

Lots of people know a good thing the minute the other fellow sees it first.

JOB E. HEDGES

JESTING *Also see:* HUMOR, WIT.

Many a true word is spoken in jest.

ENGLISH PROVERB

Judge of a jest when you have done laughing.

WILLIAM LLOYD

The jest loses its point when he who makes it is the first to laugh.

JOHANN VON SCHILLER

JOURNALISM Also see: NEWSPAPER.

Journalists do not live by words alone, although sometimes they have to eat them.

ADLAI E. STEVENSON

Get your facts first, and then you can distort 'em as you please.

MARK TWAIN

A news sense is really a sense of what is important, what is vital, what has color and life—what people are interested in. That's journalism.

BURTON RASCOE

A journalist is a grumbler, a censurer, a giver of advice, a regent of sovereigns, a tutor of nations. Four hostile newspapers are more to be feared than a thousand bayonets.

NAPOLEON BONAPARTE

Half my lifetime I have earned my living by selling words, and I hope thoughts.

WINSTON CHURCHILL

JOY Also see: ENJOYMENT, HAPPINESS, PLEASURE, SMILE.

Tranquil pleasures last the longest; we are not fitted to bear the burden of great joys.

CHRISTIAN NESTELL BOVEE

One can endure sorrow alone, but it takes two to be glad.

ELBERT HUBBARD

In this world, full often, our joys are only the tender shadows which our sorrows cast.

HENRY WARD BEECHER

Great joy, especially after a sudden change of circumstances, is apt to be silent, and dwells rather in the heart than on the tongue.

HENRY FIELDING

JUDAISM Also see: RELIGION.

The builders of Judaism utilized emotion in order to sublimate the passions, the angers, the dreams, of the people.

JOSHUA LOTH LIEBMAN

To be a Jew is a destiny.

VICKI BAUM

Judaism lives not in an abstract creed, but in its institutions.

AUERBACH

Historically the profoundest meaning of Passover is something which sets Judaism apart from other religions. It marks the birth of a nation. Out of a mass of slaves, Moses fashioned a nation and gave them a faith. From that day to this, Jews have never ceased to be a people.

PHILIP S. BERNSTEIN

JUDGMENT *Also see:* DECISION, PRUDENCE, WISDOM.

You shall judge of a man by his foes as well as by his friends.

JOSEPH CONRAD

We judge ourselves by what we feel capable of doing; others judge us by what we have done.

HENRY WADSWORTH LONGFELLOW

Everyone complains of the badness of his memory, but nobody of his judgment.

FRANÇOIS DE LA ROCHEFOUCAULD

One cool judgment is worth a thousand hasty councils. The thing to do is to supply light and not heat.

WOODROW WILSON

Hesitancy in judgment is the only true mark of the thinker.

DAGOBERT D. RUNES

The average man's judgment is so poor, he runs a risk every time he uses it.

ED HOWE

JUSTICE *Also see:* CAUSE, COURT, EQUALITY, LAW, RIGHTS.

Justice is the great interest of man on earth.

DANIEL WEBSTER

Justice is the ligament which holds civilized beings and civilized nations together.

DANIEL WEBSTER

Justice is the insurance which we have on our lives and property. Obedience is the premium which we pay for it.

WILLIAM PENN

There is no such thing as justice—in or out of court.

CLARENCE DARROW

Whenever a separation is made between liberty and justice, neither, in my opinion, is safe.

EDMUND BURKE

Though force can protect in emergency, only justice, fairness, consideration and cooperation can finally lead men to the dawn of eternal peace.

DWIGHT D. EISENHOWER

Justice is the firm and continuous desire to render to everyone that which is his due.

JUSTINIAN

Rather suffer an injustice than commit one.

ANONYMOUS

An honest man nearly always thinks justly.

JEAN JACQUES ROUSSEAU

Justice and power must be brought together, so that whatever is just may be powerful, and whatever is powerful may be just.

BLAISE PASCAL

One man's word is no man's word; we should quietly hear both sides.

JOHANN WOLFGANG VON GOETHE

KILLING . . . *See* ASSASSINATION.

KINDNESS *Also see:* CHARITY, HELP.

Human kindness has never weakened the stamina or softened the fiber of a free people. A nation does not have to be cruel in order to be tough.

FRANKLIN DELANO ROOSEVELT

The best portion of a good man's life is his little, nameless, unremembered acts of kindness and of love.

WILLIAM WORDSWORTH

We hate the kindness which we understand.

HENRY DAVID THOREAU

A kind heart is a fountain of gladness, making everything in its vicinity freshen into smiles.

WASHINGTON IRVING

Kindness is a language the dumb can speak and the deaf can hear and understand.

CHRISTIAN NESTELL BOVEE

You cannot do a kindness too soon, for you never know how soon it will be too late.

RALPH WALDO EMERSON

KING *Also see:* ARISTOCRACY, BLINDNESS.

A king is one who has "few things to desire and many things to fear."

FRANCIS BACON

Wise kings generally have wise counsellors; and he must be a wise man himself who is capable of distinguishing one.

DIOGENES

Royalty consists not in vain pomp, but in great virtues.

AGESILAUS II

Every king springs from a race of slaves, and every slave had kings among his ancestors.

PLATO

The right kind of monarchy is one where everybody goes about with the permanent conviction that the king can do no wrong.

GILBERT K. CHESTERTON

KISS *Also see:* AFFECTION, PAIN.

A kiss is a lovely trick designed by nature to stop speech when words become superfluous.

INGRID BERGMAN

It is the passion that is in a kiss that gives to it its sweetness; it is the affection in a kiss that sanctifies it.

CHRISTIAN NESTELL BOVEE

A man snatches the first kiss, pleads for the second, demands the third, takes the fourth, accepts the fifth—and endures all the rest.

HELEN ROWLAND

A peculiar proposition. Of no use to one, yet absolute bliss to two. The small boy gets it for nothing, the young man has to lie for it, and the old man has to buy it. The baby's right, the lover's privilege, and the hypocrite's mask. To a young girl, faith; to a married woman, hope; and to an old maid, charity.

V. P. I. SKIPPER

KNOWLEDGE *Also see:* CIVILIZATION, DANGER, DOUBT, DUTY, EDUCATION, POWER.

Knowledge is like money: the more he gets, the more he craves.

JOSH BILLINGS

Knowledge is knowing that we cannot know.

RALPH WALDO EMERSON

What a man knows is everywhere at war with what he wants.

JOSEPH WOOD KRUTCH

Knowledge is the small part of ignorance that we arrange and classify.

AMBROSE BIERCE

All wish to possess knowledge, but few, comparatively speaking, are willing to pay the price.

JUVENAL

LABOR *Also see:* AUTOMATION, EFFORT, EMPLOYMENT, INDUSTRY, LEISURE, MACHINE, WAGE, WORK.

Labor is man's greatest function. He is nothing, he can do nothing, he can achieve nothing, he can fulfill nothing, without working.

ORVILLE DEWEY

The fruit derived from labor is the sweetest of all pleasures.

LUC DE CLAPIERS

Excellence in any department can be attained only by the labor of a lifetime; it is not to be purchased at a lesser price.

SAMUEL JOHNSON

There is no real wealth but the labor of man.

PERCY BYSSHE SHELLEY

It is only through labor and painful effort, by grim energy and resolute courage, that we move on to better things.

THEODORE ROOSEVELT

I pity the man who wants a coat so cheap that the man or woman who produces the cloth will starve in the process.

BENJAMIN HARRISON

LANGUAGE *Also see:* CONVERSATION, LITERATURE, MUSIC, SPEECH, WORD.

Language is the blood of the soul into which thoughts run and out of which they grow.

OLIVER WENDELL HOLMES

Language is the dress of thought.

SAMUEL JOHNSON

Language is only the instrument of science, and words are but the signs of ideas.

SAMUEL JOHNSON

Think like a wise man but communicate in the language of the people.

WILLIAM BUTLER YEATS

LAUGHTER Also see: BABY, CHEERFULNESS, HUMOR, SMILE.

Those who bring sunshine to the lives of others cannot keep it from themselves.

JAMES MATTHEW BARRIE

Men show their character in nothing more clearly than by what they think laughable.

JOHANN WOLFGANG VON GOETHE

The young man who has not wept is a savage, and the old man who will not laugh is a fool.

GEORGE SANTAYANA

If you don't learn to laugh at trouble, you won't have anything to laugh at when you're old.

ED HOWE

Laughter is the sun that drives winter from the human face.

VICTOR HUGO

He laughs best who laughs last.

ENGLISH PROVERB

I can usually judge a fellow by what he laughs at.

WILSON MIZNER

LAW Also see: DISSENT, EQUALITY, GOVERNMENT.

Petty laws breed great crimes.

OUIDA

A law is valuable not because it is law, but because there is right in it.

HENRY WARD BEECHER

If we desire respect for the law, we must first make the law respectable.

LOUIS D. BRANDEIS

The best way to get a bad law repealed is to enforce it strictly.

ABRAHAM LINCOLN

It is the spirit and not the form of law that keeps justice alive.

EARL WARREN

Laws that do not embody public opinion can never be enforced.

ELBERT HUBBARD

We can not expect to breed respect for law and order among people who do not share the fruits of our freedom.

HUBERT H. HUMPHREY

LEADERSHIP *Also see:* AUTHORITY, COURAGE, HEROISM.

And when we think we lead, we are most led.

LORD BYRON

Leadership is the other side of the coin of loneliness, and he who is a leader must always act alone. And acting alone, accept everything alone.

FERDINAND EDRALIN MARCOS

Leadership: The art of getting someone else to do something you want done because he wants to do it.

DWIGHT D. EISENHOWER

If the blind lead the blind, both shall fall into the ditch.

MATTHEW 15:14

The final test of a leader is that he leaves behind him in other men the conviction and the will to carry on.

WALTER LIPPMANN

LEARNING *Also see:* DISCRETION, EDUCATION, KNOWLEDGE, STUDY, TEACHING.

The brighter you are the more you have to learn.

DON HEROLD

I've known countless people who were reservoirs of learning yet never had a thought.

WILSON MIZNER

The wisest mind has something yet to learn.

GEORGE SANTAYANA

To be proud of learning is the greatest ignorance.

JEREMY TAYLOR

I am always ready to learn, but I do not always like being taught.

WINSTON CHURCHILL

He who adds not to his learning diminishes it.

THE TALMUD

Wear your learning like your watch, in a private pocket, and do not pull it out and strike it merely to show that you have one.

LORD CHESTERFIELD

LEISURE *Also see:* IDLENESS, OPPORTUNITY, REST.

Leisure is a beautiful garment, but it will not do for constant wear.

ANONYMOUS

The end of labor is to gain leisure.

ARISTOTLE

We give up leisure in order that we may have leisure, just as we go to war in order that we may have peace.

ARISTOTLE

He does not seem to me to be a free man who does not sometimes do nothing.

CICERO

Employ thy time well, if thou meanest to gain leisure.

BENJAMIN FRANKLIN

In this theater of man's life, it is reserved only for God and angels to be lookers-on.

PYTHAGORAS

LIBERTY *Also see:* DEMOCRACY, FREEDOM of PRESS, JUSTICE, RIGHTS.

Absolute liberty is absence of restraint; responsibility is restraint; therefore, the ideally free individual is responsible to himself.

HENRY BROOKS ADAMS

Liberty, not communism, is the most contagious force in the world.

EARL WARREN

Liberty is the only thing you can't have unless you give it to others.

WILLIAM ALLEN WHITE

Liberty means responsibility. That is why most men dread it.

GEORGE BERNARD SHAW

What light is to the eyes—what air is to the lungs—what love is to the heart, liberty is to the soul of man.

ROBERT GREEN INGERSOLL

Liberty is always dangerous, but it is the safest thing we have.

HARRY EMERSON FOSDICK

LIFE *Also see:* AMUSEMENT, CERTAINTY, CHANGE, CHOICE, EMPLOYMENT, ENJOYMENT, IMMORTALITY, MAN, SOUL.

We are here to add what we can to life, not to get what we can from it.

WILLIAM OSLER

Life is not lost by dying; life is lost minute by minute, day by dragging day, in all the thousand small uncaring ways.

STEPHEN VINCENT BENÉT

The best use of life is to spend it for something that outlasts life.

WILLIAM JAMES

Life is a series of little deaths out of which life always returns.

CHARLES FEIDELSON, JR.

Life is a tragedy for those who feel, and a comedy for those who think.

JEAN DE LA BRUYÈRE

Let us so live that when we come to die even the undertaker will be sorry.

MARK TWAIN

Do not take life too seriously; you will never get out of it alive.

ELBERT HUBBARD

Life is like a cash register, in that every account, every thought, every deed, like every sale, is registered and recorded.

FULTON J. SHEEN

LIGHT

There are two kinds of light—the glow that illuminates, and the glare that obscures.

JAMES THURBER

The thing to do is supply light and not heat.

WOODROW WILSON

Light is the symbol of truth.

JAMES RUSSELL LOWELL

The pursuit of perfection, then, is the pursuit of sweetness and light.

MATTHEW ARNOLD

LITERATURE *Also see:* BOOK, LANGUAGE, PLAGIARISM, READING.

Literature is the immortality of speech.

AUGUST WILHELM VON SCHLEGEL

Great literature is simply language charged with meaning to the utmost possible degree.

EZRA POUND

Writing is the only profession where no one considers you ridiculous if you earn no money.

JULES RENARD

Literature is the art of writing something that will be read twice.

CYRIL CONNOLLY

The decline of literature indicates the decline of a nation.

JOHAN WOLFGANG VON GOETHE

Our high respect for a well-read man is praise enough of literature.

RALPH WALDO EMERSON

LOGIC *Also see:* ARGUMENT, REASON, PHILOSOPHY, SCIENCE.

Logic is the art of going wrong with confidence.

JOSEPH WOOD KRUTCH

Logic: an instrument used for bolstering a prejudice.

ELBERT HUBBARD

Logic is the anatomy of thought.

JOHN LOCKE

Man is not logical and his intellectual history is a record of mental reserves and compromises. He hangs on to what he can in his old beliefs even when he is compelled to surrender their logical basis.

JOHN DEWEY

Men are apt to mistake the strength of their felling for the strength of their argument. The heated mind resents the chill touch and relentless scrutiny of logic.

WILLIAM E. GLADSTONE

LONELINESS *Also see:* ABSENCE, DISTRUST, LEADERSHIP, SOLITUDE.

In cities no one is quiet but many are lonely; in the country, people are quiet but few are lonely.

GEOFFREY FRANCIS FISHER

People are lonely because they build walls instead of bridges.

JOSEPH F. NEWTON

Language has created the word loneliness to express the pain of being alone, and the word solitude to express the glory of being alone.

PAUL TILLICH

LOQUACITY Also see: BORE, DIPLOMACY, ELOQUENCE

He who talks much cannot talk well.

CARLO GOLDONI

Every absurdity has a champion to defend it, for error is always talkative.

OLIVER GOLDSMITH

They always talk who never think, and who have the least to say.

MATTHEW PRIOR

Speaking much is a sign of vanity, for he that is lavish with words is a niggard in deed.

SIR WALTER RALEIGH

LOSS Also see: ADVERSITY, DEFEAT, GAIN, WASTE

When wealth is lost, nothing is lost; when health is lost, something is lost; when character is lost, all is lost.

GERMAN MOTTO

It's the good loser who finally loses out.

KIN HUBBARD

The cheerful loser is the winner.

ELBERT HUBBARD

Lose an hour in the morning, and you will spend all day looking for it.

RICHARD WHATELY

LOVE Also see: AFFECTION, DEATH, DELUSION, FAITH, MARRIAGE, PASSION.

If there is anything better than to be loved it is loving.

ANONYMOUS

The way to love anything is to realize that it might be lost.

GILBERT K. CHESTERTON

Love built on beauty, soon as beauty, dies.

JOHN DONNE

To love is to place our happiness in the happiness of another.
GOTTFRIED WILHELM VON LEIBNITZ

Love gives itself; it is not bought.
HENRY WADSWORTH LONGFELLOW

It is better to have loved and lost, than not to have loved at all.
ALFRED, LORD TENNYSON

He that falls in love with himself will have no rivals.
BENJAMIN FRANKLIN

Love: the delusion that one woman differs from another.
H. L. MENCKEN

There is only one sort of love, but there are a thousand copies.
FRANÇOIS DE LA ROCHEFOUCAULD

I never knew how to worship until I knew how to love.
HENRY WARD BEECHER

There is a Law that man should love his neighbor as himself. In a few years it should be as natural to mankind as breathing or the upright gait; but if he does not learn it he must perish.
ALFRED ADLER

We are shaped and fashioned by what we love.
JOHANN WOLFGANG VON GOETHE

LOYALTY *Also see:* COUNTRY, DIPLOMACY, FIDELITY.

Loyalty means nothing unless it has at its heart the absolute principle of self-sacrifice.
WOODROW WILSON

Fidelity purchased with money, money can destroy.
SENECA

We join ourselves to no party that does not carry the American flag, and keep step to the music of the Union.
RUFUS CHOATE

My country right or wrong; when right, to keep her right; when wrong, to put her right.
CARL SCHURZ

Loyalty . . . is a realization that America was born of revolt, flourished in dissent, became great through experimentation.
HENRY S. COMMANGER

LUCK *Also see:* CHANCE, DESTINY, DIGNITY, FORTUNE.

The only sure thing about luck is that it will change.

WILSON MIZNER

Shallow men believe in luck. Strong men believe in cause and effect.

RALPH WALDO EMERSON

Chance favors the prepared mind.

LOUIS PASTEUR

Good luck is a lazy man's estimate of a worker's success.

ANONYMOUS

I believe in luck: how else can you explain the success of those you dislike?

JEAN COCTEAU

It is the mark of an inexperienced man not to believe in luck.

JOSEPH CONRAD

A pound of pluck is worth a ton of luck.

JAMES A. GARFIELD

LUXURY Also see: AVARICE, ECTRAVAGANCE, WEALTH.

War destroys men, but luxury destroys mankind; at once corrupts the body and the mind.

JOHN CROWNE

Give us the luxuries of life and we'll dispense with the necessaries.

OLIVER WENDELL HOLMES

On the soft bed of luxury most kingdoms have expired.

EDWARD YOUNG

Possessions, outward success, publicity, luxury—to me these have always been contemptible. I believe that a simple and unassuming manner of life is best for everyone, best for both the body and the mind.

ALBERT EINSTEIN

Luxury is the first, second and third cause of the ruin of republics.

EDWARD PAYSON

LYING Also see: CREDULITY, DECEIT, DISHONESTY, EXCUSES, HYPOCRISY, LOQUACITY.

You can best reward a liar by believing nothing of what he says.

ARISTIPPUS

One ought to have a good memory when he has told a lie.

CORNEILLE

The liar's punishment is not in the least that he is not believed, but that he cannot believe anyone else.

GEORGE BERNARD SHAW

Any fool can tell the truth, but it requires a man of some sense to know how to lie well.

SAMUEL BUTLER

MACHINE *Also see:* AUTOMATION, TECHNOLOGY.

One machine can do the work of fifty ordinary men. No machine can do the work of one extraordinary man.

ELBERT HUBBARD

A tool is but the extension of a man's hand, and a machine is but a complex tool. He that invents a machine augments the power of man and the well-being of mankind.

HENRY WARD BEECHER

On mechanical slavery, on the slaver of the machine, the future of the world depends.

OSCAR WILDE

To me, there is something superbly symbolic in the fact that an astronaut, sent up as assistant to a series of computers, found that he worked more accurately and more intelligently than they. Inside the capsule, man is still in charge.

ADLAI E. STEVENSON

MAJORITY *Also see:* DEMOCRACY, MINORITY.

There is one body that knows more than anybody, and that is everybody.
ALEXANDRE DE TALLEYRAND-PÉRIGORD

Any man more right than his neighbors, constitutes a majority of one.
HENRY DAVID THOREAU

The voice of the majority is no proof of justice.
JOHANN VON SCHILLER

When you get too big a majority, you're immediately in trouble.
SAM RAYBURN

It is my principle that the will of the majority should always prevail.

THOMAS JEFFERSON

MAN *Also see:* AVERAGE, BELIEF, BOOK, BOYS, CAUSE, CITIZENSHIP, CLASS, FAILURE, FATHER, FOOL, GOD, HUMAN NATURE, MACHINE, WOMAN.

Man is a reasoning rather than a reasonable animal.

ALEXANDER HAMILTON

Man is a piece of the universe made alive.

RALPH WALDO EMERSON

The ablest man I ever met is the man you think you are.

FRANKLIN DELANO ROOSEVELT

Man is a special being, and if left to himself, in an isolated condition, would be one of the weakest creatures; but associated with his kind, he works wonders.

DANIEL WEBSTER

I am the inferior of any man whose rights I trample under foot. Men are not superior by reason of the accidents of race or color. They are superior who have the best heart—the best brain. The superior man . . . stands erect by bending above the fallen. He rises by lifting others.

ROBERT GREEN INGERSOLL

MANNERS *Also see:* BEHAVIOR, COURTESY, GENTLEMAN, HASTE.

To succeed in the world, you must also be well-mannered.

VOLTAIRE

Nothing so much prevents our being natural as the desire of appearing so.

FRANÇOIS DE LA ROUCHEFOUCAULD

A man's own good breeding is the best security against other people's ill manners.

LORD CHESTERFIELD

Savages we call them because their manners differ from ours.

BENJAMIN FRANKLIN

Manners easily and rapidly mature into morals.

HORACE MANN

MARRIAGE *Also see:* ANCESTRY, BACHELOR, HUSBAND, SEX, WIFE.

The difficulty with marriage is that we fall in love with a personality, but must live with a character.

PETER DEVRIES

Marriage is that relation between man and woman in which the independence is equal, the dependence mutual, and the obligation reciprocal.

LOUIS K. ANSPACHER

Men marry to make an end; women to make a beginning.

ALEXIS DUPUY

It takes two to make a marriage a success and only one to make it a failure.

HERBERT SAMUEL

I guess the only way to stop divorce is to stop marriage.

WILL ROGERS

Well-married, a man is winged: ill-matched, he is shackled.

HENRY WARD BEECHER

A successful marriage is an edifice that must be rebuilt every day.

ANDRÉ MAUROIS

God help the man who won't marry until he finds a perfect woman, and God help him still more if he finds her.

BENJAMIN TILLETT

Marriage resembles a pair of shears, so joined that they cannot be separated; often moving in opposite directions, yet always punishing any one who comes between them.

SYDNEY SMITH

MARTYR *Also see:* HEROISM, SACRIFICE.

The way of the world is, to praise dead saints, and persecute living ones.

NATHANIEL HOWE

It is more difficult, and it calls for higher energies of soul, to live a martyr than to die one.

HORACE MANN

It is the cause and not merely the death that makes the martyr.

NAPOLEON BONAPARTE

MATURITY *Also see:* AGE.

Maturity is often more absurd than youth and very frequently is most unjust to youth.

THOMAS A. EDISON

The immature man wants to die nobly for a cause, while the mature man wants to live humanely for one.

WILHELM STEKEL

Maturity is the time of life when, if you had the time, you'd have the time of your life.

ANONYMOUS

Only the middle-aged have all their five senses in the keeping of their wits.

HERVEY ALLEN

MAXIM

Pithy sentences are like sharp nails which force truth upon our memory.

DENIS DIDEROT

Maxims are the condensed good sense of nations.

JAMES MACKINTOSH

Maxims are like lawyers who must need to see but one side of the case.

FRANK GELETT BURGESS

All maxims have their antagonist maxims; proverbs should be sold in pairs, a single one being but a half truth.

WILLIAM MATHEWS

MEANS . . . *See* END and MEANS

MEDICINE *Also see:* DISEASE, DRUGS, HEALTH, PROFESSION.

The only profession that labors incessantly to destroy the reason for its own existence.

JAMES BRYCE

God heals and the doctor takes the fee.

BENJAMIN FRANKLIN

He is the best physician who is the most ingenious inspirer of hope.

SAMUEL TAYLOR COLERIDGE

MEDITATION . . . *See* THOUGHT

MEMORY *Also see:* LYING, MONUMENT.

Memory is the cabinet of imagination, the treasury of reason, the registry of conscience, and the council chamber of thought.

ST. BASIL

Unless we remember we cannot understand.

EDWARD M. FORSTER

Those who cannot remember the past are condemned to repeat it.

GEORGE SANTAYANA

Recollection is the only paradise from which we cannot be turned out.

JEAN PAUL RICHTER

A retentive memory is a good thing, but the ability to forget is the true toke of greatness.

ELBERT HUBBARD

Every man's memory is his private literature.

ALDOUS HUXLEY

MERCY *Also see:* COMPASSION, FIRMNESS, FORGIVENESS, PITY.

Sweet mercy is nobility's true badge.

WILLIAM SHAKESPEARE

Mercy among the virtues is like the moon among the stars . . . It is the light that hovers above the judgment seat.

EDWIN HUBBEL CHAPIN

Hate shuts her soul when dove-eyed mercy pleads.

CHARLES SPRAGUE

MERIT *Also see:* CREDIT, WORTH.

If you wish your merit to be known, acknowledge that of other people.

ORIENTAL PROVERB

Contemporaries appreciate the man rather than his merit; posterity will regard the merit rather than the man.

CHARLES CALEB COLTON

The world rewards the appearance of merit oftener than merit itself.

FRANÇOIS DE LA ROCHEFOUCAULD

It never occurs to fools that merit and good fortune are closely united.

JOHANN WOLFGANG VON GOETHE

MIND *Also see:* DISEASE, INTELLIGENCE, NATION, REASON, SELF-KNOWLEDGE, UNDERSTANDING.

Commonplace minds usually condemn what is beyond the reach of their understanding.

FRANÇOIS DE LA ROCHEFOUCAULD

The mind is like the stomach. It is not how much you put into it that counts, but how much it digests.

ALBERT JAY NOCK

I not only use all the brains I have, but all that I can borrow.

WOODROW WILSON

The defects of the mind, like those of the face, grow worse as we grow old.

FRANÇOIS DE LA ROCHEFOUCAULD

Life is not a static thing. The only people who do not change their minds are incompetents in asylums, who can't, and those in cemeteries.

EVERETT M. DIRKSEN

MINORITY Also see: MAJORITY

Every new opinion, at its starting, is precisely in a minority of one.

THOMAS CARYLE

That cause is strong which has not a multitude, but one strong man behind it.

JAMES RUSSELL LOWELL

The only tyrannies from which men, women and children are suffering in real life are the tyrannies of minorities.

THEODORE ROOSEVELT

The minority of a country is never known to agree, except in its efforts to reduce and oppress the majority.

JAMES FENIMORE COOPER

The political machine works because it is a united minority acting against a divided majority.

WILL DURANT

MIRTH . . . See JOY

MISER Also see: AVARICE, GOLD, GREED, MONEY, SELFISH-NESS.

The miser, poor fool, not only starves his body, but also his own soul.

THEODORE PARKER

The happiest miser on earth is the man who saves up every friend he can make.

ROBERT EMMET SHERWOOD

The devil lies brooding in the miser's chest.

THOMAS FULLER

Misers mistake gold for good, whereas it is only a means of obtaining it.

FRANÇOIS DE LA ROCHEFOUCAULD

The miser, starving his brother's body, starves also his own soul, and at death shall creep out of his great estate of injustice, poor and naked and miserable.

THEODORE PARKER

MISERY Also see: ADVERSITY, GRIEF, PAIN, SORROW.

He that is down need fear no fall.

JOHN BUNYAN

There is no greater grief than to remember days of joy when misery is at hand.

DANTE

Man is only miserable so far as he thinks himself so.

JACOPO SANNAZARO

There are a good many real miseries in life that we cannot help smiling at, but they are the smiles that make wrinkles and not dimples.

OLIVER WENDELL HOLMES

A misery is not to be measured from the nature of the evil, but from the temper of the sufferer.

JOSEPH ADDISON

MOB Also see: RIOT, VIOLENCE

A mob is a group of persons with heads but no brains.

THOMAS FULLER

The nose of a mob is its imagination. By this, at any time, it can be quietly led.

EDGAR ALLAN POE

The mob is man voluntarily descending to the nature of the beast.

RALPH WALDO EMERSON

Get together a hundred or two men, however sensible they may be, and you are very likely to have a mob.

SAMUEL JOHNSON

The mob is the mother of tyrants.

DIOGENES

Get together a hundred or two men, however sensible they may be, and you are very likely to have a mob.

SAMUEL JOHNSON

The mob is the mother of tyrants.

DIOGENES

It is proof of a bad cause when it is applauded by the mob.

SENECA

MODERATION Also see: ABSTINENCE, BARGAIN, SELF-CONTROL.

In everything the middle road is the best; all things in excess bring trouble to men.

PLAUTUS

Moderation in temper is always a virtue; but moderation in principle is always a vice.

THOMAS PAINE

Moderation is a fatal thing: nothing succeeds like excess.

OSCAR WILDE

To go beyond the bounds of moderation is to outrage humanity.

BLAISE PASCAL

The pursuit, even of the best things, ought to be calm and tranquil.

CICERO

He will always be a slave who does not know how to live upon a little.

HORACE

MODESTY Also see: BLUSH, HUMILITY, MERIT.

Modesty is not only an ornament, but also a guard to virtue.

JOSEPH ADDISON

There's a lot to be said for the fellow who doesn't say it himself.

MAURICE SWITZER

Modesty may make a fool seem a man of sense.

JONATHAN SWIFT

It is easy for a somebody to be modest, but it is difficult to be modest when one is a nobody.

JULES RENARD

Modesty is the only sure bait when you angle for praise.

LORD CHESTERFIELD

With people of only moderate ability modesty is mere honesty; but with those who possess great talent it is hypocrisy.

ARTHUR SCHOPENHAUER

MONEY *Also see:* BORROWING, CREDIT, DEBT, DIPLOMACY, ECONOMY, FINANCE, GOLD, KNOWLEDGE, WEALTH.

He that is of the opinion money will do everything may well be suspected of doing everything for money.

BENJAMIN FRANKLIN

The safest way to double your money is to fold it over once and put it in your pocket.

KIM HUBBARD

The use of money is all the advantage there is in having it.

BENJAMIN FRANKLIN

Money often costs too much.

RALPH WALDO EMERSON

Money is not required to buy one necessity of the soul.

HENRY DAVID THOREAU

Money does all things for reward. Some are pious and honest as long as they thrive upon it, but if the devil himself gives better wages, they soon change their party.

SENECA

Put not your trust in money, but put your money in trust.

OLIVER WENDELL HOLMES

MONUMENT *Also see:* ACHIEVEMENT, GRAVE.

Deeds, not stones, are the true monuments of the great.

JOHN L. MOTLEY

The marble keeps merely a cold and sad memory of a man who would else be forgotten. No man who needs a monument ever ought to have one.

NATHANIEL HAWTHORNE

Monuments are the grappling-irons that bind one generation to another.

JOSEPH JOUBERT

If I have done any deed worthy of remembrance, that deed will be my monument. If not, no monument can preserve my memory.

AGESILAUS II

MORALITY *Also see:* ART, BOREDOM, MANNERS, VIRTUE.

Moralizing and morals are two entirely different things and are always found in entirely different people.

DON HEROLD

So far, about morals, I know only that what is moral is what you feel good after and what is immoral is what you feel bad after.

ERNEST HEMINGWAY

To denounce moralizing out of hand is to pronounce a moral judgment.

H. L. MENCKEN

All sects are different, because they come from men; morality is everywhere the same, because it comes from God.

VOLTAIRE

MORALITY . . . *See* DEATH

MOTHER *Also see:* BIRTH, BIRTH CONTROL, CHILDREN, CLEVERNESS, DESTINY, EARTH, FATHER, PARENT, WIFE, WOMAN.

Men are what their mothers made them.

RALPH WALDO EMERSON

A mother is not a person to lean on but a person to make leaning unnecessary.

DOROTHY CANFIELD FISHER

The hand that rocks the cradle is the hand that rules the world.

W. S. ROSS

God could be not everywhere, and therefore he made mothers.

JEWISH PROVERB

All that I am, or hope to be, I owe to my angel mother.

ABRAHAM LINCOLN

MURDER *Also see:* ASSASSINATION, BIRTH CONTROL.

Every unpunished murder takes away something from the security of every man's life.

DANIEL WEBSTER

Criminals do not die by the hands of the law; they die by the hands of other men.

GEORGE BERNARD SHAW

It is forbidden to kill; therefore all murderers are punished unless they kill in large numbers and to the sound of trumpets.

VOLTAIRE

The very emphasis of the commandment: Thou shalt not kill, makes it certain that we are descended from an endlessly long chain of generations of murderers, whose love of murder was in their blood as it is perhaps also in ours.

SIGMUND FREUD

MUSIC *Also see:* JAZZ.

Music is well said to be the speech of angels.

THOMAS CARLYLE

After silence that which comes nearest to expressing the inexpressible is music.

ALDOUS HUXLEY

Music is the only language in which you cannot say a mean or sarcastic thing.

LORD ERSKINE

Music is the universal language of mankind.

HENRY WADSWORTH LONGFELLOW

Music is harmony, harmony is perfection, perfection is our dream, and our dream is heaven.

AMIEL

Composers should write tunes that chauffeurs and errand boys can whistle.

THOMAS BEECHAM

MYSTERY *Also see:* SECRECY.

All is mystery; but he is a slave who will not struggle to penetrate the dark veil.

BENJAMIN DISRAELI

It is hard to say whether the doctors of law or divinity have made the greater advances in the lucrative business of mystery.

EDMUND BURKE

The most beautiful experience we can have is the mysterious. It is the fundamental emotion which stands at the cradle of true art and true science.

ALBERT EINSTEIN

It is the dim haze of mystery that adds enchantment to pursuit.

ANTOINE RIVAROL

Mystery is another name for our ignorance; if we were omniscient, all would be perfectly plain.

TRYON EDWARDS

NAME *Also see:* REPUTATION.

A person with a bad name is already half-hanged.

PROVERB

To live in mankind is far more than to live in a name.

VACHEL LINDSAY

A good name, like good will, is got by many actions and lost by one.

LORD JEFFERY

The invisible thing called a Good Name is made up of the breath of numbers that speak well of you.

LORD HALIFAX

What's in a name? That which we call a rose by any other name would smell as sweet.

WILLIAM SHAKESPEARE

Nicknames stick to people, and the most ridiculous are the most adhesive.

THOMAS C. HALIBURTON

NATION *Also see:* AMERICA, UNITED NATIONS, UNITY.

A nation is a totality of men united through community of fate into a community of character.

OTTO BAUER

The nation's honor is dearer than the nation's comfort; yes, than the nation's life itself.

WOODROW WILSON

A nation, like a person, has a mind—a mind that must be kept informed and alert, that must know itself, that understands the hopes and needs of its neighbors—all the other nations that live within the narrowing circle of the world.

FRANKLIN DELANO ROOSEVELT

No nation is fit to sit in judgment upon any other nation.

WOODROW WILSON

NATIONALISM *Also see:* CITIZENSHIP, PATRIOTISM.

We are in the midst of a great transition from narrow nationalism to international partnership.

LYNDON BAINES JOHNSON

There is a higher form of patriotism than nationalism, and that higher form is not limited by the boundaries of one's country; but by a duty to mankind to safeguard the trust of civilization.

OSCAR S. STRAUSS

Born in iniquity and conceived in sin, the spirit of nationalism has never ceased to bend human institutions to the service of dissension and distress.

THORSTEIN VEBLEN

The root of the problem is very simply stated: if there were no sovereign independent states, if the states of the civilized world were organized in some sort of federalism, as the states of the American Union, for instance, are organized, there would be no international war as we know it . . . The main obstacle is nationalism.

NORMAL ANGELL

NATURE *Also see:* ART, BEAUTY, CRUELTY, EARTH, FAMILY, FORTUNE, KISS.

The ignorant man marvels at the exceptional; the wise man marvels at the common; the greatest wonder of all is the regularity of nature.

GEORGE DANA BOARDMAN

Nature encourages no looseness, pardons no errors.

RALPH WALDO EMERSON

Nature creates ability; luck provides it with opportunity.

FRANÇOIS DE LA ROCHEFOUCAULD

Whether man is disposed to yield to nature or to oppose her, he cannot do without a correct understanding of her language.

JEAN ROSTAND

I love to think of nature as an unlimited broadcasting station, through which God speaks to us every hour, if we only will tune in.

GEORGE WASHINGTON CARVER

Man must go back to nature for information.

THOMAS PAINE

NECESSITY *Also see:* CIVILIZATION, ENDURANCE, HABIT, LUXURY, WANT.

Make yourself necessary to somebody.

RALPH WALDO EMERSON

Necessity is the mother of invention.

JONATHAN SWIFT

Our necessities are few but our wants are endless.

JOSH BILLINGS

Necessity is the plea for every infringement of human freedom. It is the argument of tyrants; it is the creed of slaves.

WILLIAM PITT

It is surprising what a man can do when he has to, and how little most men do when they don't have to.

WALTER LINN

Whatever necessity lays upon thee, endure; whatever she commands, do.

JOHANN WOLFGANG VON GOETHE

Necessity is blind until it becomes conscious. Freedom is the consciousness of necessity.

KARL MARX

NEGLECT *Also see:* IDLENESS, PROCRASTINATION.

He that thinks he can afford to be negligent is not far from being poor.

SAMUEL JOHNSON

It is the neglect of timely repair that makes rebuilding necessary.

RICHARD WHATELY

It will generally be found that men who are constantly lamenting their ill luck are only reaping the consequences of their own neglect, mismanagement, and improvidence, or want of application.

SAMUEL SMILES

NEUTRALITY *Also see:* TOLERANCE.

Neutral men are the devil's allies.

EDWIN HUBBEL CHAPLIN

Neutrality, as a lasting principle, is an evidence of weakness.

LAJOS KOSSUTH

People who demand neutrality in any situation are usually not neutral but in favor of the status quo.

MAX EASTMAN

NEWSPAPER *Also see:* FREEDOM OF THE PRESS, JOURNALISM.

Newspapers are the schoolmasters of the common people.

HENRY WARD BEECHER

A newspaper should be the maximum of information, and the minimum of comment.

RICHARD COBDEN

Newspapers are the world's mirrors.

JAMES ELLIS

We live under a government of men and morning newspapers.

WENDELL PHILLIPS

The man who reads nothing at all is better educated than the man who reads nothing but newspapers.

THOMAS JEFFERSON

Were it left to me to decide whether we should have a government without newspapers or newspapers without government, I should not hesitate a moment to prefer the latter.

THOMAS JEFFERSON

NOVELTY *Also see:* ORIGINALITY, VARIETY.

It is not only old and early impressions that deceive us; the charms of novelty have the same power.

BLAISE PASCAL

Novelty is the great parent of pleasure.

ROBERT SOUTH

Some degree of novelty must be one of the materials in almost every instrument which works upon the mind; and curiosity blends itself, more or less, with all our pleasures.

EDMUND BURKE

In science, as in common life, we frequently see that a novelty in system, or in practice, cannot be duly appreciated till time has sobered the enthusiasm of its advocates.

MAUD

NUCLEAR WARFARE *Also see:* TECHNOLOGY, WAR.

We've opened a door—maybe a treasure house, maybe only the realization of a maniac's dream of destruction.

JOHN ANDERSON

People who talk of outlawing the atomic bomb are mistaken—what needs to be outlawed is war.

LESLIE RICHARD GROVES

Idealists maintain that all nations should share the atomic bomb. Pessimists maintain that they will.

PUNCH

The hydrogen bomb is history's exclamation point. It ends an age-long sentence of manifest violence.

MARSHALL MCLUHAN

We develop weapons, not to wage war, but to prevent war. Only in the clear light of this greater truth can we properly examine the lesser matter of the testing of our nuclear weapons.

DWIGHT D. EISENHOWER

OBEDIENCE *Also see:* CHILDREN, DUTY, JUSTICE.

Wicked men obey from fear; good men, from love.

ARISTOTLE

The only safe ruler is he who has learned to obey willingly.

THOMAS A. KEMPIS

There are two kinds of men who never amount to much: those who cannot do what they are told, and those who can do nothing else.

CYRUS H. CURTIS

OBLIGATION . . . *See* DUTY

OBSCURITY . . . *See* AMBIGUITY

OBSERVATION *Also see:* PERCEPTION, SCIENCE.

Observation—activity of both eyes and ears.

HORACE MANN

If I were to prescribe one process in the training of men which is fundamental to success in any direction, it would be thoroughgoing training in the habit of observation. It is a habit which every one of us should be seeking ever more to perfect.

EUGENE G. GRACE

Every man who observes vigilantly and resolves steadfastly grows unconsciously into genius.

EDWARD G. BULWER-LYTTON

OPINION *Also see:* BELIEF, FORCE, FREEDOM, IDEA, JUDG-MENT, MINORITY, OPPRESSION, PREJU-DICE.

The foolish and the dead alone never change their opinions.

JAMES RUSSELL LOWELL

People do not seem to realize that their opinion of the world is also a confession of character.

RALPH WALDO EMERSON

He that never changes his opinions, never corrects his mistakes, and will never be wiser on the morrow than he is today.

TRYON EDWARDS

Opinions cannot survive if one has no chance to fight for them.

THOMAS MANN

Public opinion is a weak tyrant, compared with our private opinion—what a man thinks of himself, that is which determines, or rather indicates his fate.

HENRY DAVID THOREAU

OPPORTUNITY *Also see:* ABILITY, ACHIEVEMENT, CHANCE, CIVILIZATION, FORTUNE, LUCK.

A wise man will make more opportunities than he finds.

FRANCIS BACON

You will never "find" time for anything. If you want time you must make it.

CHARLES BUXTON

Do not wait for extraordinary circumstances to do good; try to use ordinary situations.

JEAN PAUL RICHTER

The commonest form, one of the most often neglected, and the safest opportunity for the average man to seize, is hard work.

ARTHUR BRISBANE

OPPRESSION *Also see:* ABUSE, CRUELTY, TYRANNY.

You can't hold a man down without staying down with him.

BOOKER T. WASHINGTON

A desire to resist oppression is implanted in the nature of man.

TACITUS

He that would make his own liberty secure must guard even his enemy from oppression; for if he violates this duty, he establishes a precedent that will reach to himself.

THOMAS PAINE

OPTIMISM *Also see:* CHEERFULNESS, PESSIMISSM, TRADITION.

In these times you have to be an optimist to open your eyes in the morning.

CARL SANDBURG

The only limit to our realization of tomorrow will be our doubts of today.

FRANKLIN DELANO ROOSEVELT

There is no sadder sight than a young pessimist, except an old optimist.

MARK TWAIN

Optimist: a proponent of the doctrine that black is white.

AMBROSE BIERCE

The optimist proclaims that we live in the best of all possible worlds; and the pessimist fears this is true.

JAMES BRANCH CABELL

The habit of looking on the bright side of every event is worth more than a thousand pounds a year.

SAMUEL JOHNSON

ORDER *Also see:* CIVILIZATION, DISCOVERY, EFFICIENCY.

A place for everything, everything in its place.

BENJAMIN FRANKLIN

The art of progress is to preserve order amid change, and to preserve change and order.

ALFRED NORTH WHITEHEAD

He who has no taste for order, will be often wrong in his judgment, and seldom considerate or conscientious in his actions.

JOHANN KASPAR LAVATER

ORIGINALITY *Also see:* CREATIVITY, FASHION, INVENTION, PLAGIARISM.

Orginality is simply a pair of fresh eyes.

THOMAS WENTWORTH HIGGINSON

It is better to create than to be learned; creating is the true essence of life.

BARTHOLD GEORG NIEBUHR

The merit of originality is not novelty, it is sincerity. The believing man is the original man; he believes for himself, not for another.

THOMAS CARLYLE

Originality is nothing but judicious imitation.

VOLTAIRE

OSTENTATION *Also see:* PRETENSION, PRIDE.

Ostentation is the signal flag of hypocrisy.

EDWIN HUBBLE CHAPIN

Whatever is done without ostentation, and without the people being witnesses of it, is in my opinion, most praiseworthy: not that the public eye should be entirely avoided, for good actions desire to be placed in the light; but notwithstanding this, the greatest theater for virtue is conscience.

CICERO

Pride is the master sin of the devil, and the devil is the father of lies.

EDWIN HUBBEL CHAPIN

That which is given with pride and ostentation is rather an ambition than a bounty.

SENECA

The charity that hastens to proclaim its good deeds, ceases to be charity, and is only pride and ostentation.

WILLIAM HUTTON

PAIN *Also see:* SUFFERING.

Pain adds rest unto pleasure, and teaches the luxury of health.

MARTIN F. TUPPER.

The pain of the mind is worse than the pain of the body.

PUBLILIUS SYRUS

Pain dies quickly, and lets her weary prisoners go; the fiercest agonies have shortest reign.

WILLIAM CULLEN BRYANT

Pain and pleasure, like light and darkness, succeed each other.

LAURENCE STERNE

Pain is life—the sharper, the more evidence of life.

CHARLES LAMB

Man endures pain as an undeserved punishment; woman accepts it as a natural heritage.

ANONYMOUS

PARDON . . . *See* FORGIVENESS

PARENTS

The joys of parents are secret, and so are their griefs and fears.

FRANCIS BACON

The first half of our lives is ruined by our parents and the second half by our children.

CLARENCE DARROW

We never know the love of the parent till we become parents ourselves.
HENRY WARD BEECHER

The most important thing a father can do for his children is to love their mother.
THEODORE M. HESBURGH

How many hopes and fears, how many ardent wishes and anxious apprehensions are twisted together in the threads that connect the parent with the child!
SAMUEL GRISWOLD GOODRICH

PARTY Also see: GOVERNMENT, POLITICS.

He serves his party best who serves the country best.
RUTHERFORD B. HAYES

Any party which takes credit for the rain must not be surprised if its opponents blame it for the drought.
DWIGHT W. MORROW

I know my Republican friends were glad to see my wife feeding an elephant in India. She gave him sugar and nuts. But of course the elephant wasn't satisfied.
JOHN FITZGERALD KENNEDY

The best system is to have one party govern and the other party watch.
THOMAS B. REED

Party honesty is party expediency.

GROVER CLEVELAND

PASSION Also see: ANGER, DESIRE, EMOTION, ENTHUSIASM, PATIENCE, POETRY.

Act nothing in furious passion. It's putting to sea in a storm.
THOMAS FULLER

Passion is universal humanity. Without it religion, history, romance and art would be useless.
HONORÉ DE BALZAC

The passions are like fire, useful in a thousand ways and dangerous only in one, through their excess.
CHRISTIAN NESTELL BOVEE

He only employs his passion who can make no use of his reason.

CICERO

Our passions are like convulsion fits, which, though they make us stronger for the time, leave us the weaker ever after.

JONATHAN SWIFT

He submits to be seen through a microscope, who suffers himself to be caught in a fit of passion.

JOHANN KASPAR LAVATER

PAST *Also see:* FUTURE, HISTORY, PRESENT.

I tell you the past is a bucket of ashes.

CARL SANDBURG

Those who cannot remember the past are condemned to repeat it.

GEORGE SANTAYANA

The free world must now prove itself worthy of its own past.

DWIGHT D. EISENHOWER

Study the past if you would divine the future.

CONFUCIUS

The present contains nothing more than the past, and what is found in the effect was already in the cause.

HENRI BERGSON

PATIENCE *Also see:* ANGER, ENDURANCE.

Adopt the pace of nature: her secret is patience.

RALPH WALDO EMERSON

He that can have patience can have what he will.

BENJAMIN FRANKLIN

They also serve who only stand and wait.

JOHN MILTON

Our patience will achieve more than our force.

EDMUND BURKE

Everything comes to him who hustles while he waits.

THOMAS A. EDISON

Patience is bitter, but its fruit is sweet.

JEAN JACQUES ROUSSEAU

Patience and time do more than strength or passion.

JEAN DE LA FONTAINE

PATRIOTISM *Also see:* CITIZENSHIP, COUNTRY, NATIONAL-
ISM.

Patriotism is easy to understand in America; it means looking out for
yourself by looking out for your country.

CALVIN COOLIDGE

I only regret that I have but one life to give for my country.

NATHAN HALE

Ask not what your country can do for you: Ask what you can do for
your country.

JOHN FITZGERALD KENNEDY

Love of country is like love of woman—he loves her best who seeks to
bestow on her the highest good.

FELIX ADLER

A man's country is not a certain area of land, of mountains, rivers, and
woods, but it is a principle; and patriotism is loyalty to that principle.

GEORGE WILLIAM CURTIS

You'll never have a quiet world till you knock the patriotism out of the
human race.

GEORGE BERNARD SHAW

A man's feet must be planted in his country, but his eyes should survey
the world.

GEORGE SANTAYANA

PEACE *Also see:* BLOOD, DISARMAMENT, HOME, LEISURE,
LOYALTY, WAR.

Peace, in international affairs, is a period of cheating between two periods
of fighting.

AMBROSE BIERCE

If they want peace, nations should avoid the pin-pricks that precede
cannonshots.

NAPOLEON BONAPARTE

Peace is rarely denied to the peaceful.

JOHANN VON SCHILLER

Peace is the one condition of survival in this nuclear age.

ADLAI E. STEVENSON

We seek peace, knowing that peace is the climate of freedom.

DWIGHT D. EISENHOWER

If we are to live together in peace, we must come to know each other better.

LYNDON BAINES JOHNSON

PERCEPTION *Also see:* SCIENCE, UNDERSTANDING.

Only in quiet waters things mirror themselves undistorted. Only in a quiet mind is adequate perception of the world.

HANS MARGOLIUS

The heart has eyes which the brain knows nothing of.

CHARLES H. PARKHURST

To see what is right, and not do it, is want of courage, or of principle.

CONFUCIUS

The clearsighted do not rule the world, but they sustain and console it.

AGNES REPPLIER

PERFECTION

Trifles make perfection, and perfection is no trifle.

MICHELANGELO

Aim at perfection in everything, though in most things it is unattainable. However, they who aim at it, and persevere, will come much nearer to it than those whose laziness and despondency make them give it up as unattainable.

LORD CHESTERFIELD

Perfection is attained by slow degrees; it requires the hand of time.

VOLTAIRE

No good work whatever can be perfect, and the demand for perfection is always a sign of a misunderstanding of the ends of art.

JOHN RUSKIN

This is the very perfection of a man, to find out his own imperfections.

ST. AUGUSTINE

The artist who aims at perfection in everything achieves it in nothing.

DELACROIX

It is reasonable to have perfection in our eye that we may always advance toward it, though we know it can never be reached.

SAMUEL JOHNSON

PERSEVERANCE *Also see:* DIGNITY, DILIGENCE, ENDURANCE, PATIENCE, PURPOSE.

The difference between perseverance and obstinacy is, that one often comes from a strong will, and the other from a strong won't.

HENRY WARD BEECHER

Consider the postage stamp, my son. It secures success through its ability to stick to one thing till it gets there.

JOSH BILLINGS

We make way for the man who boldly pushes past us.

CHRISTIAN NESTELL BOVEE

There is no failure except in no longer trying. There is no defeat except from within, no really insurmountable barrier save our own inherent weakness of purpose.

KIN HUBBARD

Perseverance is more prevailing than violence; and many things which cannot be overcome when they are together yield themselves up when taken little by little.

PLUTARCH

PERSONALITY *Also see:* CHARACTER, INDIVIDUALITY, MATURITY.

Everyone is a moon, and has a dark side which he never shows to anybody.

MARK TWAIN

Some persons are likeable in spite of their unswerving integrity.

DON MARQUIS

If you have anything really valuable to contribute to the world it will come through the expression of your own personality, that single spark of divinity that sets you off and makes you different from every other living creature.

BRUCE BARTON

Personality is to a man what perfume is to a flower.

CHARLES M. SCHWAB

PESSIMISM *Also see:* CYNIC, OPTIMISM, SKEPTICISM, TRADITION.

A pessimist is one who feels bad when he feels good for fear he'll feel worse when he feels better.

ANONYMOUS

Cheer up, the worst is yet to come.

PHILANDER JOHNSON

PHILOSOPHY *Also see:* DISCRETION, GOD, REASON, RELIGION, SCIENCE, THEORY.

Philosophy: unintelligible answers to insoluble problems.

HENRY BROOKS ADAMS

The philosophy of one century is the common sense of the next.

HENRY WARD BEECHER

All philosophy lies in two words, sustain and abstain.

EPICTETUS

Philosophy is an unusually ingenious attempt to think fallaciously.

BERTRAND RUSSELL

Philosophy is the science which considers truth.

ARISTOTLE

Philosophy, when superficially studied, excites doubt; when thoroughly explored, it dispels it.

FRANCIS BACON

PITY *Also see:* COMPASSION, SYMPATHY.

Pity is best taught by fellowship in woe.

SAMUEL TAYLOR COLERIDGE

Compassion is the only one of the human emotions the Lord permitted Himself and it has carried the divine flavor ever since.

DAGOBERT D. RUNES

We pity in others only those evils which we have ourselves experienced.

JEAN JACQUES ROUSSEAU

Pity is not natural to man. Children and savages are always cruel. Pity is acquired and improved by the cultivation of reason. We may have uneasy sensations from seeing a creature in distress, without pity; but we have not pity unless we wish to relieve him.

SAMUEL JOHNSON

PLAGIARISM *Also see:* ORIGINALITY, WRITER.

When you take stuff from one writer, it's plagiarism; but when you take it from many writers, it's research.

WILSON MIZNER

About the most originality that any writer can hope to achieve honestly is to steal with good judgment.

JOSH BILLINGS

Literature is full of coincidences, which some love to believe are plagiarisms. There are thoughts always abroad in the air which it takes more wit to avoid than to hit upon.

OLIVER WENDELL HOLMES

A certain awkwardness marks the use of borrowed thoughts; but as soon as we have learned what to do with them, they become our own.

RALPH WALDO EMERSON

Every man is a borrower and a mimic, life is theatrical and literature a quotation.

RALPH WALDO EMERSION

PLEASURE *Also see:* ANXIETY, CHEERFULNESS, COURTESY, JOY.

That man is the richest whose pleasures are the cheapest.

HENRY DAVID THOREAU

In diving to the bottom of pleasure we bring up more gravel than pearls.

HONORÉ DE BAIZAC

We tire of those pleasures we take, but never of those we give.

JOHN PETIT-SENN

The average man does not get pleasure out of an idea because he thinks it is true; he thinks it is true because he gets pleasure out of it.

H. L. MENCKEN

Whenever you are sincerely pleased you are nourished.

RALPH WALDO EMERSON

To make pleasures pleasant shorten them.

CHARLES BUXTON

POETRY *Also see:* ARTIST.

With me poetry has not been a purpose, but a passion.

EDGAR ALLAN POE

Writing free verse is like playing tennis with the net down.

ROBERT FROST

When power leads man toward arrogance, poetry reminds him of his limitations. When power narrows the areas of man's concern, poetry reminds him of the richness and diversity of his existence. When power corrupts, poetry cleanses.

JOHN FITZGERALD KENNEDY

Poetry comes nearer to vital truth than history.

PLATO

Poetry is the utterance of deep and heart-felt truth—the true poet is very near the oracle.

EDWIN HUBBEL CHAPIN

POLITICS *Also see:* DEFEAT, GOVERNMENT, INDEPENDENCE, PARTY, POWER, PROFESSION, PROSPERITY, REVOLUTION.

Politics is a profession; a serious, complicated and, in its true sense, a noble one.

DWIGHT D. EISENHOWER

Politics is too serious a matter to be left to the politicians.

CHARLES DE GAULLE

Politics is the conduct of public affairs for private advantage.

AMBROSE BIERCE

A politician thinks of the next election; a statesman, of the next generation.

J. F. CLARKE

Politicians are the same all over. They promise to build a bridge even where there is no river.

NIKITA KHRUSHCHEV

The political world is stimulating. It's the most interesting thing you can do. It beats following the dollar.

JOHN FITZGERALD KENNEDY

POLLUTION *Also see:* CONSERVATION.

Among these treasures of our land is water—fast becoming our most valuable, most prized, most critical resource. A blessing where properly used—but it can bring devastation and ruin when left uncontrolled.

DWIGHT D. EISENHOWER

We in Government have begun to recognize the critical work which must be done at all levels—local, State and Federal—in ending in the pollution of our waters.

ROBERT F. KENNEDY

The American people have a right to air that they and their children can breathe without fear.

LYNDON BAINES JOHNSON

As soils are depleted, human health, vitality and intelligence go with them.

LOUIS BROMFIELD

POPULARITY *Also see:* FAME, REPUTATION.

Avoid popularity if you would have peace.

ABRAHAM LINCOLN

Popular opinion is the greatest lie in the world.

THOMAS CARLYLE

Popularity is exhausting. The life of the party almost always winds up in a corner with an overcoat over him.

WILSON MIZNER

True popularity is not the popularity which is followed after, but the popularity which follows after.

LORD MANSFIELD

To his dog, every man is Napoleon; hence the constant popularity of dogs.

ALDOUS HUXLEY

Whatever is popular deserves attention.

JAMES MACKINTOSH

Avoid popularity; it has many snares, and no real benefit.

WILLIAM PENN

POPULATION *Also see:* BIRTH, BIRTH CONTROL.

We have been God-like in our planned breeding of our domesticated plants and animals, but we have been rabbit-like in our unplanned breeding of ourselves.

ARNOLD JOSEPH TOYNBEE

The hungry world cannot be fed until and unless the growth of its resources and the growth of its population come into balance. Each man and woman—and each nation—must make decisions of conscience and policy in the face of this great problem.

LYNDON BAINES JOHNSON

POVERTY *Also see:* AVARICE, LUXURY, PRIDE, TAX, WANT.

Poverty is the step-mother of genius.

JOSH BILLINGS

Poverty often deprives a man of all spirit and virtue; it is hard for an empty bag to stand upright.

BENJAMIN FRANKLIN

I thank fate for having made me born poor. Poverty taught me the true value of the gifts useful to life.

ANATOLE FRANCE

For every talent that poverty has stimulated it has blighted a hundred.

JOHN W. GARDNER

In a country well governed, poverty is something to be ashamed of. In a country badly governed, wealth is something to be ashamed of.

CONFUCIUS

Hard as it may appear in individual cases, dependent poverty ought to be held disraceful.

THOMAS ROBERT MALTHUS

The child was diseased at birth, stricken with a hereditary ill that only the most vital men are able to shake off. I mean poverty—the most deadly and prevalent of all diseases.

EUGENE O'NEILL

POWER *Also see:* ABUSE, AUTHORITY, BEAUTY, DESIRE, FORCE, PARTY, PATIENCE, POETRY, VIOLENCE.

Most powerful is he who has himself in his own power.

SENECA

We cannot live by power, and a culture that seeks to live by it becomes brutal and sterile. But we can die without it.

MAX LERNER

Man is born to seek power, yet his actual condition makes him a slave to the power of others.

HANS J. MORGENTHAU

I know of nothing sublime which is not some modification of power.

EDMUND BURKE

There is no knowledge that is not power.

RALPH WALDO EMERSON

We often say how impressive power is. But I do not find it impressive at all. The guns and the bombs, the rockets and the warships, are all symbols of human failure. They are necessary symbols. They protect what we cherish. But they are witness to human folly.

LYNDON BAINES JOHNSON

Power will intoxicate the best hearts, as wine the strongest heads. No man is wise enough, nor good enough to be trusted with unlimited power.

CHARLES CALEB COLTON

PRAISE *Also see:* FLATTERY, MODESTY.

When we disclaim praise, it is only showing our desire to be praised a second time.

FRANÇOIS DE LA ROCHEFOUCAULD

Get someone else to blow your horn and the sound will carry twice as far.

WILL ROGERS

He who praises everybody, praises nobody.

SAMUEL JOHNSON

I can live for two months on a good compliment.

MARK TWAIN

PRAYER

Practical prayer is harder on the soles of your shoes than on the knees of your trousers.

AUSTIN O'MALLEY

Certain thoughts are prayers. There are moments when, whatever be the attitude of the body, the soul is on its knees.

VICTOR HUGO

No man every prayed heartily without learning something.

RALPH WALDO EMERSON

God hears no more than the heart speaks; and if the heart be dumb, God will certainly be deaf.

THOMAS BROOKS

Pray as if everything depended on God, and work as if everything depended upon man.

FRANCIS CARDINAL SPELLMAN

Prayer is a confession of one's own unworthiness and weakness.

MAHATMA GANDHI

PREACHING Also see: SIN.

Only the sinner has a right to preach.

CHRISTOPHER MORLEY

The world is dying for want, not of good preaching, but of good hearing.

GEORGE DANA BOARDMAN

One of the proofs of the divinity of our gospel is the preaching it has survived.

WOODROW WILSON

The minister's brain is often the "poor-box" of the church.

EDWIN PERCY WHIPPLE

The test of a preacher is that his congregation goes away saying, not "What a lovely sermon" but, "I will do something!"

ST. FRANCIS DE SALES

The best of all the preachers are the men who live their creeds.

EDGAR A. GUEST

PREJUDICE *Also see:* BIGOTRY, INTOLERANCE, QUESTION, RACE.

To lay aside all prejudices, is to lay aside all principles. He who is destitute of principles is governed by whims.

FRIEDRICH H. JACOBI

Prejudice, which sees what it pleases, cannot see what is plain.

AUBREY T. DE VERA

A prejudice is a vagrant opinion without visible means of support.

AMBROSE BIERCE

When dealing with people, remember you are not dealing with creatures of logic, but with creatures of emotion, creatures bristling with prejudice and motivated by pride and vanity.

DALE CARNEGIE

The time is past when Christians in America can take a long spoon and hand the gospel to the black man out the back door.

MORDECAI W. JOHNSON

He that is possessed with a prejudice is possessed with a devil, and one of the worst kinds of devils, for it shuts out the truth, and often leads to ruinous error.

TRYON EDWARDS

PRESENT *Also see:* PAST, TIME.

He to whom the present is the only thing that is present, knows nothing of the age in which he lives.

OSCAR WILDE

The future is purchased by the present.

SAMUEL JOHNSON

Those who live to the future must always appear selfish to those who live to the present.

RALPH WALDO EMERSON

PRESIDENT

No man will every bring out of the Presidency the reputation which carries him into it.

THOMAS JEFFERSON

I seek the Presidency not because it offers me a chance to be somebody but because it offers a chance to do something.

RICHARD M. NIXON

The American presidency will demand more than ringing manifestos issued from the rear of battle. It will demand that the President place himself in the very thick of the fight; that he care passionately about the fate of the people he leads . . .

JOHN FITZGERALD KENNEDY

President means chief servant.

MAHATMA GANDHI

My most fervent prayer is to be a President who can make it possible for every boy in this land to grow to manhood by loving his country—instead of dying for it.

LYNDON BAINES JOHNSON

When I was a boy I was told that anybody could become President; I'm beginning to believe.

CLARENCE DARROW

PRETENSION *Also see:* OSTENTATION, PRIDE, SCANDAL, SELF-CONFIDENCE.

The only good in pretending is the fun we get out of fooling ourselves that we fool somebody.

BOOTH TARKINGTON

The hardest tumble a man can make is to fall over his own bluff.

AMBROSE BIERCE

When there is much pretension, much has been borrowed; nature never pretends.

JOHANN KASPAR LAVATER

Pretension almost always overdoes the original, and hence exposes itself.

HOSEA BALLOU

We had better appear what we are, than affect to appear what we are not.

FRANÇOIS DE LA ROCHEFOUCAULD

PRIDE *Also see:* OSTENTATION, PRETENSION, RIVALRY, TAX, VANITY.

There is this paradox in pride—it makes some men ridiculous, but prevents others from becoming so.

CHARLES CALEB COLTON

Pride is an admission of weakness; it secretly fears all competition and dreads all rivals.

FULTON J. SHEEN

The infinitely little have a pride infinitely great.

VOLTAIRE

To be proud and inaccessible is to be timid and weak.

JEAN BAPTISTE MASILLON

Pride is seldom delicate; it will please itself with very mean advantages.

SAMUEL JOHNSON

PRIVACY Also see: COMMUNICATION, LONELINESS, SOLITUDE.

Privacy is the right to be alone—the most comprehensive of rights, and the right most valued by civilized man.

LOUIS D. BRANDEIS

Modern Americans are so exposed, peered at, inquired about, and spied upon as to be increasingly without privacy—members of a naked society and denizens of a goldfish bowl.

EDWARD V. LONG

Far from the madding crowd's ignoble strife.

THOMAS GRAY

PROCRASTINATION Also see: ACTION, IDLENESS, NEGLECT.

Procrastination is the art of keeping up with yesterday.

DON MARQUIS

Even if you're on the right track—you'll get run over if you just sit there.

ARTHUR GODFREY

Never leave that till tomorrow which you can do today.

BENJAMIN FRANKLIN

Putting off an easy thing makes it hard, and putting off a hard one makes it impossible.

GEORGE H. LORIMER

PRODUCTION Also see: ECONOMY, EFFICIENCY, INDUSTRY, LABOR.

Production is the only answer to inflation.

CHESTER BOWLES

The goose lays the golden egg. Payrolls make consumers.

GEORGE HUMPHEY

It is one of the greatest errors to put any limitation upon production . . .
We have not the power to produce more than there is a potential to
consume.

LOUIS D. BRANDEIS

Unless each man produces more than he receives, increases his output,
there will be less for him than all the others.

BERNARD M. BARUCH

PROFANITY *Also see:* WICKEDNESS.

Nothing is greater, or more fearful sacrilege than to prostitute the great
name of God to the petulancy of an idle tongue.

JEREMY TAYLOR

The foolish and wicked practice of profane cursing and swearing is a
vice so mean and low that every person of sense and character detests
and depises it.

GEORGE WASHINGTON

Profaneness is a brutal vice. He who indulges in it is no gentleman.

EDWIN HUBBEL CHAPIN

PROFESSION *Also see:* MEDICINE, POLITICS.

I hold every man a debtor to his profession.

FRANCIS BACON

Medicine is my lawful wife and literature my mistress; when I get tired
of one, I spend the night with the other.

ANTON CHEKHOV

In all professions each affects a look and an exterior to appear what he
wishes the world to believe that he is. Thus we may say that the whole
world is made up of appearances.

FRANÇOIS DE LA ROCHEFOUCAULD

We forget that the most successful statesmen have been professionals.
Lincoln was a professional politician.

FELIX FRANKFURTER

PROFIT . . . *See* GAIN

PROGRESS *Also see:* AMERICA, BEHAVIOR, DIFFERENCE, DIF-FICULTY, DISCONTENT, EDUCATION, IMPROVEMENT, ORDER, SELF-IMPROVEMENT.

He that is good, will infallibly become better, and he that is bad, will as certainly become worse; for vice, virtue and time are three things that never stand still.

CHARLES CALEB COLTON

All that is human must retrograde if it does not advance.

EDWARD GIBBON

The reasonable man adapts himself to the world, but the unreasonable man tries to adapt the world to him—therefore, all progress depends upon the unreasonable man.

SAMUEL BUTLER

Social advance depends as much upon the process through which it is secured as upon the result itself.

JANE ADDAMS

Speak softly, and carry a big stick; you will go far.

THEODORE ROOSEVELT

Those who work most for the world's advancement are the ones who demand least.

HENRY DOHERTY

PROMISE . . . *See* VOW

PROPAGANDA *Also see:* ART, DECEIT, RELIGION, TRUTH, WORD.

Propaganda must not serve the truth, especially insofar as it might bring out something favorable for the opponent.

ADOLF HITLER

Some of mankind's most terrible misdeeds have been committed under the spell of certain magic words or phrases.

JAMES BRYANT CONANT

A propagandist is a specialist in selling attitudes and opinions.

HANS SPEIER

We have made the Reich by propaganda.

JOSEPH PAUL GOEBBELS

Today the world is the victim of propaganda because people are not intellectually competent. More than anything the United States needs effective citizens competent to do their own thinking.

WILLIAM MATHER LEWIS

PROPERTY *Also see:* WEALTH.

Mine is better than ours.

BENJAMIN FRANKLIN

Private property began the instant somebody had a mind of his own.

E. E. CUMMINGS

Property is the fruit of labor; property is desirable; it is a positive good in the world.

ABRAHAM LINCOLN

Ultimately property rights and personal rights are the same thing.

CALVIN COOLIDGE

What we call real estate—the solid ground to build a house on—is the broad foundation on which nearly all the guilt of this world rests.

NATHANIAL HAWTHORNE

It is preoccupation with possession, more than anything else, that prevents men from living freely and nobly.

BERTRAND RUSSELL

PROSPERITY *Also see:* ADVERSITY, ADVICE, WEALTH.

Prosperity makes friends, adversity tries them.

PUBLILIUS SYRUS

Prosperity is something the businessmen created for politicians to take credit for.

BRUNSWICK (GA.) PILOT

The prosperous man is never sure that he is loved for himself.

LUCAN

Prosperity is the surest breeder of insolence I know.

MARK TWAIN

When prosperity comes, do not use all of it.

CONFUCIUS

PROVIDENCE *Also see:* GOD, FATE.

There are many scapegoats for our sins, but the most popular is providence.

MARK TWAIN

Friends, I agree with you in Providence; but I believe in the Providence of the most men, the largest purse, and the longest cannon.

ABRAHAM LINCOLN

God's providence is on the side of clear heads.

HENRY WARD BEECHER

The longer I live, the more convincing proofs I see of this truth, that God governs in the affairs of man; and if a sparrow cannot fall to the ground without his notice, is it probable that an empire can rise without his aid?

BENJAMIN FRANKLIN

PRUDENCE *Also see:* MODERATION, QUESTION, WISDOM

The prudence of the best heads is often defeated by the tenderness of the best of hearts.

HENRY FIELDING

It is by the goodness of God that in our country we have those three unspeakably precious things: freedom of speech, freedom of conscience, and the prudence never to practice either.

MARK TWAIN

Prudence is an attitude that keeps life safe, but does not often make it happy.

SAMUEL JOHNSON

There is nothing more imprudent than excessive prudence.

CHARLES CALEB COLTON

PSYCHOLOGY *Also see:* MIND

Anybody who is 25 or 30 years old has physical scars from all sorts of things, from tuberculosis to polio. It's the same with the mind.

MOSES R. KAUFMAN

Psychoanalysis has changed American psychology from a diagnostic to a therapeutic science, not because so many patients are cured by the psychoanalytic technique, but because of the new understanding of psychiatric patients it has given us, and the new and different concept of illness and health.

KARL A. MENNINGER

PUBLIC *Also see:* PUBLICITY, TASTE

If there's anything a public servant hates to do it's something for the public.

KIN HUBBARD

In a free and republican government, you cannot restrain the voice of the multitude.

GEORGE WASHINGTON

That miscellaneous collection of a few wise and many foolish individuals, called the public.

JOHN STUART MILL

The public have neither shame nor gratitude.

WILLIAM HAZLITT

The public is a ferocious beast: one must either chain it up or flee from it.

VOLTAIRE

PUBLICITY *Also see:* ADVERTISING, NEWSPAPER.

Without publicity there can be no public support, and without public support every nation must decay.

BENJAMIN DISRAELI

Publicity, publicity, PUBLICITY is the greatest moral factor and force in our public life.

JOSEPH PULITZER

Modern business and persons and organizations that seek publicity must recognize their obligations to the public and to the press.

HENRY F. WOODS, JR.

PUNCTUALITY

I could never think well of a man's intellectual or moral character, if he was habitually unfaithful to his appointments.

NATHANIEL EMMONS

Unfaithfulness in the keeping of an appointment is an act of clear dishonesty. You may as well borrow a person's money as his time.

HORACE MANN

Punctuality is one of the cardinal business virtues: always insist on it in your subordinates.

DON MARQUIS

PUNISHMENT *Also see:* CRIME, DISCONTENT, LYING, PAIN, SIN.

We are not punished for our sins, but by them.

ELBERT HUBBARD

If punishment makes not the will supple it hardens the offender.

JOHN LOCKE

It is as expedient that a wicked man be punished as that a sick man be cured by a physician; for all chastisement is a kind of medicine.

PLATO

Crime and punishment grow out of one stem.

RALPH WALDO EMERSON

PURPOSE *Also see:* AIM, FIRMNESS, IDEAL, INSTINCT, SUCCESS.

The secret of success is constancy to purpose.

BENJAMIN DISRALLI

Great minds have purposes, others have wishes.

WASHINGTON IRVING

Only the consciousness of a purpose that is mightier than any man and worthy of all men can fortify and inspirit and compose the souls of men.

WALTER LIPPMANN

The good man is the man who, no matter how morally unworthy he has been, is moving to become better.

JOHN DEWEY

PURSUIT *Also see:* ADVENTURE, ENTHUSIASM, MYSTERY.

The rapture of pursuing is the prize the vanquished gain.

HENRY WADSWORTH LONGFELLOW

The crowning fortune of a man is to be born to some pursuit which finds him employment and happiness, whether it be to make baskets, or broadswords, or canals, or statues, or songs.

RALPH WALDO EMERSON

Men tire themselves in pursuit of rest.

LAURENCE STERNE

QUALITY *Also see:* PUBLIC, VALUE, WORTH.

We are never so ridiculous by the qualities we have, as by those we affect to have.

FRANÇOIS DE LA ROCHEFOUCAULD

It is the quality of our work which will please God and not the quantity.
MAHATMA GANDHI

Nothing endures but personal qualities.
WALT WHITMAN

I think there is only one quality worse than hardness of heart, and that is softness of head.
THEODORE ROOSEVELT

Many individuals have, like uncut diamonds, shining qualities beneath a rough exterior.
JUVENAL

QUARREL *Also see:* ANGER, ARGUMENT, CHEERFULNESS, COWARDICE.

When chickens quit quarreling over their food they often find that there is enough for all of them. I wonder if it might not be the same with the human race.
DON MARQUIS

People generally quarrel because they cannot argue.
GILBERT K. CHESTERTON

He that blows the coals in quarrels he has nothing to do with has no right to complain if the sparks fly in his face.
BENJAMIN FRANKLIN

Two cannot fall out if one does not choose.
SPANISH PROVERB

A long dispute means that both parties are wrong.
VOLTAIRE

I never take my own side in a quarrel.
ROBERT FROST

In quarreling the truth is always lost.
PUBLILIUS SYRUS

QUESTION *Also see:* CONVERSATION, CURIOSITY, DOUBT.

No man really becomes a fool until he stops asking questions.
CHARLES STEINMETZ

A fool may ask more questions in an hour than a wise man can answer in seven years.
ENGLISH PROVERB

No question is so difficult to answer as that to which the answer is obvious.

GEORGE BERNARD SHAW

Man will not live without answers to his questions.

HANS MORGENTHAU

Judge a man by his questions rather than his answers.

VOLTAIRE

He must be very ignorant for he answers every question he is asked.

VOLTAIRE

A prudent question is one-half of wisdom.

FRANCIS BACON

QUIET *Also see:* REST, SILENCE.

The good and the wise lead quiet lives.

EURIPIDES

To have a quiet mind is to possess one's mind wholly; to have a calm spirit is to possess one's self.

HAMILTON MABIE

An inability to stay quiet is one of the conspicuous failings of mankind.

WALTER BAGEHOT

God gives quietness at last.

JOHN GREENLEAF WHITTIER

Quiet is what home would be without children.

ANONYMOUS

Stillness of person and steadiness of features are signal marks of good breeding.

OLIVER WENDELL HOLMES

QUOTATION *Also see:* MAXIM, PLAGIARISM, WRITER.

The profoundest thought or passion sleeps as in a mine, until an equal mind and heart finds and publishes it.

RALPH WALDO EMERSON

He presents me with what is always an acceptable gift who brings me news of a great thought before unknown. He enriches me without impoverishing himself.

RALPH WALDO EMERSON

Certain brief sentences are peerless in their ability to give one the feeling that nothing remains to be said.

JEAN ROSTAND

Next to the originator of a good sentence is the first quoter of it.

RALPH WALDO EMERSON

RACE *Also see:* DIGNITY, PREJUDICE.

Mere connection with what is known as a superior race will not permanently carry an individual forward unless the individual has worth.

BOOKER T. WASHINGTON

The difference of race is one of the reasons why I fear war may always exist; because race implies difference, difference implies superiority, and superiority leads to predominance.

BENJAMIN DISRAELI

The existence of any pure race with special endowments is a myth, as is the belief that there are races all of whose members are foredoomed to eternal inferiority.

FRANZ BOAS

A heavy guilt rests upon us for what the whites of all nations have done to the colored peoples. When we do good to them, it is not benevolence—it is atonement.

ALBERT SCHWEITZER

At the heart of racism is the religious assertion that God made a creative mistake when He brought some people into being.

FRIEDRICH OTTO HERTZ

When white and black and brown and every other color decide they're going to live together as Christians, then and only then are we going to see an end to these troubles.

BARRY M. GOLDWATER

RADICAL *Also see:* EXTREMES, REBELLION, REVOLUTION, VIOLENCE.

A radical is one who speaks the truth.

CHARLES A. LINDBERGH

If a man is right, he can't be too radical; if he is wrong, he can't be too conservative.

JOSH BILLINGS

A radical man is a man with both feet firmly planted in the air.

FRANKLIN DELANO ROOSEVELT

I am trying to do two things: dare to be a radical and not a fool, which is a matter of no small difficulty.

JAMES A. GARFIELD

RANK *Also see:* ANCESTRY, CLASS.

It is an interesting question how far men would retain their relative rank if they were divested of their clothes.

HENRY DAVID THOREAU

Rank and riches are chains of gold, but still chains.

GIOVANNI RUFFINI

To be vain of one's rank or place, is to show that one is below it.

STANISLAS I

What men prize most is a privilege, even if it be that of chief mourner at a funeral.

JAMES RUSSELL LOWELL

READING *Also see:* BOOK, LITERATURE, NEWSPAPER.

I divide all readers into two classes: those who read to remember and those who read to forget.

WILLIAM LYON PHELPS

Reading is to the mind what exercise is to the body.

JOSEPH ADDISON

We should be as careful of the books we read, as of the company we keep. The dead very often have more power than the living.

TRYON EDWARDS

No entertainment is so cheap as reading, nor any pleasure so lasting.

MARY WORTLEY MONTAGU

Reading is a basic tool in the living of a good life.

MORTIMER J. ADLER

Read the best books first, or you may not have a chance to read them all.

HENRY DAVID THOREAU

REALITY *Also see:* APPEARANCE, DREAM, ILLUSION, TRUTH.

Facts are facts and will not disappear on account of your likes

JAWAHARLAL NEHRU

A theory must be tempered with reality.

JAWAHARLAL NEHRU

I accept reality and dare not question it.

WALT WHITMAN

The realist is the man, who having weighed all the visible factors in a given situation and having found that the odds are against him, decides that fighting is useless.

RAOUL DE SALES

REASON *Also see:* ANGER, ARGUMENT, COMMON SENSE, FORCE, HEART, LOGIC, MIND, TEMPER, UNDERSTANDING.

Most of our so-called reasoning consists in finding arguments for going on believing as we already do.

JAMES ROBINSON

Reason has never failed men. Only force and repression have made the wrecks in the world.

WILLIAM ALLEN WHITE

Man has received direct from God only one instrument wherewith to know himself and to know his relation to the universe—he has no other—and that instrument is reason.

LEO TOLSTOI

Man is a reasoning rather than a reasonable animal.

ALEXANDER HAMILTON

An appeal to the reason of the people has never been known to fail in the long run.

JAMES RUSSELL LOWELL

Error of opinion may be tolerated where reason is left free to admit it.

THOMAS JEFFERSON

Reason can in general do more than blind force.

GALLUS

Many are destined to reason wrongly; others, not to reason at all; and others, to persecute those who do reason.

VOLTAIRE

REBELLION *Also see:* DISSENT, OPPRESSION, REVOLUTION, RIOT, TREASON.

Rebellion against tyrants is obedience to God.

BENJAMIN FRANKLIN

As long as the world shall last there will be wrongs, and if no man objected and no man rebelled, those wrongs would last forever.

CLARENCE DARROW

An oppressed people are authorized whenever they can to rise and break their fetters.

HENRY CLAY

Men seldom, or rather never for a length of time and deliberately, rebel against anything that does not deserve rebelling against.

THOMAS CARLYLE

It doesn't take a majority to make a rebellion; it takes only a few determined leaders and a sound cause.

H. L. MENCKEN

REFLECTION . . . *See* THOUGHT

REFORM *Also see:* IMPROVEMENT, PROGRESS.

Nothing so needs reforming as other people's habits.

MARK TWAIN

Reform must come from within, not from without. You cannot legislate for virtue.

JAMES CARDINAL GIBBONS

What is a man born for but to be a reformer, a remaker of what has been made, a denouncer of lies, a restorer of truth and good?

RALPH WALDO EMERSON

The church is always trying to get other people to reform; it might not be a bad idea to reform itself.

MARK TWAIN

I think I am better than the poeple who are trying to reform me.

ED HOWE

REGRET *Also see:* REMORSE.

Regret is an appalling waste of energy; you can't build on it; it's only good for wallowing in.

KATHERINE MANSFIELD

I only regret that I have but one life to give for my country.

NATHAN HALE

For of all sad words of tongue or pen, the saddest are these: "It might have been!"

JOHN GREENLEAF WHITTIER

RELIGION *Also see:* CHRISTIANITY, CHURCH and STATE, CON-

SCIENCE, HEAVEN, HYPROCRISY, JUDA-
ISM, PREACHING.

All religions must be tolerated, for every man must get to heaven in his own way.

FREDERICK THE GREAT

Many have quarreled about religion that never practiced it.

BENJAMIN FRANKLIN

Religion is the sum of the expansive impulses of a being.

HENRY H. ELLIS

Every man, either to his terror or consolation, has some sense of religion.

JAMES HARRINGTON

Science without religion is lame; religion without science is blind.

ALBERT EINSTEIN

Measure not men by Sundays, without regarding what they do all the week after.

THOMAS FULLER

To swallow and follow, whether old doctrine or new propaganda, is a weakness still dominating the human mind.

CHARLOTTE P. GILBERT

Our hope of immortality does not come from any religions, but nearly all religions come from that hope.

ROBERT GREEN INGERSOLL

You can change your faith without changing gods, and vice versa.

STANISLAW J. LEC

REMORSE *Also see:* GRIEF, GUILT, REGRET.

Remorse is the pain of sin.

THEODORE PARKER

To be left alone, and face to face with my own crime, had been just retribution.

HENRY WADSWORTH LONGFELLOW

Remorse is the echo of a lost virtue.

EDWARD G. BULLWER-LYTTON

Remorse: beholding heaven and feeling hell.

GEORGE MOORE

REPENTANCE *Also see:* CONFESSION, GUILT, SIN.

It is much easier to repent of sins that we have committed than to repent of those that we intend to commit.

JOSH BILLINGS

Of all acts of man repentance is the most divine. The greatest of all faults is to be conscious of none.

THOMAS CARLYLE

True repentance is to cease from sinning.

AMBROSE OF MILAN

Bad men are full of repentance.

ARISTOTLE

Great is the difference betwixt a man's being frightened at, and humbled for his sins.

THOMAS FULLER

REPETITION Also see: LOQUACITY.

Iteration, like friction, is likely to generate heat instead of progress.

GEORGE ELIOT

There is no absurdity so palpable but that it may be firmly planted in the human head if you only begin to inculcate it before the age of five, by constantly repeating it with an air of great solemnity.

ARTHUR SCHOPENHAUER

REPUTATION Also see: CHARACTER, FAME, NAME, PERSONALITY, SLANDER.

A reputation once broken may possibly be repaired, but the world will always keep their eyes on the spot where the crack was.

JOSEPH HALL

Good will, like a good name, is got by many actions, and lost by one.

LORD JEFFREY

Associate with men of good quality if you esteem your own reputation; for it is better to be alone than in bad company.

GEORGE WASHINGTON

A doctor's reputation is made by the number of eminent men who die under his care.

GEORGE BERNARD SHAW

The two most precious things this side of the grave are our reputation and our life. But it is to be lamented that the most contemptible whisper may deprive us of the one, and the weakest weapon of the other.

CHARLES CALEB COLTON

What people say behind your back is your standing in the community.

ED HOWE

RESENTMENT . . . *See* DISCONTENT

RESIGNATION *Also see:* ENDURANCE, RETIREMENT.

Resignation is the courage of Christian sorrow.

ALEXANDER VINET

A wise man cares not for what he cannot have.

JACK HERBERT

For after all, the best thing one can do when it's raining is to let it rain.

HENRY WADSORTH LONGFELLOW

What is called resignation is confirmed desperation.

HENRY DAVID THOREAU

We cannot conquer fate and necessity, yet we can yield to them in such a manner as to be greater than if we could.

WALTER S. LANDOR

RESOLUTION *Also see:* AIM, FIRMNESS, PURPOSE, SECURITY, VOW.

The block of granite which is an obstacle in the pathway of the weak, becomes a stepping-stone in the pathway of the strong.

THOMAS CARLYLE

Either I wil find a way, or I will make one.

PHILIP SIDNEY

It is always during a passing state of mind that we make lasting resolutions.

MARCEL PROUST

Resolve to perform what you ought; perform without fail what you resolve.

BENJAMIN FRANKLIN

Resolve and thou are free.

HENRY WADSWORTH LONGFELLOW

RESPECT *Also see:* ADMIRATION, TYRANNY.

I must respect the opinions of others even if I disagree with them.

HERBERT HENRY LEHMAN

I don't know what a scoundrel is like, but I know what a respectable man is like, and it's enough to make one's flesh creep.

J. M. MAISTRE

Men are respectable only as they respect.

RALPH WALDO EMERSON

RESPONSIBILITY *Also see:* DISCIPLINE, DUTY, RIGHTS.

Responsibility is the thing people dread most of all. Yet it is the one thing in the world that develops us, give us manhood or womanhood fibre.

FRANK CRANE

Responsibility educates.

WENDELL PHILLIPS

Every human being has a work to carry on within, duties to perform abroad, influence to exert, which are peculiarly his, and which no conscience but his own can teach.

WILLIAM ELLERY CHANNING

The only way to get rid of responsibilities is to discharge them.

WALTER S. ROBERTSON

Responsibility is the price of greatness.

WINSTON CHURCHILL

REST *Also see:* SLEEP.

Eternal rest sounds comforting in the pulpit; well, you try it once, and see how heavy time will hang on your hands.

MARK TWAIN

Rest is a good thing, but boredom is its brother.

VOLTAIRE

Rest: the sweet sauce of labor.

PLUTARCH

Put off thy cares with thy clothes; so shall thy rest strengthen thy labor, and so thy labor sweeten thy rest.

FRANCIS QUARLES

RESULT *Also see:* ABILITY, CAUSE, END and MEANS.

Results! Why, man, I have gotten a lot of results. I know several thousand things that won't work.

THOMAS A. EDISON

It has been my observation and experience, and that of my family, that nothing human works out well.

DON MARQUIS

The man who gets the most satisfactory results is not always the man with the most brilliant single mind, but rather the man who can best coordinate the brains and talents of his associates.

W. ALTON JONES

RETIREMENT *Also see:* LABOR, RESIGNATION, REST, WORK.

The worst of work nowadays is what happens to people when they cease to work.

GILBERT K. CHESTERTON

Don't think of retiring from the world until the world will be sorry that you retire.

SAMUEL JOHNSON

The best time to start thinking about your retirement is before the boss does.

ANONYMOUS

A man is known by the company that keeps him on after retirement age.

ANONYMOUS

REVENGE . . . *See* VENGEANCE

REVERIE *Also see:* DREAM, ILLUSION.

Sit in reverie and watch the changing color of the waves that break upon the idle seashore of the mind.

HENRY WADSWORTH LONGFELLOW

To lose one's self in reverie, one must be either very happy, or very unhappy. Reverie is the child of extremes.

ANTOINE RIVAROL

Reverie is when ideas float in our mind without reflection or regard of the understanding.

JOHN LOCKE

Do anything rather than give yourself to reverie.

WILLIAM ELLERY CHANNING

REVOLUTION *Also see:* CHANGE, GOVERNMENT, TYRANNY, VIOLENCE.

Revolution: in politics, an abrupt change in the form of misgovernment.
AMBROSE BIERCE

Revolutions are not trifles, but spring from trifles.
ARISTOTLE

Make revolution a parent of settlement, and not a nursery of future revolutions.
EDMUND BURKE

Those who make peaceful revolution impossible will make violent revolution inevitable.
JOHN FITZGERALD KENNEDY

Any people anywhere being inclined and having the power have the right to rise up and shake off the existing government, and force a new one that suits them better.
ABRAHAM LINCOLN

Revolutions have never lightened the burden of tyranny: they have only shifted it to another shoulder.
GEORGE BERNARD SHAW

It is impossible to predict the time and progress of revolution. It is governed by its own more or less mysterious laws.
LENIN

REWARD Also see: ACHIEVEMENT, AMBITION, SUCCESS.

The reward of a thing well done is to have done it.
RALPH WALDO EMERSON

No man, who continues to add something to the material, intellectual and moral well-being of the place in which he lives, is left long without proper reward.
BOOKER T. WASHINGTON

He that does good for good's sake seeks neither paradise nor reward, but he is sure of both in the end.
WILLIAM PENN

Not in rewards, but in the strength to strive, the blessing lies.
J. T. TOWBRIDGE

The effects of our actions may be postponed but they are never lost. There is an inevitable reward for good deeds and an inescapable punishment for bad. Meditate upon this truth, and seek always to earn good wages from Destiny.
WU MING FU

No person was ever honored for what he received. Honor has been the reward for what he gave.
CALVIN COOLIDGE

Let the motive be in the deed and not in the event. Be not one whose motive for action is the hope of reward.

KREESHNA

RIDICULE *Also see:* ABSURDITY, IRONY, JESTING, SARCASM.

Mockery is the weapon of those who have no other.

HUBERT PIERIOT

Ridicule is the first and last argument of fools.

CHARLES SIMMONS

Resort is had to ridicule only when reason is against us.

THOMAS JEFFERSON

Ridicule is the language of the devil.

THOMAS CARLYLE

Man learns more readily and remembers more willingly what excites his ridicule than what deserves esteem and respect.

HORACE

RIGHTS *Also see:* CUSTOM, DIGNITY, EQUALITY, FREEDOM OF THE PRESS, PRIVACY, PROPERTY, WAGE.

Many a person seems to think it isn't enough for the government to guarantee him the pursuit of happiness. He insists it also run interference for him.

ANONYMOUS

No man was ever endowed with a right without being at the same time saddled with a responsibility.

GERALD W. JOHNSON

We hold these truths to be self-evident, that all men are created equal, that they are endowed by their Creator with certain unalienable rights, that among these are life, liberty, and the pursuit of happiness.

THOMAS JEFFERSON

No man has a right to do what he pleases, except when he pleases to do right.

CHARLES SIMMONS

In giving rights to others which belong to them, we give rights to ourselves and to our country.

JOHN FITZGERALD KENNEDY

From the equality of rights springs identity of our highest intersts; you cannot subvert your neighbor's rights without striking a dangerous blow at your own.

CARL SHURZ

RIOT Also see: MOB, REBELLION, REVOLUTION, VIOLENCE.

No nation, no matter how enlightened, can endure criminal violence. If we cannot control it, we are admitting to the world and to ourselves that our laws are no more than a facade that crumbles when the winds of crisis rise.

ALAN BIBLE

The poor suffer twice at the rioter's hands. First, his destructive fury scars their neighborhood; second, the atmosphere of accomodation and consent is changed to one of hostility and resentment.

LYNDON BAINES JOHNSON

If we sort to lawlessness, the only thing we can hope for is civil war, untold bloodshed, and the end of our dreams.

ARCHIE LEE MOORE

RISK Also see: DANGER.

The policy of being too cautious is the greatest risk of all.

JAWAHARLAL NEHRU

The willingness to take risks is our grasp of faith.

GEORGE E. WOODBERRY

Don't be afraid to take a big step if one is indicated; you can't cross a chasm in two small jumps.

WILLIAM LLOYD GEORGE

Every nobel acquisition is attended with its risks; he who fears to encounter the one must not expect to obtain the other.

METASTASIO

Risk is a part of God's game, alike for men and nations.

GEORGE E. WOODBERRY

Who bravely dares must sometimes risk a fall.

TOBIAS G. SMOLLETT

RIVALRY Also see: AMBITION, JEALOUSY, SUCCESS.

In ambition, as in love, the successful can afford to be indulgent toward their rivals.

CHRISTIAN NESTELL BOVEE

If we devote our time disparaging the products of our business rivals, we hurt business generally, reduce confidence, and increase discontent.

EDWARD N. HURLEY

It is the privilege of posterity to set matters right between those antagonists who, by their rivalry for greatness, divided a whole age.

JOSEPH ADDISON

Competition is the keen cutting edge of business, always shaving away at costs.

HENRY FORD II

Anybody can win unless there happens to be a second entry.

GEORGE ADE

RUMOR . . . *See* GOSSIP

SACRIFICE *Also see:* COMPROMISE, HEROISM, MARTYR.

Good manners are made up of petty sacrifices.

RALPH WALDO EMERSON

In this world it is not what we take up, but what we give up, that makes us rich.

HENRY WARD BEECHER

One-half of knowing what you want is knowing what you must give up before you get it.

SIDNEY HOWARD

They never fail who die in a great cause.

LORD BYRON

No sacrifice short of individual liberty, individual self-respect, and individual enterprise is too great a price to pay for permanent peace.

CLARK H. MINOR

SADNESS . . . *See* SORROW

SAFETY *Also see:* SECURITY, SELF-RESPECT, VIGILANCE.

It is better to be safe than sorry.

AMERICAN PROVERB

A ship in harbor is safe, but that is not what ships are built for.

JOHN A. SHEDD

He that's secure is not safe.

BENJAMIN FRANKLIN

Let the people know the truth and the country is safe.

ABRAHAM LINCOLN

SARCASM *Also see:* CRITICISM, HUMOR, IRONY, RIDICULE.

Sarcasm is the language of the devil, for which reason I have long since as good as renounced it.

THOMAS CARLYLE

Blows are sarcasms turned stupid.

GEORGE ELIOT

A sneer is the weapon of the weak.

JAMES RUSSELL LOWELL

To "leave a sting within a brother's heart."

EDWARD YOUNG

SCANDAL *Also see:* GOSSIP, REPUTATION, SLANDER.

There is so much good in the worst of us, and so much bad in the best of us, that it hardly becomes any one of us to talk about the rest of us.

ANONYMOUS

Everybody says it, and what everybody says must be true.

JAMES FENIMORE COOPER

How awful to reflect that what people say of us is true.

LOGAN P. SMITH

The objection of the scandalmonger is not that she tells of racy doings, but that she pretends to be indignant about them.

H. L. MENCKEN

Scandal: gossip made tedious by morality.

OSCAR WILDE

Scandal dies sooner of itself, than we could kill it.

BENJAMIN RUSH

SCHOOL . . . *See* EDUCATION

SCIENCE *Also see:* ART, ARTIST, FASHION, IMAGINATION, NOVELTY, RELIGION.

Science is nothing but perception.

PLATO

Every great advance in science has issued from a new audacity of imagination.

JOHN DEWEY

It stands to the everlasting credit of science that by acting on the human mind it has overcome man's insecurity before himself and before nature.

ALBERT EINSTEIN

Science is simply common sense at its best—that is, rigidly accurate in observation, and merciless to fallacy in logic.

THOMAS HUXLEY

It will free man from his remaining chains, the chains of gravity which still tie him to this planet. It will open to him the gates of heaven.

WERNHER VON BRAUN

SECRECY *Also see:* TRUST.

To keep your secret is wisdom; but to expect others to keep it is folly.

SAMUEL JOHNSON

I usually get my stuff from people who promised somebody else that they would keep it a secret.

WALTER WINCHELL

Secrets are things we give to others to keep for us.

ELBERT HUBBARD

Where secrecy or mystery begins, vice or roguery is not far off.

SAMUEL JOHNSON

Trust him not with your secrets, who, when left alone in your room, turns over your papers.

JOHANN KASPAR LAVATER

SECURITY *Also see:* COUNTRY, MURDER, REWARD, WAGE.

Too many people are thinking of security instead of opportunity.

JAMES F. BYRNES

Each one of us requires the spur of insecurity to force us to do our best.

HAROLD W. DODDS

Happiness has many roots, but none more important than security.

E. R. STETTINIUS, JR.

Security is the priceless product of freedom. Only the strong can be secure, and only in freedom can men produce those material resources which can secure them from want at home and against aggression from abroad.

B. E. HUTCHINSON

Security is mostly a superstition. It does not exist in nature, nor do the children of men as a whole experience it. Avoiding danger is no safer in the long run than outright exposure. Life is either a daring adventure, or nothing.

HELEN KELLER

In no direction that we turn do we find ease or comfort. If we are honest and if we have the will to win we find only danger, hard work and iron resolution.

WENDELL K. WILLKIE

SELF-CONFIDENCE Also see: BEHAVIOR, CONFIDENCE, RES-OLUTION.

Do not attempt to do a thing unless you are sure of yourself; but do not relinquish it simply because someone else is not sure of you.

STEWART E. WHITE

Calm self-confidence is as far from conceit as the desire to earn a decent living is remote from greed.

CHANNING POLLOCK

The history of the world is full of men who rose to leadership, by sheer force of self-confidence, bravery and tenacity.

MAHATMA GANDHI

They can conquer who believe they can.

VERGIL

SELF-CONTROL Also see: BEHAVIOR, CHARACTER, QUIET.

It is by presence of mind in untried emergencies that the native metal of man is tested.

JAMES RUSSELL LOWELL

The best time for you to hold your tongue is the time you feel you must say something or bust.

JOSH BILLINGS

Such power there is in clear-eyed self-restraint.

JAMES RUSSELL LOWELL

SELF-IMPROVEMENT Also see: CHANGE, HABIT, PURPOSE, REFORM.

There is no use whatever trying to help people who do not help themselves. You cannot push anyone up a ladder unless he be willing to climb himself.

ANDREW CARNEGIE

I tell you that as long as I can conceive something better than myself I cannot be easy unless I am striving to bring it into existence or clearing the way for it.

GEORGE BERNARD SHAW

People seldom improve when they have no other model but themselves to copy after.

OLIVER GOLDSMITH

All of us, who are worth anything, spend our manhood in unlearning the follies, or expiating the mistakes of our youth.

PERCY BYSSHE SHELLEY

SELFISHNESS *Also see:* AVARICE, GALLANTRY.

The man who lives by himself and for himself is likely to be corrupted by the company he keeps.

CHARLES H. PARHKURST

He who lives only to benefit himself confers on the world a benefit when he dies.

TERTULLIAN

Selfishness is the greatest curse of the human race.

WILLIAM E. GLADSTONE

Next to the very young, the very old are the most selfish.

WILLIAM MAKEPEACE THACKERAY

SELF-KNOWLEDGE *Also see:* HEROISM, QUIET, REASON, REVERIE.

It's not only the most difficult thing to know one's self, but the most inconvenient.

JOSH BILLINGS

We know what we are, but know not what we may be.

WILLIAM SHAKESPEARE

He that knows himself, knows others; and he that is ignorant of himself, could not write a very profound lecture on other men's heads.

CHARLES CALEB COLTON

Other men's sins are before our eyes; our own are behind our backs.

SENECA

SELF-RESPECT *Also see:* LOYALTY, PRIDE, SACRIFICE.

It is necessary to the happiness of a man that he be mentally faithful to himself.

THOMAS PAINE

Never violate the sacredness of your individual self-respect.

THEODORE PARKER

He that respects himself is safe from others; He wears a coat of mail that none can pierce.

HENRY WADSWORTH LONGFELLOW

No more duty can be urged upon those who are entering the great theater of life than simple loyalty to their best convictions.

EDWIN HUBBEL CHAPIN

SELF-SACRIFICE *Also see:* GENEROSITY, HEROISM, LOYALTY, REWARD, SACRIFICE.

Self-sacrifice is the real miracle out of which all the reported miracles grow.

RALPH WALDO EMERSON

Many men have been capable of doing a wise thing, more a cunning thing, but very few a generous thing.

ALEXANDER POPE

Self-sacrifice is never entirely unselfish, for the giver never fails to receive.

DOLORES E. MCGUIRE

For anything worth having one must pay the price; and the price is always work, patience, love, self-sacrifice—no paper currency, no promises to pay, but the gold of real service.

JOHN BURROUGHS

The men and women who have the right ideals . . . are those who have the courage to strive for the happiness which comes only with labor and effort and self-sacrifice, and those whose join in life springs in part from power of work and sense of duty.

THEODORE ROOSEVELT

SENSUALITY *Also see:* GLUTTON, REVERIE, SEX, SOUL, VICE.

The body of a sensualist is the coffin of a dead soul.

CHRISTIAN NESTELL BOVEE

Sensual pleasures are like soap bubbles, sparkling effervescent. The pleasures of intellect are calm, beautiful, sublime, ever enduring.

JOHN H. AUGHEY

If sensuality were happiness, beasts were happier than men; but human felicity is lodged in the soul, not in the flesh.

SENECA

All sensuality is one, though it takes many forms, as all purity is one. It is the same whether a man eat, or drink, or cohabit, or sleep sensually. They are but one appetite, and we only need to see a person do any one of these things to know how great a sensualist he is.

HENRY DAVID THOREAU

Human brutes, like other beasts, find snares and poison in the provision of life, and are allured by their appetites to their destruction.

JONATHAN SWIFT

SENTIMENT *Also see:* EMOTION, PASSION, REVERIE.

A sentimentalist is simply one who desires to have the luxury of an emotion without paying for it.

OSCAR WILDE

Sentimentality is the only sentiment that rubs you the wrong way.

W. SOMERSET MAUGHAM

He who molds the public sentiment . . . makes statues and decisions possible or impossible to make.

ABRAHAM LINCOLN

Society is infested by persons who, seeing that the sentiments please, counterfeit the expression of them. These we call sentimentalists—talkers who mistake the description for the thing, saying for having.

RALPH WALDO EMERSON

Sentimentality—that's what we call the sentiment we don't share.

GRAHAM GREENE

Sentiment is the poetry of the imagination.

ALPHONSE DE LAMARTINE

SEX *Also see:* BIRTH, SENSUALITY.

Sex has become one of the most discussed subjects of modern times. The Victorians pretended it did not exist; the moderns pretend that nothing else exists.

FULTON J. SHEEN

Sex is a flame which uncontrolled may scorch; properly guided, it will light the torch of eternity.

JOSEPH FETTERMAN

Some things are better than sex, and some are worse, but there's nothing exactly like it.

W. C. FIELDS

Sex lies at the roof of life, and we can never learn to reverence life until we know how to understand sex.

HAVELOCK ELLIS

The sexes were made for each other, and only in the wise and loving union of the two is the fullness of health and duty and happiness to be expected.

WILLIAM HALL

SILENCE *Also see:* CONVERSATION, LOQUACITY, UNDER-STANDING.

Silence is the ultimate weapon of power.

CHARLES DE GAULLE

Silence is one of the hardest arguments to refute.

JOSH BILLINGS

Silence is foolish if we are wise, but wise if we are foolish.

CHARLES CALEB COLTON

Still waters run deep.

ENGLISH PROVERB

Blessed is the man who, having nothing to say, abstains from giving wordy evidence of the fact.

GEORGE ELIOT

If you keep your mouth shut you will never put your foot in it.

AUSTIN O'MALLEY

If you don't say anything, you won't be called on to repeat it.

CALVIN COOLIDGE

SIMPLICITY *Also see:* BREVITY, TASTE, TRUTH.

When thought is too weak to be simply expressed, it's clear proof that it should be rejected.

LUC DE CLAPIERS

Nothing is more simple than greatness; indeed, to be simple is to be great.

RALPH WALDO EMERSON

Everything should be made as simple as possible, but not simpler.

ALBERT EINSTEIN

The whole is simpler than the sum of its parts.

WILLARD GIBBS

Simplicity is the glory of expression.

WALT WHITMAN

SIN *Also see:* DEATH, EVIL, GUILT, HUMANITY, PREACHING, PROVIDENCE, PUNISHMENT, REMORSE, RE-PENTANCE, WICKEDNESS.

He that falls into sin is a man; that grieves at it, is a saint; that boasteth of it, is a devil.

THOMAS FULLER

He that is without sin among you, let him cast the first stone.

JOHN 8:7

Men are not punished for their sins, but by them.

ELBERT HUBBARD

Sin is not harmful because it is forbidden, but it is forbidden because it is hurtful.

BENJAMIN FRANKLIN

Man-like it is to fall into sin; fiendlike it is to dwell therein.

HENRY WADSWORTH LONGFELLOW

Only the sinner has a right to preach.

CHRISTOPHER MORLEY

There is no sin except stupidity.

OSCAR WILDE

SINCERITY . . . *See* HONESTY

SKEPTICISM *Also see:* CREDULITY, CYNIC, DOUBT, PESSI-MISM.

Skeptics are never deceived.

FRENCH PROVERB

Skepticism, riddling the faith of yesterday, prepared the way for the faith of tomorrow.

ROMAIN ROLLAND

The path of sound credence is through the thick forest of skepticism.

GEORGE JEAN NATHAN

Skepticism is the chastity of the intellect.

GEORGE SANTAYANA

Skepticism: the mark and even the pose of the educated mind.

JOHN DEWEY

Great intellects are skeptical.

NIETZSCHE

SLANDER *Also see:* GOSSIP, INJURY, REPUTATION, SCANDAL.

To murder character is as truly a crime as to murder the body: the tongue of the slanderer is brother to the dagger of the assassin.

TRYON EDWARDS

I hate the man who builds his name on the ruins of another's fame.

JOHN GAY

Never throw mud. You may miss your mark, but you will have dirty hands.

JOSEPH PARKER

Slander is the revenge of a coward, and dissimulation of his defense.

SAMUEL JOHNSON

Character assassination is at once easier and surer than physical assault; and it involves far less risk for the assassin. It leaves him free to commit the same deed over and over again, and may, indeed, win him the honors of a hero even in the country of his victims.

ALAN BARTH

The worthiest people are the most injured by slander, as is the best fruit which the birds have been pecking at.

JONATHON SWIFT

SLEEP *Also see:* REST, SUCCESS.

Sleep she as sound as careless infancy.

WILLIAM SHAKESPEARE

It is a delicious moment, certainly, that of being well-nestled in bed and feeling that you shall drop gently to sleep. The good is to come, not past; the limbs are tired enough to render the remaining in one posture delightful; the labor of the day is gone.

LEIGH HUNT

Living is a disease from which sleep gives us relief eight hours a day.

CHAMFORT

Sleep is the twin of death.

HOMER

SMILE *Also see:* BEAUTY, CHEERFULNESS, KINDNESS.

Smiles form the channels of a future tear.

LORD BYRON

Wrinkles should merely indicate where smiles have beeen.

MARK TWAIN

Wear a smile and have friends; wear a scowl and have wrinkles. What do we live for if not to make the world less difficult for each other?

GEORGE ELIOT

There are many kinds of smiles, each having a distinct character. Some announce goodness and sweetness, others betray sarcasm, bitterness and pride; some soften the countenance by their languishing tenderness, others brighten by their spiritual vivacity.

JOHANN KASPAR LAVATER

SMOKING Also see: HABIT.

To cease smoking is the easiest thing I ever did; I ought to know because I've done it a thousand times.

MARK TWAIN

Much smoking kills live men and cures dead swine.

GEORGE D. PRENTICE

I tried to stop smoking cigarettes by telling myself I just didn't want to smoke, but I didn't believe myself.

BARBARA KELLY

The best way to stop smoking is to carry wet matches.

ANONYMOUS

SOCIETY Also see: CLASS, HUMANITY, HUMOR, MAN, POVERTY, SENTIMENT.

Society is like a lawn where every roughness is smoothed, every bramble eradicated, and where the eye is delighted by the smiling verdure of a velvet surface.

WASHINGTON IRVING

To get into the best society nowadays, one has either to feed people, amuse people, or shock people.

OSCAR WILDE

One great society alone on earth: the noble living and the noble dead.

WILLIAM WORDSWORTH

The pillars of truth and the pillars of freedom—they are the pillars of society.

HENRIK IBSEN

SOLDIER *Also see:* CITIZENSHIP, COURAGE, DRAFT, DUTY, WAR.

A good soldier, like a good horse, cannot be of a bad color.

OLIVER WENDELL HOLMES

I want to see you shoot the way you shout.

THEODORE ROOSEVELT

Every citizen should be a soldier. This was the case with the Greeks and Romans, and must be that of every free state.

THOMAS JEFFERSON

Theirs is not to make reply, Theirs is not to reason why, Theirs is but to do and die.

ALFRED, LORD TENNYSON

But in a larger sense we cannot dedicate, we cannot consecrate, we cannot hallow this ground. The brave men, living and dead, who struggled here, have consecrated it far above our poor power to add or detract.

ABRAHAM LINCOLN

SOLITUDE *Also see:* LONELINESS.

I live in that solitude which is painful in youth, but delicious in the years of maturity.

ALBERT EINSTEIN

Solitude, though it may be silent as light, is like light, the mightiest of agencies; for solitude is essential to man.

THOMAS DE QUINCEY

I never found a companion that was so companionable as solitude.

HENRY DAVID THOREAU

It is easy in the world to live after the world's opinions; it is easy in solitude to live after your own; but the great man is he who in the midst of the crowd keeps with perfect sweetness the independence of solitude.

RALPH WALDO EMERSON

The right to be alone—the most comprehensive of rights, and the right most valued by civilized man.

LOUIS D. BRANDEIS

SORROW *Also see:* AFFLICTION, GRIEF, GUILT, HUMOR, RESIGNATION.

Into each life some rain must fall.

HENRY WADSWORTH LONGFELLOW

There can be no rainbow without a cloud and a storm.

J. H. VINCENT

Sorrow makes men sincere.

HENRY WARD BEECHER

The world is so full of care and sorrow that it is a gracious debt we owe to one another to discover the bright crystals of delight hidden in somber circumstances and irksome tasks.

HELEN KELLER

Out of suffering have emerged the strongest souls.

EDWIN HUBBEL CHAPIN

Earth has no sorrow that heaven cannot heal.

THOMAS MOORE

Where there is sorrow, there is holy ground.

OSCAR WILDE

SOUL *Also see:* BODY, CONFESSION, CONSCIENCE, CRIME, DRESS, HEAVEN, INFLUENCE, MISER, NEGLECT, PRAYER, PURPOSE, SENSUALITY.

The one thing in the world, of value, is the active soul.

RALPH WALDO EMERSON

The soul, like the body, lives by what it feeds on.

JOSIAH GILBERT HOLLAND

Most people sell their souls and live with a good conscience on the proceeds.

LOGAN P. SMITH

My mind is inescapable of conceiving such a thing as a soul. I may be in error, and man may have a soul; but I simply do not believe it.

THOMAS A. EDISON

The wealth of a soul is measured by how much it can feel; its poverty by how little.

WILLIAM ROUNSEVILLE ALGER

SPACE *Also see:* SCIENCE, TECHNOLOGY.

Here's one small step for a man . . . one giant leap for mankind.

NEIL ARMSTRONG

There is beauty in space, and it is orderly. There is no weather, and there is regularity. It is predictable . . . Everything in space obeys the laws of physics. If you know these laws and obey them, space will treat you kindly. And don't tell me man doesn't belong out there. Man belongs wherever he wants to go.

WERNHER VON BRAUN

The moon and other celestial bodies should be free for exploration and use by all countries. No country should be permitted to advance a claim of sovereignty.

LYNDON BAINES JOHNSON

The sky is no longer the limit.

RICHARD M. NIXON

God has no intention of setting a limit to the efforts of man to conquer space.

PLUS XII

SPECULATION Also see: BUSINESS, FINANCE.

Speculation is only a word covering the making of money out of the manipulation of prices, instead of supplying goods and services.

HENRY FORD

A speculator is a man who observes the future, and acts before it occurs.

BERNARD M. BARUCH

If there were no bad speculations there could be no good investments; if there were no wild ventures there would be no brilliantly successful enterprises.

F. W. HIRST

There will always be speculation of some kind. If you throw it out of an organized exchange, you throw it out into the street.

H. C. EMERY

SPEECH Also see: ELOQUENCE, LANGUAGE, LOQUACITY, MUSIC.

Speak softly, and carry a big stick.

THEODORE ROOSEVELT

It usually takes more than three weeks to prepare a good impromptu speech.

MARK TWAIN

Speak clearly, if you speak at all; carve every word before you let it fall.

OLIVER WENDELL HOLMES

Half the world is composed of people who have something to say and can't, and the other half who have nothing to say and keep on saying it.

ROBERT FROST

Speech is power: speech is to persuade, to convert, to compel.

RALPH WALDO EMERSON

We speak little if not egged on by vanity.

FRANÇOIS DE LA ROCHEFOUCAULD

Speech is human nature itself, with none of the artificiality of written language.

ALFRED NORTH WHITEHEAD

SPIRIT *Also see:* COWARDICE, CULTURE, ENERGY, ENTHUSI-
ASM, ZEAL.

One truth stands firm. All that happens in world history rests on something spiritual. If the spiritual is strong, it creates world history. If it is weak, it suffers world history.

ALBERT SCHWEITZER

It must be of the spirit if we are to save the flesh.

DOUGLAS MACARTHUR

Great men are they who see that the spiritual is stronger than any material force.

RALPH WALDO EMERSON

There are only two forces in the world, the sword and the spirit. In the long run the sword will always be conquered by the spirit.

NAPOLEON BONAPARTE

He that loseth wealth, loseth much; he that loseth friends, loseth more; but he that loseth his spirit loseth all.

SPANISH MAXIM

STRENGTH *Also see:* CHEERFULNESS, RESOLUTION, REWARD,
WILL.

O, it is excellent to have a giant's strength, but it is tyrannous to use it like a giant.

WILLIAM SHAKESPEARE

Don't hit at all if it is honorably possible to avoid hitting, but never hit soft.

THEODORE ROOSEVELT

We acquire the strength we have overcome.

RALPH WALDO EMERSON

Concentration is the secret of strength.

RALPH WALDO EMERSON

I wish to preach not the doctrine of ignoble ease, but the doctrine of strenuous life.

THEODORE ROOSEVELT

Don't expect to build up the weak by pulling down the strong.

CALVIN COLLIDGE

STRESS . . . *See* ANXIETY

STUDY *Also see:* LEARNING, SELF-IMPROVEMENT, THOUGHT.

No student knows his subject: the most he knows is where and how to find out the things he does not know.

WOODROW WILSON

The world's great men have not commonly been great scholars, nor its great scholars great men.

OLIVER WENDELL HOLMES

The mind of the scholar, if he would leave it large and liberal, should come in contact with other minds.

HENRY WADSWORTH LONGFELLOW

There are more men ennobled by study than by nature.

CICERO

I would live to study, and not study to live.

FRANCIS BACON

The more we study the more we discover our ignorance.

PERCY BYSSHE SHELLEY

SUCCESS *Also see:* ACHIEVEMENT, AMBITION, CONFIDENCE, DEFEAT, ENEMY, LUCK, POPULARITY, REWARD, VICTORY.

If A equals success, then the formula is A equals X plus Y and Z, with X being work, Y play, and Z keeping your mouth shut.

ALBERT EINSTEIN

If man has good corn, or wood, or boards, or pigs to sell, or can make better chairs or knives, crucibles, or church organs, than anybody else, you will find a broad, hard-beaten road to his house, tho it be in the woods.

RALPH WALDO EMERSON

There is only one success—to spend your life in your own way.

CHRISTOPHER MORLEY

Try not to become a man of success but rather try to become a man of value.

ALBERT EINSTEIN

The gent who wakes up and finds himself a success hasn't been asleep.

WILSON MIZNER

SUFFERING *Also see:* ABSENCE, AFFLICTION, FEAR, PAIN, RE-
WARD, SORROW.

I have suffered too much in this world not to hope for another.

JEAN JACQUES ROUSSEAU

It requires more courage to suffer than to die.

NAPOLEON BONAPARTE

It is a glorious thing to be indifferent to suffering, but only to one's own suffering.

ROBERT LYND

The salvation of the world is in man's suffering.

WILLIAM FAULKNER

Suffering becomes beautiful when anyone bears great calamities with cheerfulness, not through insensibility but through greatness of mind.

ARISTOTLE

We are healed of a suffering only by experiencing it in full.

MARCEL PROUST

SUPERSTITION *Also see:* BELIEF, CREDULITY, IDOLATRY, IG-
NORANCE, SECURITY.

Superstition is a senseless fear of God.

CICERO

Superstition is . . . religion which is incongruous with intelligence.

JOHN TYNDALL

Superstition is the poison of the mind.

JOSEPH LEWIS

Superstition, idolatry, and hypocrisy have ample wages, but truth goes begging.

MARTIN LUTHER

Superstition is the religion of feeble minds.

EDMUND BURKE

Superstitions are, for the most part, but the shadows of great truths.

TRYON EDWARDS

SUSPICION *Also see:* DISTRUST, DOUBT, GUILT.

Suspicions which may be unjust need not be stated.

ABRAHAM LINCOLN

The less we know the more we suspect.

JOSH BILLINGS

The louder he talked of his honor, the faster we counted our spoons.

RALPH WALDO EMERSON

A woman of honor should not expect of others things she would not do herself.

MARGUERITE DE VALOIS

SYMPATHY *Also see:* COMPASSION, KINDNESS, MERCY, PITY.

Sympathy is a virtue unknown in nature.

PAUL EIPPER

Harmony of aim, not identity of conclusion, is the secret of sympathetic life.

RALPH WALDO EMERSON

A sympathetic heart is like a spring of pure water bursting forth from the mountain side.

ANONYMOUS

TACT *Also see:* COURTESY, DIPLOMACY, DISCRETION, GALLANTRY.

Tact: the ability to describe others as they see themselves.

ABRAHAM LINCOLN

Be kind and considerate to others, depending somewhat upon who they are.

DON HEROLD

Tact is one of the first mental virtues, the absence of which is often fatal to the best of talents; it supplies the place of many talents.

WILLIAM GILMORE SIMMS

Don't flatter yourself that friendship authorizes you to say disagreeable things to your intimates. The nearer you come into relation with a person, the more necessary do tact and courtesy become.

OLIVER WENDELL HOLMES

TALENT . . . *See* ABILITY

TALKING . . . *See* LOQUACITY

TASTE *Also see:* DESIRE, TEMPER, VARIETY, VULGARITY.

Taste is the feminine of genius.

EDWARD FITZGERALD

I would rather be able to appreciate things I cannot have than to have things I am not able to appreciate.

ELBERT HUBBARD

Partial culture runs to the ornate; extreme culture to simplicity.

CHRISTIAN NESTELL BOVEE

Taste is, so to speak, the microscope of the judgment.

JEAN JACQUES ROUSSEAU

Bad taste is a species of bad morals.

CHRISTIAN NESTELL BOVEE

TAX *Also see:* CENSURE, GOVERNMENT.

Death and taxes are inevitable.

THOMAS C. HALIBURTON

The income tax has made more liars out of the American people than gold has.

WILL ROGERS

The power to tax involves the power to destroy.

JOHN MARSHALL

For every benefit you receive a tax is levied.

RALPH WALDO EMERSON

The tax collector must love poor people—he's creating so many of them.

BILL VAUGHAN

To tax and to please, no more than to love and to be wise, is not given to men.

EDMUND BURKE

Taxes are the sinews of the state.

CICERO

TEACHING *Also see:* EDUCATION, KNOWLEDGE, LEARNING.

You cannot teach a man anything; you can only help him find it within himself.

GALILEO

One good schoolmaster is worth a thousand priests.

ROBERT GREEN INGERSOLL

Knowledge exists to be impaired.

RALPH WALDO EMERSON

The teacher is one who makes two ideas grow where only one grew before.

ELBERT HUBBARD

The man who can make hard things easy is the educator.

RALPH WALDO EMERSON

A teacher affects eternity; he can never tell where his influence stops.

HENRY BROOKS ADAMS

TECHNOLOGY Also see: SCIENCE, SPACE.

The economic and technological triumphs of the past few years have not solved as many problems as we thought they would, and, in fact, have brought us new problems we did not forsee.

HENRY FORD II

What is more difficult, to think of an encampment on the moon or of Harlem rebuilt? Both are now within the reach of our resources. Both now depend upon human decision and human will.

ADLAI E. STEVENSON

As nuclear and other technological achievements continue to mount, the normal life span will continue to climb. The hourly productivity of the worker will increase.

DWIGHT D. EISENHOWER

TELEVISION Also see: COMMUNICATION.

Television is now so desperately hungry for material that they're scraping the top of the barrel.

GORE VIDAL

Time has convinced me of one thing: Television is for appearing on—not for looking at.

NOEL COWARD

I hate television. I hate it as much as peanuts. But I can't stop eating peanuts.

ORSON WELLS

TEMPER *Also see:* ANGER, MISERY, MODERATION, SELF-CON-
TROL

The worst-tempered people I've ever met were people who knew they
were wrong.

WILSON MIZNER

A tart temper never mellows with age; and a sharp tongue is the only
edged tool that grows keener with constant use.

WASHINGTON IRVING

Man is a rational animal who always loses his temper when called upon
to act in accordance with the dictates of reason.

OSCAR WILDE

Men lose their tempers in defending their taste.

RALPH WALDO EMERSON

TEMPTATION *Also see:* COWARDICE, DESIRE, PASSION, SELF-
CONTROL.

Few men have virtue to withstand the highest bidder.

GEORGE WASHINGTON

I can resist anything except temptation.

OSCAR WILDE

There are several good protections against temptations, but the surest is
cowardice.

MARK TWAIN

He who cannot resist temptation is not a man.

HORACE MANN

The only way to get rid of a temptation is to yield to it.

OSCAR WILDE

As the Sandwich-Islander believes that the strength and valor of the enemy
he kills passes into himself, so we gain the strength of the temptations
we resist.

RALPH WALDO EMERSON

THEOLOGY *Also see:* ATHEISM, CHRISTIANITY, HELL, JUDA-
ISM, RELIGION.

My theology, briefly, is that the universe was dictated but not signed.

CHRISTOPHER MORLEY

Theology is a science of mind applied to God.

HENRY WARD BEECHER

The best theology is rather a devine life than a divine knowledge.

JEREMY TAYLOR

Theology is but our ideas of truth classified and arranged.

HENRY WARD BEECHER

As the grave grows nearer my theology is growing strangely simple, and it begins and ends with Christ as the only Savior of the lost.

HENRY BENJAMIN WHIPPLE

Let us put theology out of religion. Theology has always sent the worst to heaven, the best to hell.

ROBERT GREEN INGERSOLL

THEORY *Also see:* FACTS, PHILOSOPHY, REALITY.

Science is organized common sense where many a beautiful theory was killed by an ugly fact.

THOMAS HUXLEY

A little experience often upsets a lot of theory.

CADMAN

There can be no theory of any account unless it corroborate with the theory of the earth.

WALT WHITMAN

I never once made a discovery . . . I speak without exaggeration that I have constructed three thousand different theories in connection with the electric light . . . Yet in only two cases did my experiments prove the truth of my theory.

THOMAS A. EDISON

A theory is no more like a fact than a photograph is like a person.

ED HOWE

In scientific work, those who refuse to go beyond fact rarely get as far as fact.

THOMAS HUXLEY

THOUGHT *Also see:* ACTION, DISSENT, LANGUAGE, LOGIC, PLAGIARISM, POLITICS, PROPAGANDA, QUOTATION, REVERIE, SELF-KNOWL-EDGE, STUDY.

Great thoughts reduced to practice become great acts.

WILLIAM HAZLITT

You are today where your thoughts have brought you; you will be to-morrow where your thoughts take you.

JAMES ALLEN

The soul of God is poured into the world through the thoughts of men.

RALPH WALDO EMERSON

I've known countless people who were reservoirs of learning, yet never had a thought.

WILSON MIZNER

Learning without thought is labor lost.

CONFUCIUS

THRIFT . . . *See* ECONOMY

TIME *Also see:* BUSY, EFFICIENCY, ETERNITY, HASTE, OPPORTUNITY, PRESENT, PUNCTUALITY, REST, WASTE.

Lost time is never found again.

JOHN H. AUGHEY

Dost thou love life? Then do not squander time, for that is the stuff life is made of.

BENJAMIN FRANKLIN

As if you could kill time without injuring eternity.

HENRY DAVID THOREAU

Time is like money; the less we have of it to spare the further we make it go.

JOSH BILLINGS

Lost, yesterday, somewhere between sunrise and sunset, two golden hours, each set with sixty diamond minutes. No reward is offered for they are gone forever.

HORACE MANN

TOLERANCE *Also see:* INTOLERANCE, LIBERTY, RIGHTS.

Tolerance is another word for difference.

W. SOMERSET MAUGHAM

No man has a right in America to treat any other man "tolerantly" for tolerance is the assumption of superiority. Our liberties are equal rights of every citizen.

WENDELL K. WILLKIE

It is easy to be tolerant of the principles of other people if you have none of your own.

HERBERT SAMUEL

Tolerance is the oil which takes the friction out of life.

WILBERT E. SCHEER

Tolerance comes with age. I see no fault committed that I myself could not have committed at some time or other.

JOHANN WOLFGANG VON GOETHE

I have seen gross intolerance shown in support of tolerance.

SAMUEL TAYLOR COLERIDGE

TRADITION *Also see:* CUSTOM.

Traditionalists are pessimists about the future and optimists about the past.

LEWIS MUMFORD

It takes an endless amount of history to make even a little tradition.

HENRY JAMES

Tradition does not mean that the living are dead, but that the dead are living.

GILBERT K. CHESTERTON

Tradition is an important help to history, but its statements should be carefully scrutinized before we rely on them.

JOSEPH ADDISON

TRAGEDY *Also see:* ADVERSITY, DESIRE, LIFE, SORROW.

The tragedy of life is not so much what men suffer, but rather what they miss.

THOMAS CARLYLE

There are two tragedies in life: one is to lose your heart's desire, the other is to gain it.

GEORGE BERNARD SHAW

The world is a comedy to those who think, a tragedy to those who feel.

HORACE WALPOLE

TRANQUILITY . . . *See* PEACE

TRAVEL *Also see:* ADVENTURE, SPACE, WORLD.

The world is a book, and those who do not travel, read only a page.

ST. AUGUSTINE

A man travels the world over in search of what he needs, and returns home to find it.

GEORGE MOORE

The man who gets out alone can start today; but he who travels with another must wait till that other is ready.

HENRY DAVID THOREAU

The traveler sees what he sees, the tourist sees what he has come to see.

GILBERT K. CHESTERTON

TREASON *Also see:* INGRATITUDE, REBELLION.

We are a rebellious nation. Our whole history is treason; our blood was attained before we were born; our creeds were infidelity to the mother church; our constitution treason to our fatherland.

THEODORE PARKER

Is there not some chosen curse, some hidden thunder in the stores of heaven, red with uncommon wrath, to blast the man who owes his greatness to his country's ruin!

JOSEPH ADDISON

There is something peculiarly sinister and insidious in even a charge of disloyalty. Such a charge all too frequently places a strain on the reputation of an individual which is indelible and lasting, regardless of the complete innocence later proved.

JOHN LORD O'BRIAN

Write on my gravestone: "Infidel, Traitor."—infidel to every church that compromises with wrong; traitor to every government that oppresses the people.

WENDELL PHILLIPS

TRIFLES *Also see:* AFFECTION, SIMPLICITY.

Little things affect little minds.

BENJAMIN DISRAELI

It is the little bits of things that fret and worry us; we can dodge an elephant, but we can't dodge a fly.

JOSH BILLINGS

Little strokes fell great oaks.

BENJAMIN FRANKLIN

The creation of a thousand forests is in one acorn.

RALPH WALDO EMERSON

A small leak will sink a great ship.

BENJAMIN FRANKLIN

There is nothing too little for so little a creature as man. It is by studying little things that we attain the great art of having as little misery and as much happiness as possible.

SAMUEL JOHNSON

Trifles make perfection—and perfection is no trifle.

MICHELANGELO

TROUBLE ... *See* ANXIETY

TRUST *Also see:* CONFIDENCE, CREDIT, DISHONESTY, ILLUSION, MONEY, SECRECY, SYMPATHY, WEALTH.

When a man has no reason to trust himself, he trusts in luck.

ED HOWE

Put your trust in God, but keep your powder dry.

OLIVER CROMWELL

Trust men and they will be true to you; treat them greatly and they will show themselves great.

RALPH WALDO EMERSON

Woe to the man whose heart has not learned while young to hope, to love—and to put its trust in life.

JOSEPH CONRAD

You may be deceived if you trust too much, but you will live in torment if you don't trust enough.

FRANK CRANE

TRUTH *Also see:* BIBLE, BIGOTRY, CHILDREN, DIPLOMACY, ENEMY, ERROR, GOSSIP, LYING, MAXIM, PHILOSOPHY, PREJUDICE, PROPAGANDA, RADICAL, REFORM, SAFETY, SCANDAL, SUPERSTITION, TIME.

Rather than love, than money, than fame, give me truth.

HENRY DAVID THOREAU

Men occasionally stumble over the truth, but most of them pick themselves up and hurry off as if nothing happened.

WINSTON CHURCHILL

Never tell the truth to people who are not worthy of it.

MARK TWAIN

Truth is always served by great minds, even if they fight it.

JEAN ROSTAND

Everyone wishes to have truth on his side, but not everyone wishes to be on the side of truth.

RICHARD WHATELY

When you want to fool the world, tell the truth.

OTTO VON BISMARK

The pure and simple truth is rarely pure and never simple.

OSCAR WILDE

The truth is more important than the facts.

FRANK LLOYD WRIGHT

The greatest homage we can pay to truth, is to use it.

JAMES RUSSELL LOWELL

It is easier to perceive error than to find truth, for the former lies on the surface and is easily seen, while the latter lies in the depth, where few are willing to search for it.

JOHANN WOLFGANG VON GOETHE

Truth is the property of no individual but is the treasure of all men.

RALPH WALDO EMERSON

The greatest friend of truth is Time, her greatest enemy is Prejudice, and her constant companion is Humility.

CHARLES CALEB COLTON

It is man that makes truth great, not truth that makes man great.

CONFUCIUS

As scarce as truth is, the supply has always been in excess of the demand.

JOSH BILLINGS

TYRANNY Also see: COMMUNISM, CONSCIENCE, DESTINY, MOB, REBELLION, REVOLUTION, UNITY.

Every tyrant who has lived has believed in freedom—for himself.

ELBERT HUBBARD

Tyranny and anarchy are never far asunder.

JEREMY BENTHAM

Hateful is the power, and pitiable is the life, of those who wish to be feared rather than loved.

CORNELIUS NEPOS

Resistance to tyrants is obedience to God.

THOMAS JEFFERSON

Tyrants are seldom free; the cares and the instruments of their tyranny enslave them.

GEORGE SANTAYANA

There is a secret pride in every human heart that revolts at tyranny. You may order and drive an individual, but you cannot make him respect you.

WILLIAM HAZLITT

UGLINESS *Also see:* BEAUTY

Better an ugly face than an ugly mind.

JAMES ELLIS

There is a sort of charm in ugliness, if the person has some redeeming qualities and is only ugly enough.

JOSH BILLINGS

Heaven sometimes hedges a rare character about with ungainliness and odium, as the burr that protects the fruit.

RALPH WALDO EMERSON

UNDERSTANDING *Also see:* ANGER, COMMUNICATION, MIND, PERCEPTION, PITY, REVERIE, WORD.

Understanding is a two-way street.

ELEANOR ROOSEVELT

Whatever you cannot understand, you cannot possess.

JOHANN WOLFGANG VON GOETHE

There is a great difference between knowing and understanding: you can know a lot about something and not really understand it.

CHARLES F. KETTERING

The improvement of understanding is for two ends: first, our own increase of knowledge; secondly, to enable us to deliver that knowledge to others.

JOHN LOCKE

UNHAPPINESS . . . *See* SORROW

UNION *Also see:* ECONOMICS, LABOR, WORK.

The labor movement's basic purpose is to achieve a better life for its members. A union that fails in this purpose has failed utterly.

NEW YORK TIMES

We must hang together or assuredly we shall hang separately.

BENJAMIN FRANKLIN

The trade union movement represents the organized economic power of the workers . . . It is in reality the most potent and the most direct social insurance the workers can establish.

SAMUEL GOMPERS

All for one; one for all.

ALEXANDER DUMAS

UNITED NATIONS

The United Nations is our one great hope for a peaceful and free world.

RALPH BUNCHE

This organization is created to prevent you from going to hell. It isn't created to take you to heaven.

HENRY CABOT LODGE

The whole basis of the United Nations is the right of all nations—great or small—to have weight, to have vote, to be attended to, to be a part of the twentieth century.

ADLAI E. STEVENSON

We have actively sought and are actively seeking to make the United Nations an effective instrument of international cooperation.

DEAN ACHESON

The United Nations is designed to make possible lasting freedom and independence for all its members.

HARRY S. TRUMAN

UNITY Also see: LOYALTY, MARRIAGE, STRENGTH.

Men's hearts ought not to be set against one another, but set with one another, and all against evil only.

THOMAS CARLYLE

There are no problems we cannot solve together, and very few that we can solve by ourselves.

LYNDON BAINES JOHNSON

We cannot be separated in interest or divided in purpose. We stand together until the end.

WOODROW WILSON

One country, one constitution, one destiny.

DANIEL WEBSTER

We come to reason, not to dominate. We do not seek to have our way, but to find a common way.

LYNDON BAINES JOHNSON

A house divided against itself cannot stand.

ABRAHAM LINCOLN

United we stand, divided we fall.

G. P. MORRIS

UNIVERSE Also see: EARTH, MAN, SCIENCE, SPACE, TECHNOLOGY.

The Universe is but one vast symbol of God.

THOMAS CARLYLE

The universe is one of God's thoughts.

JOHANN VON SCHILLER

The universe is duly in order, everything in its place.

WALT WHITMAN

An infinite universe is at each moment opened to our view. And this universe is the sign and symbol of infinite Power, Intelligence, Purity, Bliss, and Love.

WILLIAM ELLERY CHANNING

We are all fellow passengers on a dot of earth. And each of us, in the span of time, has really only a moment among our companions.

LYNDON BAINES JOHNSON

UNIVERSITY Also see: EDUCATION, TEACHING.

The university most worthy of rational admiration is that one in which your lonely thinker can feel himself lonely, most positively furthered, and most richly fed.

WILLIAM JAMES

The task of a university is the creation of the future, so far as rational thought and civilized modes of appreciation can affect the issue.

ALFRED NORTH WHITEHEAD

This institution will be based on the illimitable freedom of the human mind. For here we are not afraid to follow truth wherever it may lead, not tolerate error as long as reason is left free to combat it.

THOMAS JEFFERSON

A university should be a place of light, of liberty, and of learning.

BENJAMIN DISRAELI

VACATION *Also see:* REST, VARIETY.

No man needs a vaction so much as the man who has just had one.

ELBERT HUBBARD

If some people didn't tell you, you'd never know they'd been away on a vacation.

KIN HUBBARD

A period of travel and relaxation when you take twice the clothes and half the money you need.

ANONYMOUS

VALOR . . . . *See* COURAGE

VALUE *Also see:* CIVILIZATION, MERIT, SUCCESS, WORTH.

Some values are . . . like sugar on the doughnut, legitimate, desirable, but insufficient, apart from the doughnut itself. We need substance as well as frosting.

RALPH T. FLEWELLING

I conceive that the great part of the miseries of mankind are brought upon them by false estimates they have made of the value of things.

BENJAMIN FRANKLIN

What we obtain too cheap, we esteem too lightly; it is dearness only that gives everything its value.

THOMAS PAINE

The value of a principle is the number of things it will explain; and there is no good theory of disease which does not at once suggest a cure.

RALPH WALDO EMERSON

Nothing can have value without being an object of utility.

KARL MARX

All that is valuable in human society depends upon the opportunity for development accorded the individual.

ALBERT EINSTEIN

VANITY *Also see:* CURIOSITY, FAME, FAULT, LONELINESS, LO-
QUACITY, RANK, SPEECH.

A vain man finds it wise to speak good or ill of himself; a modest man does not talk of himself.

JEAN DE LA BRUYÈRE

It is our own vanity that makes the vanity of others intolerable to us.

FRANÇOIS DE LA ROCHEFOUCAULD

Vanity as an impulse has without doubt been of far more benefit to civilization than modesty has ever been.

WILLIAM E. WOODWARD

To be a man's own fool is bad enough; but the vain man is everybody's.

WILLIAM PENN

The highest form of vanity is love of fame.

GEORGE SANTAYANA

A man who is not a fool can rid himself of every folly except vanity.

JEAN JACQUES ROUSSEAU

The only cure for vanity is laughter, and the only fault that's laughable is vanity.

HENRI BERGSON

VARIETY *Also see:* CHANGE, ORIGINALITY.

Variety's the very spice of life, that gives it all its flavor.

WILLIAM COWPER

Variety of mere nothings gives more pleasure than uniformity of something.

JEAN PAUL RICHTER

It takes all sorts to make a world.

ENGLISH PROVERB

The most delightful pleasures cloy without variety.

PUBLILIUS SYRUS

Sameness is the mother of disgust, variety the cure.

PETRARCH

VENGEANCE *Also see:* ANGER, HATE, INJURY, SLANDER.

Vengeance has no foresight.

NAPOLEON BONAPARTE

Revenge is the abject pleasure of an abject mind.

JUVENAL

Avenge not yourselves, but rather give place unto wrath; for it is written, Vengeance is mine; I will repay, saith the Lord.

ROMANS 12:19

Revenge if an act of passion; vengeance of justice. Injuries are revenged; crimes are avenged.

JOSEPH JOUBERT

VICE *Also see:* CRIME, CRUELTY, EVIL, FANATICISM, PROFANITY, SELFISHNESS, SIN, WICKEDNESS.

This is the essential evil of vice, that it debases man.

EDWIN HUBBEL CHAPIN

One big vice in a man is apt to keep out a great many smaller ones.

BRET HARTE

Vices are often habits rather than passions.

ANTOINE RIVAROL

It has been my experience that folks who have no vices have very few virtues.

ABRAHAM LINCOLN

Men wish to be saved from the mischiefs of their vices, but not from their vices.

RALPH WALDO EMERSON

It is but a step from companionship to slavery when one associates with vice.

HOSEA BALLOU

Our faith comes in moments; our vice is habitual.

WILLIAM ELLERY CHANNING

There will be vice as long as there are men.

TACITUS

VICTORY *Also see:* CHARACTER, DEFEAT, SUCCESS, WAR.

One may know how to gain a victory, and know not how to use it.

BARCA

The greatest conquerer is he who overcomes the enemy without a blow.

CHINESE PROVERB

We should wage war not to win war, but to win peace.

PAUL HOFFMAN

Victories that are easy are cheap. Those only are worth having which come as the result of hard fighting.

HENRY WARD BEECHER

The god of victory is said to be one-handed, but peace gives victory on both sides.

RALPH WALDO EMERSON

It is fatal to enter any war without the will to win it.

DOUGLAS MACARTHUR

VIGILANCE *Also see:* CAUTION, PRUDENCE, WISDOM.

Eternal vigilance is the price of liberty.

THOMAS JEFFERSON

He is most free from danger, who, even when safe, is on his guard.

PUBLILIUS SYRUS

There is a significant Latin proverb; to wit; Who will guard the guards?

JOSH BILLINGS

They that are on their guard and appear ready to receive their adversaries, are in much less danger of being attacked than the supine, secure and negligent.

BENJAMIN FRANKLIN

Experience should teach us to be most on our guard to protect liberty when the government's purposes are beneficent.

LOUIS D. BRANDEIS

VIOLENCE *Also see:* HATE, PERSEVERANCE, REVOLUTION, RIOT, TELEVISION, WAR.

Nothing good ever comes of violence.

MARTIN LUTHER

Degeneracy follows every autocratic system of violence, for violence inevitably attracts moral inferiors. Time has proven that illustrious tyrants are succeeded by scoundrels.

ALBERT EINSTEIN

There is a violence that liberates, and a violence that enslaves; there is a violence that is moral and a violence that is immoral.

BENITO MUSSOLINI

It is organized violence on top which creates individual violence at the bottom. It is the accumulated indignation against organized wrong, organized crime, organized injustice, which drives the political offender to act.

EMMA GOLDMAN

Violence cannot build a better society. Disruption and disorder nourish repression, not justice. They strike at the freedom of every citizen. The community cannot—it will not—tolerate coercion and mob rule.

COMMISSION ON CIVIL DISORDER, 1968

VIRTUE Also see: ARISTOCRACY, INNOCENCE, MERCY, MODESTY, WORTH.

Virtue is like a rich stone, best plain set.

FRANCIS BACON

If you can be well without health, you may be happy without virtue.

EDMUND BURKE

Perfect virtue is to do unwitnessed that which we should be capable of doing before all the world.

FRANÇOIS DE LA ROCHEFOUCAULD

The person who talks most of his own virtue is often the least virtuous.

JAWAHARLAL NEHRU

Virtue consists, not in abstaining from vice, but in not desiring it.

GEORGE BERNARD SHAW

The only reward of virtue is virtue.

RALPH WALDO EMERSON

VISION Also see: BLINDNESS, COURAGE, CYNIC, EYE, IDEAL, IMAGINATION, TOLERANCE, WONDER.

It is never safe to look into the future with eyes of fear.

EDWARD H. HARRIMAN

No man that does not see visions will ever realize any high hope or undertake any high enterprise.

WOODROW WILSON

The farther back you can look, the farther forward you are likely to see.

WINSTON CHURCHILL

Where there is no vision a people perish.

RALPH WALDO EMERSON

You see things and you say "Why?"; but I dream things that never were and I say "Why not?"

GEORGE BERNARD SHAW

VOICE Also see: DISSENT, PUBLIC, SPEECH, VIOLENCE, WORD.

The sweetest of all sounds is that of the voice of the woman we love.

JEAN DE LA BRUYÈRE

There is no index so sure as the voice.

TANCRED

A man's style is his mind's voice. Wooden minds, wooden voices.

RALPH WALDO EMERSON

It is the still small voice that the soul heeds; not the deafening blasts of doom.

WILLIAM D. HOWELLS

The human voice is the organ of the soul

HENRY WADSWORTH LONGFELLOW

VOTE *Also see:* AMERICA, CITIZENSHIP, DEMOCRACY, POLITICS.

Where annual elections end, there slavery begins.

JOHN QUINCY ADAMS

Vote for the man who promises least—he'll be the least disappointing.

BERNARD BARUCH

Always vote for principle, though you may vote alone, and you may cherish the sweetest reflection that your vote is never lost.

JOHN QUINCY ADAMS

The future of this republic is in the hands of the American voter.

DWIGHT D. EISENHOWER

Giving every man a vote has no more made men wise and free than Christianity has made them good.

H. L. MENCKEN

When a fellow tells me he's bipartisan, I know he's going to vote against me.

HARRY S. TRUMAN

There can no longer be anyone too poor to vote.

LYNDON BAINES JOHNSON

VOID . . . *See* ABSENCE

VOW *Also see:* MARRIAGE, POLITICS, RESOLUTION.

Your capacity to keep your vow will depend on the purity of your life.

MAHATMA GANDHI

Hasty resolutions are of the nature of vows, and to be equally avoided.

WILLIAM PENN

A vow is fixed and unalterable determination to do a thing, when such a determination is related to something noble which can only uplift the man who makes the resolve.

MAHATMA GANDHI

VULGARITY *Also see:* ABUSE, AMBITION, HASTE, PROFANITY, TELEVISION, TASTE.

Vulgarity is more obvious in satin than in homespun.

NATHANIEL P. WILLIS

Vulgarity is the conduct of other people, just as falsehoods are the truths of other people.

OSCAR WILDE

By vulgarity I mean that vice of civilization which makes man ashamed of himself and his next of kin, and pretend to be somebody else.

SOLOMON SCHECHTER

A thing is not vulgar merely because it is common.

WILLIAM HAZLITT

WAGE *Also see:* CAPITALISM, EMPLOYMENT, LABOR, REWARD, UNION.

Low wages are not cheap wages.

LOUIS D. BRANDEIS

It is but a truism that labor is most productive where its wages are largest. Poorly paid labor is inefficient labor, the world over.

HENRY GEORGE

No business which depends for existence on paying less than living wages to its workers has any right to continue in this country.

FRANKLIN DELANO ROOSEVELT

The high wage begins down in the shop. If it is not created there it cannot get into pay envelopes. There will never be a system invented which will do away with the necessity for work.

HENRY FORD

"A fair day's wage for a fair day's work": it is as just a demand as governed men ever made of governing. It is the everlasting right of man.

THOMAS CARLYLE

Men who do things without being told draw the most wages.

EDWIN H. STUART

WANT *Also see:* DESIRE, INDEPENDENCE, NECESSITY, POVERTY, SECURITY, SPEECH, WASTE.

Our necessities never equal our wants.

BENJAMIN FRANKLIN

The keener the want the lustier the growth.

WENDELL PHILLIPS

It is not from nature, but from education and habits, that our wants are chiefly derived.

HENRY FIELDING

He can feel no little wants who is in pursuit of grandeur.

JOHANN KASPAR LAVATER

The fewer our wants, the nearer we resemble the gods.

SOCRATES

WAR *Also see:* BLOOD, CAUSE, CIVILIZATION, DIPLOMACY, DISARMAMENT, HEROISM, NUCLEAR WAR-FARE, PEACE, POWER, RACE, SOLDIER, UNITED NATIONS, YOUTH.

Soldiers usually win the battles and generals get the credit for them.

NAPOLEON BONAPARTE

The tragedy of war is that it uses man's best to do man's worst.

HARRY EMERSON FOSDICK

I don't know whether war is an interlude during peace, or peace is an interlude during war.

GEORGES CLEMENCEAU

War is the science of destruction.

JOHN ABBOTT

No one can guarantee success in war, but only deserve it.

WINSTON CHURCHILL

When people speak to you about a preventive war, you tell them to go and fight it. After my experience, I have come to hate war. War settles nothing.

DWIGHT D. EISENHOWER

The essence of war is violence. Moderation in war is imbecility.

JOHN A. FISHER

There was never a good war, or a bad peace.

BENJAMIN FRANKLIN

Only two great groups of animals, men and ants, indulge in highly organized mass warfare.

CHARLES H. MASKINS

There is no such things as an inevitable war. If war comes it will be from failure of human wisdom.

ANDREW B. LAW

War is hell.

WILLIAM TECUMSEH SHERMAN

The next World War will be fought with stones.

ALBERT EINSTEIN

Diplomats are just as essential in starting a war as soldiers are in finishing it.

WILL ROGERS

I have never advocated war except as a means of peace.

ULYSSESS S. GRANT

WASTE *Also see:* LOSS, PURSUIT, REFORM, REGRET, WAGE.

Waste neither time nor money, but make the best use of both. Without industry and frugality, nothing will do, and with them everything.

BENJAMIN FRANKLIN

The waste of life occasioned by trying to do too many things at once is appalling.

ORISON S. MARDEN

Short as life is, we make it still shorter by the careless waste of time.

VICTOR HUGO

A man who dares to waste one hour of life has not discovered the value of life.

CHARLES DARWIN

Waste is worse than loss. The time is coming when every person who lays claim to ability will keep the question of waste before him constantly. The scope of thrift is limitless.

THOMAS A. EDISON

WEAKNESS *Also see:* COWARDICE, CRUELTY, NEUTRALITY, PRIDE.

There are two kinds of weakness, that which breaks and that which bends.

JAMES RUSSELL LOWELL

Better make a weak man your enemy than your friend.

JOSH BILLINGS

Our strength grows out of our weakness.

RALPH WALDO EMERSON

A weak mind is like a microscope, which magnifies trifling things but cannot receive great ones.

LORD CHESTERFIELD

You cannot run away from weakness; you must some time fight it out or perish; and if that be so, why not now, and where you stand?

ROBERT LOUIS STEVENSON

What is bad? All that proceeds from weakness.

NIETZSCHE

WEALTH *Also see:* CAPITALISM, LOSS, MONEY, OPPORTUNITY, PROSPERITY, VALUE.

Surplus wealth is a sacred trust which its possessor is bound to administer in his lifetime for the good of the community.

ANDREW CARNEGIE

It is sheer madness to live in want in order to be wealthy when you die.

JUVENAL

The gratification of wealth is not found in mere possession or in lavish expenditure, but in its wise application.

MIGUEL DE CERVANTES

There's nothing so comfortable as a small bankroll. A big one is always in danger.

WILSON MIZNER

He is richest who is content with the least, for content is the wealth of nature.

SOCRATES

Without a rich heart wealth is an ugly beggar.

RALPH WALDO EMERSON

WEATHER

Sunshine is delicious, rain is refreshing, wind braces up, snow is exhilarating; there is no such thing as bad weather, only different kinds of good weather.

JOHN RUSKIN

Don't knock the weather, nine-tenths of the people couldn't start a conversation if it didn't change once in a while.

KIN HUBBARD

Everybody talks about the weather but nobody does anything about it.

CHARLES DUDLEY WARNER

Change of weather is the discourse of fools.

THOMAS FULLER

WICKEDNESS Also see: EVIL, PROFANITY, PUNISHMENT, REPENTANCE, SIN.

To see and listen to the wicked is already the beginning of wickedness.

CONFUCIUS

It is a statistical fact that the wicked work harder to reach hell than the righteous do to enter heaven.

JOSH BILLINGS

The sun also shines on the wicked.

SENECA

The world loves a spice of wickedness.

HENRY WADSWORTH LONGFELLOW

No wickedness proceeds on any grounds of reason.

LIVY

God bears with the wicked, but not forever.

MIGUEL DE CERVANTES

There is wickedness in the intention of wickedness, even though it be not perpetrated in the act.

CICERO

WIFE Also see: ACHIEVEMENT, COMPLIMENT, FIDELITY, HUSBAND, MARRIAGE, MOTHER.

I chose my wife, as she did her wedding gown, for qualities that would wear well.

OLIVER GOLDSMITH

Wives are young men's mistresses, companions for middle age, and old men's nurses.

FRANCIS BACON

Of all the home remedies, a good wife is best.

KIN HUBBARD

Heaven will be no heaven to me if I do not meet my wife there.

ANDREW JACKSON

All married women are not wives.

JAPANESE PROVERB

A wife is a gift bestowed upon man to reconcile him to the loss of paradise.

JOHANN WOLFGANG VON GOETHE

A wife is essential to great longevity; she is the receptacle of half a man's cares, and two-thirds of his ill-humor.

CHARLES READE

WILL Also see: AIM, DESIRE, PURPOSE, RESOLUTION, TECHNOLOGY, VICTORY.

People do not lack strength; they lack will.

VICTOR HUGO

Great souls have wills; feeble ones have only wishes.

CHINESE PROVERB

To deny the freedom of the will is to make morality impossible.

JAMES A. FROUDE

Will is character in action.

WILLIAM MCDOUGALL

Strength does not come from physical capacity. It comes from an indomitable will.

MAHATMA GANDHI

No action will be considered blameless, unless the will was so, for by the will the act was dictated.

SENECA

WISDOM Also see: COMMON SENSE, JUDGMENT, KNOWLEDGE, LEARNING, QUESTION.

The wisest man is generally he who thinks himself the least so.

NICOLAS BOILEAU-DESPRÉAUX

One of the greatest pieces of economic wisdom is to know what you do not know.

JOHN KENNETH GALBRAITH

It is unwise to be too sure of one's own wisdom. It is healthy to be reminded that the strongest might weaken and the wisest might err.

MAHATMA GANDHI

It is more easy to be wise for others than for ourselves.

FRANÇOIS DE LA ROCHEFOUCAULD

Nine-tenths of wisdom consists in being wise in time.

THEODORE ROOSEVELT

The older I grow the more I distrust the familiar doctrine that age brings wisdom.

H. L. MENCKEN

WIT *Also see:* FOOL, HUMOR, INSANITY, JESTING, MATURITY.

If it were not for the company of fools, a witty man would often be greatly at a loss.

FRANÇOIS DE LA ROCHEFOUCAULD

Wit is the salt of conversation, not the food.

WILLIAM HAZLITT

The next best thing to being witty one's self, is to be able to quote another's wit.

CHRISTIAN NESTELL BOVEE

A wise man will live as much within his wit as within his income.

LORD CHESTERFIELD

Wit makes its own welcome, and levels all distinctions. No dignity, no learning, no force of character, can make any stand against good wit.

RALPH WALDO EMERSON

WOMAN *Also see:* DRESS, SEX, WIFE.

There is nothing enduring in life for a woman except what she builds in a man's heart.

JUDITH ANDERSON.

The way to fight a woman is with your hat. Grab it and run.

JOHN BARRYMORE

She is not made to be the admiration of all, but the happiness of one.

EDMUND BURKE

Being a woman is a terribly difficult task since it consists principally in dealing with men.

JOSEPH CONRAD

A woman's guess is much more accurate than a man's certainty.

RUDYARD KIPLING

Of all the rights of women, the greatest is to be a mother.

LIN YUTANG

A beautiful lady is an accident of nature. A beautiful old lady is a work of art.

LOUIS NIZER

WONDER *Also see:* CURIOSITY, DOUBT, PHILOSOPHY, VISION

The world will never starve for want of wonders, but for want of wonder.
GILBERT K. CHESTERTON

It was through the feeling of wonder that men now and at first began to philosophize.
ARISTOTLE

He who can no longer pause to wonder and stand rapt in awe, is as good as dead; his eyes are closed.
ALBERT EINSTEIN

As knowledge increases, wonder deepens.
CHARLES MORGAN

Men love to wonder and that is the seed of our science.
RALPH WALDO EMERSON

WORDS *Also see:* BREVITY, DIFFERENCE, JOURNALISM, LAN-GUAGE, LOQUACITY, POETRY, PROPA-GANDA, SPEECH.

One great use of words is to hide our thoughts.
VOLTAIRE

Eating words has never given me indigestion.
WINSTON CHURCHILL

The finest words in the world are only vain sounds, if you cannot comprehend them.
ANATOLE FRANCE

A thousand words will not leave so deep an impression as one deed.
HENRIK IBSEN

The safest words are always those which bring us most directly to facts.
CHARLES H. PARKHURST

Without knowing the force of words, it is impossible to know men.
CONFUCIUS

Suit the action to the word, the word to the action.
WILLIAM SHAKESPEARE

WORK *Also see:* AUTOMATION, DILIGENCE, EFFORT, INDUS-TRY, LABOR, RETIREMENT, WAGE, ZEAL.

Nothing is really work unless you would rather be doing something else.

JAMES MATTHEW BARRIE

A man is a worker. If he is not that he is nothing.

JOSEPH CONRAD

Work is the meat of life, pleasure the dessert.

BERTIE CHARLES FORBES

I like work; it fascinates me. I can sit and look at it for hours.

JEROME K. JEROME

Work is the greatest thing in the world, so we should always save some of it for tomorrow.

DON HEROLD

The world is filled with willing people; some willing to work, the rest willing to let them.

ROBERT FROST

Labor disgraces no man, but occasionally men disgrace labor.

ULYSSES S. GRANT

WORLD Also see: CITIZENSHIP, COUNTRY, EARTH, RETIRE-MENT, UNIVERSE.

The world gets better every day—then worse again in the evening.

KIN HUBBARD

The world always had the same bankrupt look, to foregoing ages as to us.

RALPH WALDO EMERSON

He who imagines he can do without the world deceives himself much; but he who fancies the world cannot do without him is still more mistaken.

FRANÇOIS DE LA ROCHEFOUCAULD

The only fence against the world is a thorough knowledge of it.

JOHN LOCKE

We can only change the world by changing men.

CHARLES WELLS

The world is not growing worse and it is not growing better—it is just turning around as usual.

FINLEY PETER DUNNE

WORRY Also see: ANXIETY, AUTOMATION, FEAR, TRIFLES.

The freedom now desired by many is not freedom to do and dare but freedom from care and worry.

JAMES TRUSLOW ADAMS

Worry is interest paid on trouble before it is due.

WILLIAM RALPH INGE

I have lost everything, and I am so poor now that I really cannot afford to let anything worry me.

JOSEPH JEFFERSON

As a cure for worrying, work is better than whiskey.

RALPH WALDO EMERSON

Worry is the interest paid by those who borrow trouble.

GEORGE LYON

Don't tell me that worry doesn't do any good. I know better. The things I worry about don't happen.

ANONYMOUS

There is nothing that wastes the body like worry, and one who has any faith in God should be ashamed to worry about anything whatsoever.

MAHATMA GANDHI

The reason why worry kills more people than work is that more people worry than work.

ROBERT FROST

WORTH *Also see:* MERIT, QUALITY, RACE, RESPECT.

I believe in the supreme worth of the individual and in his right to life, liberty, and the pursuit of happiness.

JOHN D. ROCKEFELLER

It's not what you pay a man, but what he costs you that counts.

WILL ROGERS

For anything worth having one must pay the price; and the price is always work, patience, love, self-sacrifice.

JOHN BURROUGHS

He is rich or poor according to what he is, not according to what he has.

HENRY WARD BEECHER

Where is quality is the thing sought after, the thing of supreme quality is cheap, whatever the price one has to pay for it.

WILLIAM JAMES

WRITER *Also see:* AMBIGUITY, BOOK, HISTORY, JOURNALISM, LITERATURE, POETRY, QUOTATION, TRUTH, WORD.

Talent alone cannot make a writer. There must be a man behind the book.

RALPH WALDO EMERSON

Nothing gives an author so much pleasure as to find his works respectfully quoted by other learned authors.

BENJAMIN FRANKLIN

Your manuscript is both good and original, but the part that is good is not original, and the part that is original is not good.

SAMUEL JOHNSON

The most original authors are not so because they advance what is new, but because they put what they have to say as if it had never been said before.

JOHANN WOLFGANG VON GOETHE

Every compulsion is put upon writers to become safe, polite, obedient, and sterile.

SINCLAIR LEWIS

You become a good writer just as you become a good joiner: by planning down your sentences.

ANATOLE FRANCE

WRITING . . . *See* JOURNALISM

WRONG *Also see:* APATHY, CRUELTY, ERROR, EVIL, FOOL, FRAUD, SIN, VICE, WICKEDNESS.

It is better to suffer wrong than to do it, and happier to be sometimes cheated than not to trust.

SAMUEL JOHNSON

Wrong is but falsehood put in practice.

WALTER S. LANDOR

There are few people who are more often in the wrong than those who cannot endure to be so.

FRANÇOIS DE LA ROCHEFOUCAULD

The man who says "I may be wrong, but—" does not believe there can be any such possibility.

KIN HUBBARD

YEARS . . . *See* AGE

YOUTH *Also see:* AGE, AMERICA, BOYS, CHILDREN, DEBT, DISAPPOINTMENT, GIRLS, MATURITY, SELF-IMPROVEMENT, SENSUALITY.

It is not possible for civilization to flow backwards while there is youth in the world.

HELEN KELLER

Youth is the first victim of war; the first fruit of peace. It takes 20 years or more of peace to make a man; it takes only 20 seconds of war to destroy him.

BAUDOUIN I

Older men declare war. But it is the youth that must fight and die.

HERBERT HOOVER

For God's sake, give me the young man who has brains enough to make a fool of himself.

ROBERT LOUIS STEVENSON

It is better to be a young June-bug than an old bird of paradise.

MARK TWAIN

Youth is that period when a young boy knows everything but how to make a living.

CAREY WILLIAMS

The Youth of a Nation are the trustees of posterity.

BENJAMIN DISRAELI

Youth is a wonderful thing: what a crime to waste it on children.

GEORGE BERNARD SHAW

In youth we run into difficulties, in old age difficulties run into us.

JOSH BILLINGS

Youth comes but once in a lifetime.

HENRY WADSWORTH LONGFELLOW

ZEAL *Also see:* AMBITION, ENTHUSIASM, FANATICISM, PURPOSE, SPIRIT, WILL.

Zeal without humanity is like a ship without a rudder, liable to be stranded at any moment.

OWEN FELLTHAM

The greatest dangers to liberty lurk in insidious encroachment by men of zeal, well-meaning, but without understanding.

LOUIS D. BRANDEIS

Experience shows that success is due less to ability than to zeal. The winner is he who gives himself to his work, body and soul.

CHARLES BUXTON

Zeal is very blind, or badly regulated, when it encroaches upon the rights of others.

QUESNEL

There is no greater sign of a general decay of virtue in a nation, than a want of zeal in its inhabitants for the good of their country.

JOSEPH ADDISON

Zeal is fit only for wise men but is found mostly in fools

ANCIENT PROVERB

NOTES

NOTES

NOTES